TO
THE
FINISH
LINE

TO THE FINISH LINE

A World Champion Triathlete's Guide to Your Perfect Race

CHRISSIE WELLINGTON

CONSTABLE

CONSTABLE

First published in Great Britain in 2017 by Constable

1 3 5 7 9 10 8 6 4 2

Copyright © Chrissie Wellington with Immediate Media Company Bristol Limited, 2017

The moral right of the author has been asserted.

A CIP catalogue record for this book
is available from the British Library.

ISBN: 978-1-47212-497-5

Designed by Sian Rance and Emil Dacanay at D. R. ink

Illustrations by Stephen Dew (pages 104, 144, 160 and 162–7)

Printed and bound in China by C&C Offset Printing Co. Ltd.

Papers used by Constable are from well-managed forests and other responsible sources.

Constable
An imprint of
Little, Brown Book Group
Carmelite House
50 Victoria Embankment
London EC4Y 0DZ

An Hachette UK Company
www.hachette.co.uk

www.littlebrown.co.uk

Disclaimer: Regular exercise is one of the healthiest habits you can have. But, even for healthy individuals, there will always be an element of risk. This is the case for triathlon – an endurance sport which places physical demands on the body. If you have any concerns about your ability to undertake triathlon and/or have pre-existing medical conditions, you should consult a health care professional. Ultimately you, the athlete, should listen to your body and use common sense.

For Esme.
You are our sunshine.

CONTENTS

ACKNOWLEDGEMENTS

This book started as a seed of an idea, germinated during a long ride in the Somerset countryside. And like a seed it has grown and blossomed, in ways I never even envisaged. Although the guidance in this book is based on my own personal experiences and I take full responsibility for its contents, I couldn't have crossed the publication finish line alone. As with triathlon, I am indebted to so many people, some of whom I have worked with, consulted and referred to within the book and others who have unconditionally supported from the shadows. Writing this guide has been a true labour of love, and I am indebted to all those who have answered endless emails, provided answers to my many questions, calmed me down when anxiety levels have escalated and read through countless drafts.

I particularly want to thank my wonderful family, close and extended, for always being there for me; my friends near and far; the coaches and other experts I have had the privilege to work with and learn so much from; and the hundreds of others who have helped me on my journey from triathlon rookie to four-time Ironman World Champion. This includes the thousands of triathlon age groupers for whom this book is principally written. I hope that the contents go some way in giving back to you and to a sport that has gifted me so much.

Of course, for any professional or retired athlete sponsorship is vital. TYR Sport and Brooks, in particular, provide support that continues to this day.

I would also like to give a special mention to parkrun, who have offered me the opportunity to grow, learn and live my passion since retiring from professional sport – their work demonstrates that physical activity and volunteering really can transform lives. As with the other charities for which I am a patron, I am honoured to be involved with your wonderful work and will do whatever I can to support you.

My deepest gratitude goes to Helen Webster and Liz Barrett of *220 Triathlon* magazine, along with the rest of the 220 staff, who gave me the platform all those years ago to share my thoughts and ideas and hopefully help inspire many more people to chase their sporting dreams. Their support has never wavered, not least in the production of this book. A special mention to the 'K-Team' members – Katy Campbell and coach Matt Edwards, who I was so privileged to work with in 2014 and 2015. My sincere thanks are also extended to Andreas Campomar and Claire Chesser of Constable, Rolf Zettersten and Kate Hartson of Hachette and Jonathan Conway of Jonathan Conway Literary Agency for enabling me to translate the seed of an idea into published reality. Heartfelt appreciation also goes to my friend and coach Dave Scott, as well as Mike Taylor, Asker Jeukendrup, Kate Percy and Andy Kirkland whose support has been absolutely invaluable. And to the wonderful Tim Heming, who patiently and painstakingly read through repeated drafts, and to whom I am forever indebted.

The last word is saved for my incredible husband Tom, who is my absolute rock, best friend and soul mate, and to our wonderful daughter Esme Grace – the light of our lives.

Your support enables me to cross my own personal finish lines and for that I am eternally grateful.

INTRODUCTION

BECOMING A CHAMPION

M̲ention the word 'triathlon' 20 years ago and you would probably have been met with a blank stare. Back then, triathlon was perceived as the sole province of muscle-bound masochists. Thankfully times have changed. Triathlon made it on to the Olympic stage in Sydney in 2000, and ever since has been one of the world's fastest growing sports. Triathlons of all shapes and sizes (see the Annex for more details on different types of triathlon) are appearing on our television screens and reported on in newspapers, triathlon clubs are spreading like wildfire and the annual race calendar is chock-full.

It wasn't until I was in my mid-twenties, and with a demanding full-time job, that I had my first foray into triathlon, and a few years later I was fortunate enough to start making a living out of the sport with which I'd quickly fallen in love. I was driven by a desire to know – to find out what I was capable of and how good I could be. I never

OPPOSITE: Victory at the Ironman World Championship, 2008.

want to look back on my life and think 'what if'. Triathlon presented me with a fantastic challenge truly to be the best that I could be, and I was determined to rise to it.

There is a multitude of benefits to triathlon. Combining three different disciplines spices up training and racing; you never get bored. Plus the range of events – from relays to sprints to long-distance triathlons – means there is something to suit every slow or fast twitch-muscle fibre. Then there are the numerous health benefits, the chance to travel and, best of all, you can share all this pleasure and pain with the thousands of others who have taken up the challenge of swim, bike and run.

One of my most treasured memories is of my first Ironman World Championship in Kona, Hawaii, when I watched in awe as competitors ran, walked, staggered and crawled their way across the line. There were people of all ages, from 18-year-old students to 80-year-old grandparents, to daughters, wives, husbands, fathers . . . even those who have been on the brink of death and survived. I realised then that each triathlete has a unique and special story to tell, but they are all united by one thing – the journey to that hallowed finish line.

Never in a million years did I think that I would be where I am today – writing this book as a four-time Ironman World Champion. It still baffles me to think about the paths I have travelled and the experiences I have been fortunate to have along the way. I see life as being like a tree – branching in a range of wonderful ways, and triathlon is one of the most prominent branches; one which changed my life for ever.

I achieved more than I ever thought possible in the sport, but after Challenge Roth in 2011 and the World Championship later that year I instinctively knew that I'd reached my personal pinnacle. A crash I had only two weeks prior to the latter race had left me with wounds all over the left side of my body, and internal bruising that caused intense pain. Yet it was the race I had always dreamed of; the one where I dug to the depths and battled with my valiant competitors to cross that finish line in first place, conquering fears, adversity and self-doubt. It was my perfect race, even though – paradoxically – the build-up and the race itself were fraught with imperfections. I felt utterly complete. I felt liberated. I'd achieved my holy grail. It was now time to carve out a new path, and one that didn't have triathlon as the axis around which everything revolved.

Since retiring from professional triathlon in 2012, I've continued to add new branches to my own personal tree; whether that be collaborating with the UK government to inform the development of sport and physical activity policy,

working for parkrun and setting up the successful junior parkrun series of events, lobbying for gender equality in sport (and, specifically, successfully calling for a women's race at the Tour de France), throwing myself into different endurance events or giving birth to our daughter, my proudest achievement to date.

Although I am no longer a professional athlete, not a day goes by when I don't think about triathlon and the fantastic opportunities it offered me as well as the thousands who take up the challenge every year. The triathlon door is now open to all, and I am living proof that anything truly is possible with some passion, self-belief, support and a lot of hard work.

I want to seize the wonderful opportunity that I have to inspire and encourage others to take up the sport or push that bar a little bit higher, and it is to this quest that I now dedicate my life.

High fives at junior parkrun.

Me pounding the pavements in Boulder, Colorado in 2010.

In 2015, I headed out on my bike to the hills of Somerset (aka the Mendips). It was a glorious day and I felt free, psychologically 'light' and at peace. I often find that this is when I am struck by my best ideas.

I have written for *220 Triathlon* since 2008. The prose has taken various forms, from ramblings about whatever tickles my fancy, to answering readers' questions and more recently as a mentor to novice triathlete, Katy Campbell. It was during this ride that a bolt of inspiration hit. I had a collection of articles that aimed to inspire, enthuse and inform readers about all things triathlon-related: contributions that have hopefully enabled the reader to understand the mind and body of a champion and, in turn, learn from what I, and my fellow professionals, do.

I have also had the privilege of delivering countless presentations and seminars on all manner of subjects related in some way to my triathlon journey. During these presentations, I have conveyed some of the important lessons that I have learned and been asked a wide variety of questions by people in the audience, which I've done my very best to answer. I have also received countless emails and social media messages requesting my advice on all manner of issues, which, again, I have tried to answer as comprehensively as possible.

I realised that, if brought together, all of these articles, presentations, emails and conversations could enable people, no matter their ability, to act like champions in their daily triathlon lives and provide a guide for getting to whatever finish line they set their sights on.

The reality is that there is no single ingredient or magic wand that can turn an athlete into a champion. But what does being a champion truly mean? Is it crossing the finish line with your arms aloft and a smile on your face? Is it demolishing your personal best? Or is it a title that can only be bestowed on those who have won a significant sporting event?

" I want to inspire and encourage others to push that bar a little bit higher. "

In my view, anyone can become a champion, if you *act* like one. As an athlete, you don't just perform on race day, you demonstrate the behaviour and habits of a champion on a daily basis. Day in and day out. Put another way, champions are defined not by achieving their goal but by their willingness to try.

And so this book was born. This isn't a compilation of all the material I have written or presentations that I have delivered. Nor is it my (very entertaining!) autobiography, *A Life Without Limits*, which I published in 2012. Nor is it simply a dull, dry training bible with tables of swim, bike and run plans or academic-sounding ramblings on hourly percentages of carbohydrate consumption. It is much more than that. In creating this book, I wanted to bring triathlon to life: to make it accessible to everyone – no matter his or her ability. I wanted to create a book filled with tips, practical advice and information, but also musings on other issues related to triathlon, sport and life in general. Along with the best of my articles in *220 Triathlon*, I have added a wealth of new material from which triathletes of all standards can benefit.

The book is based on a holistic perspective that sees triathlon training and racing as being so much more than swim, bike and run, and includes advice and information on, for example, goal setting, strength and conditioning, psychology, nutrition, rest and recovery and effective race preparation, as well as on my latest topic of interest, pre- and post-natal exercise.

> " Champions are defined not by achieving their goal but by their willingness to try. "

Each chapter comprises separate sections, some being Q & As, snapshots from my mentee Katy's triathlon journey and blogged reflections on a few of the most important races of my career. I have been incredibly fortunate to work with many fantastic coaches, advisors and mentors, some of whom have contributed to the book, offering their own perspectives on my training and providing expertise on specific topics. Six-time Ironman World Champion and my coach, Dave Scott, has provided insight and wisdom throughout. I have also leaned on Mike Taylor for his bike-fitting expertise, Professor Asker Jeukendrup as my sports-nutrition guru, and consulted with Kate Percy, creator of delicious and nutritious athlete-focused recipes. Like a sponge, over my triathlon career and indeed my life, I've absorbed a wealth of information, lessons and experiences that I can now share.

I have divided triathletes into three broad categories: beginner, intermediate and advanced. However, while you might be new to triathlon, you may have come from an established single sport background. It's important that for each discipline you train dependent on your current skill, experience and fitness levels. For example, an advanced runner may need to follow a beginner's programme in the water. It's also worth remembering that often the biggest gains can be made in our weakest discipline. We all feel most secure when reverting to our strengths, but don't fall into that all-too-comfortable trap. The aim is to reach the finish line in the least amount of time, not to focus on your strongest discipline in order to achieve the fastest individual swim, bike or run split.

Each triathlete has a different story to tell, and each one of us will seek different ways to improve, but we are all united by one thing – the journey to the finish line. Whether you are targeting a super-sprint or Ironman, my hope is that this book will help guide you on a wonderful triathlon adventure and to write your own sporting success story.

Good luck, and never stop believing in all you can achieve!

CHAPTER ONE
GOAL SETTING

Y ou may be reading this as a non-triathlete trying to decide whether or not to do a triathlon; or contemplating whether or not to do an Ironman having previously focused on Olympic distance; maybe even thinking you might have what it takes to be a professional athlete. Or, alternatively, you might be at a crossroads in your career, your studies or your personal life and uncertain about whether or not to embark on a new adventure.

I believe that life is so much richer, more fulfilling, if we follow our passions; when we are able to find, and then pursue, activities/sports/jobs that make us smile, that challenge us, that widen our circle of friends, that make our hearts sing.

We might not always know what these passions are, and that's when we need to summon up the courage to explore, to venture, to take a leap of faith. If I hadn't chosen to have a go at triathlon in 2004, I would never have realised my passion for the sport: I would have been forever blind to my capabilities and to something that, as it transpired, had the capacity to give me so much.

This chapter offers advice on finding and then following your passion in triathlon by setting ambitious goals, and a seasonal plan based on these, to maximise your enjoyment and potential in this amazing sport.

OPPOSITE: Welcoming the final finisher as he crosses the line at Challenge Roth.

FACE FEARS: FINDING YOUR PASSION

My initial plan after graduating from the University of Birmingham in 1998 was to become a solicitor. A London-based law firm offered me a two-year training contract and financial support to undertake the obligatory law-conversion course. That course was due to start in September 1999, and in the interim I decided to go travelling. I bought a round-the-world ticket and left the UK in November 1998 for Africa, thereafter journeying to New Zealand, Australia and several countries in Asia. I returned not after nine months, as planned, but almost two years later. This trip changed the direction my life would take.

It was a friend I made in Africa, Jude, who encouraged me to question my choice to pursue law, look deep inside myself and work out what my passion really was. Through introspection, I realised that I had chosen the legal profession, not because I was truly passionate about it, but because I felt I ought to: because I had been academically successful, and wanted a label with which to define myself career-wise. I realised that my true interest – ever since I was a young girl – lay in international development. After much soul searching, I decided to renege on my contract with the law firm and instead embark on a Masters in development studies. It was a fork in the road and, this time, my passion was my compass.

Fast forward a few years to 2006 and I encountered another such fork. This time it was after having won the World Age Group Championship. I had to decide whether or not to give up my job as a government policy advisor on international development and become a full-time triathlete. It wasn't an easy decision. Yes, my love for triathlon was growing with every week of training and every race I did. Yet, it was still uncharted territory. I didn't know much about the professional side of the sport and what being a professional athlete entailed. And I was scared. Scared of what people would think of me. Scared of not being able to make a living and support myself financially. Scared that I may give up everything and not enjoy the lifestyle. Scared of the unknown and, ultimately, fearful of failure.

However, I never want to look back and think 'what if'. I never want to be left wondering what might have been. To me the biggest failure of all is the failure to try. Hence, despite the fears, nervousness and anxiety, I decided to leave my job, take the plunge, follow my passion and travel down the unfamiliar path of professional triathlon.

I'm sure that many of us experience such emotions at some point, or points, in our lives. We are worried about making changes, anxious about how we will be perceived, nervous about trying something new. We can either let those emotions impede us, or we can look our fears in the face and follow an existing passion or embark on a journey that could potentially catalyse a new one.

" On reflection, I'm so glad I chose the path that scared me. "

I often think about what would have been had I decided to stay as a civil servant. I would not be sitting here as four-time Ironman World Champion, and nor would I have had the wealth of opportunities that this title has afforded me. On reflection, I'm so glad I chose the path that scared me.

So, if you are reading this and facing a crossroads in your life or have a nagging feeling that something needs to change, spend some time on introspection. Think about occasions in your life when you have been happiest, and the reasons behind this; or something that may have piqued your interest but you never pursued. There doesn't have to be a huge flame: a little spark is enough to start a fire burning. Then vow to take that one step forward: to try. That way you'll never be left wondering. You'll have your answer. You'll be following a passion.

Assuming that, for you, triathlon or endurance sport is what lights your fire, the next step is to set yourself a goal to give your passionate pursuit some clear direction and focus, and it is to that subject that we will now turn.

Q & A: Picking a Winner – Choosing Your 'A' Race

Q 'I want to do a triathlon next year but there are so many races to choose from! How do I decide which one would suit me best?'

FIONA SMYTH

A It's always hard to 'pick a winner', isn't it? I'm not referring to my father's sage advice when he (repeatedly) caught me with my finger up my nose, but instead to the difficult decision about what triathlon you throw yourself into. If you had entered the sport in the 1970s or 1980s there would only have been a handful of triathlons to choose from, in addition to dayglo Lycra and Dave Scott handlebar moustaches (and that's just for the girls) being de rigueur. In fact, you could probably have participated in all of the triathlons in the UK over the course of a year, so few and far between were the events. How times have changed. Fast-forward a few decades and dayglo went out of fashion (and is now apparently back in), aerobars are more common than handlebars and the triathlon calendar is bursting at the seams.

Q&A

> " 'A' hopefully stands for 'awesome' but it's generally used to denote the event that is the focus of your season. "

Whether a novice or a seasoned veteran, you only have to look at a credible triathlon website to see super-sprints, sprints, Olympic-distance races, half Ironmans, Ironmans, aquathlons, duathlons, bonker-thons that go beyond Ironman distance . . . You name it, there's a 'thon for you.

There's the chance that you may simply enjoy the process of triathlon training without ever wanting to race. That's perfectly fine; however, for those reading this whose goal is to do a triathlon of whatever distance, it's likely that you'll want to select an 'A' race – 'A' hopefully stands for 'awesome' but it's generally used to denote the event that is the focus of your season. Of course, it's possible to have a couple of A races spread throughout the season. I felt that I could realistically and successfully peak for three races throughout the course of the year, essentially having about three months to prepare for each. I therefore prioritised the Ironman World Championship in October but also selected a couple of other Ironmans, one in the northern hemisphere spring and one in the summer, which I considered high priority.

So, if you're planning a triathlon season, what factors come into play in deciding what your 'awesome' race should be?

Race distance

Decide what distance you want to focus your efforts on. If you're a novice, there's nothing to say that your first race has to be a short-course triathlon. I know quite a few athletes who have thrown caution to the wind and made their first A race an Ironman event, but I would advise doing some shorter races beforehand to help you prepare effectively.

Course

Even for races of the same distance, the type of swim, bike and run course will be different. For example, the swim can be in a pool or in open water. If open water, it could be in the sea (which could be rough or calm), a lake or a canal – with a variety of water temperatures. Bike courses can be hilly or flat or a mix of both. The run can be on the road or on hard-packed trails and, again, can be bumpy or pancake flat. There are also races that are multi-lap and those that have a single lap for each discipline. Race choice is down to personal preference and once you have made that decision you can tailor your training to suit.

Timing

Think about what time of year you want to race. This is strongly linked to your current fitness level, your goal for the A race and how long it will take you to reach your desired standard. It usually takes considerably longer to prepare for an Ironman than it does a super-sprint, but much depends on your athletic background. You may also need time to save money to pay for everything associated with this crazy sport, as well as the next factor – the weather.

Weather conditions

You may have a preference for a particular type of weather conditions in which to race. I personally love it when the temperature climbs (and luckily for me Hawaii is rather more tropical than your average British summer) and usually underperform in colder conditions when my polar-bear competitors thrive. Hence, I chose races where warmer weather was almost guaranteed. This is linked to the location but also the time of year. If you want to race in the UK and prefer warmer weather, then you may want to hedge your bets and enter a race that's between May and

August (although granted this is no guarantee that there won't be biblical rain and/or single-digit temperatures). If you don't want to train in the cold, it may be sensible to avoid entering a race that's in the early part of the year (if you live in the northern hemisphere) as it would mean training in freezing conditions or inside. You might want to take a look at the heat acclimatisation section on page 322 if you fancy racing in the heat yet live in a place where rain/cloud/snow features strongly.

Altitude

Think carefully before you enter races at a higher altitude, particularly those above 1,500m, as this can impact you physiologically, especially if you're not acclimatised.

Location

Do you want to do an event in the UK or travel abroad? If the former, do you want to race close to home or venture to far-flung parts of the country – maybe somewhere you've never been, such as Tenby, for instance? The same applies if you want to go overseas. Do you fancy racing in Europe, or have you always wanted to go to the triathlon mecca that is Timbuktu? The decision is obviously linked to many other factors, including cost, travel time, whether you want a holiday afterwards (I hear Tenby is very nice) and if you would like family and friends to be able to attend. Racing in or near a big city might appear to have its advantages, but some of the most revered races can be found in places slightly off the beaten track, in part because the local communities fully embrace the sport.

Budget

If your wallet isn't supersized, then you'll probably be watching your pennies. Travelling to Timbuktu is far more expensive than getting to Tenby. Of course, racing abroad also means transporting your bike without it resembling a mangled mess (see page 230 for more information about pre-race preparation). You'll also want to consider the cost of race entry, as this can vary considerably even for events of the same distance. Bear in mind that just because you have paid an eye-wateringly large race fee, it's no guarantee that the race will be run to a higher standard than cheaper alternatives.

Brand

There are many different race organisers out there, from the local triathlon clubs to big global corporations and everything in between. If you're focusing on Olympic

distance, think about whether you want to race an International Triathlon Union (ITU)-organised event or are happy doing the local triathlon arranged by John or Jane Bloggs. If you want to do an Ironman race, there is a similarly large range of options: from the official 'Ironman' branded series of events, i.e. owned by the World Triathlon Corporation (WTC); those organised by other large global companies, such as Challenge; or races put on by smaller, national or local operators that may be less costly and offer a slightly different Ironman race experience.

Atmosphere and extras

Races vary wildly in terms of the atmosphere, the number of competitors, the pre- and post-race support and activities, the goodies you get (e.g. a finisher's medal, a race T-shirt), the number of spectators and so forth. For me, racing was a performance and I relished plying my trade in front of a crowd – one of the many reasons I loved Challenge Roth, where hundreds of thousands of people line the streets, celebrating, cheering and drinking beer. I also thrived on the jubilant, emotive and inspirational finish-line atmosphere; especially the music and firework show finale to celebrate the last finisher. Think about what really motivates you and will drive you to great heights, and do some research to ensure you get exactly what you want.

Support by friends and family

This is linked to location and timing. If it's vital that your friends and family come and watch, cheer and tell you that you look 'awesome'/'gorgeous'/'knackered'/'downright dreadful', then make sure you enter a race to which they can travel easily and where they can manoeuvre around the course to see you in action.

Reputation

Did previous participants like the event? Was the route well marshalled or did everyone go off-course and end up in Timbuktu rather than Tenby? Was the atmosphere good or was it a total damp squib? I suggest chatting to friends and reading previous race reports. Of course, such feedback and reviews are always subjective but they can give a flavour of what an event is like.

Qualification

Find out whether you need to qualify to enter the race. For example, unless you have a) been totally awesome and been awarded a slot through a previous performance or b) earned a place by virtue of being bonkers enough to clock up

loads of Ironman finishes, unfortunately you won't be racing at the Ironman World Championship. Likewise, if you want to compete for your country, for example at the ITU World Age Group Championship, you'll need to qualify and, if you aren't able to do so, there is little point in making it your A race.

The world truly is our oyster when it comes to doing any type of 'thon. Only you can decide what criteria matter in picking your A-race winner. Importantly, be passionate, excited and energised about the goal and the reasons behind it – rather than simply doing something because you feel you ought to or because everyone else is doing it.

There are many underlying motives for swimming, cycling and running towards your finish line but here are a few of the most popular:

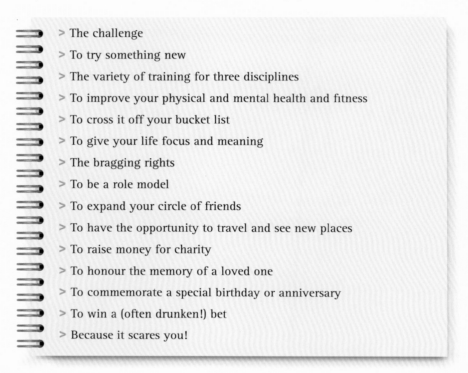

> The challenge

> To try something new

> The variety of training for three disciplines

> To improve your physical and mental health and fitness

> To cross it off your bucket list

> To give your life focus and meaning

> The bragging rights

> To be a role model

> To expand your circle of friends

> To have the opportunity to travel and see new places

> To raise money for charity

> To honour the memory of a loved one

> To commemorate a special birthday or anniversary

> To win a (often drunken!) bet

> Because it scares you!

So select that A race, commit (literally and also mentally) by entering and then make that goal – and your motives – tangible by writing them down and telling friends, family and Facebook; and, as we will see in Chapter 8, use this as motivational fuel for your fire.

Crucially, enjoy every single minute of the journey, whether you're aiming for tri-terrific Tenby or Timbuktu. ●

A RACING ROADMAP: PLANNING YOUR RACE SEASON

For most of us, training is not simply a means to look buff, meet a Lycra lover, buy lots of overpriced paraphernalia or eat syrupy concoctions out of little foil pouches. We train to race. However, unless you have superhuman talents it's very unusual for a novice to commence triathlon training in May and be able to race, successfully, in June. That's why triathlon is often viewed as a lifestyle sport – it's one that has to be done year-round in order to reap the rewards. Whether you're a newbie or a seasoned, long-in-the-triathlon-tooth veteran, enjoying the sport and achieving your goals means hatching a personal roadmap for the year ahead.

Start off by acquiring a decent calendar. Being an old-school Luddite, I like this to be the pen and paper variety (it's best not to wait until March, even though they are bound to be virtually free as stationers rid themselves of said almanacs). The importance of 'having it off' and taking a break is covered elsewhere (Chapter 10), so I'll focus here on the remainder of the year and, specifically, how to proactively plan your race schedule.

As well as my usual three Ironman distance races per year, I would throw in some half Ironmans and a couple of other events (say, a 10km road race or an Olympic-distance event) for added spice. A little fly in the chamois cream is that planning a season (and a tailored training programme) is very different for a pro than it is an age grouper, and a pro's schedule won't and shouldn't bear any resemblance to your own reality. I would bet my bottom dollar, or any dollar in fact, that a racing roadmap like mine would leave you fatigued, injured or retired with the notion that lawn bowls is a much more attractive proposition.

SELECT YOUR A RACE

First, select your A race or races, using the handy tips on page 24. To recap, an A race is a priority event where you want to perform at your best. This could be anything from completing your first sprint distance race, to getting a PB or winning your age group at the World Championship. This is the axis around which your season revolves. Insert this race into your new, full-priced calendar, adding a big star or smiley face as necessary. I would suggest that amateur athletes have no more than two A races per season, otherwise you risk losing focus and underperforming at the key time; reaching for the stars and grabbing a handful of gravel instead.

As a pro, I liked to have a block of about ten to 12 weeks to prepare for my A race. However, bear in mind that I had a certain level of fitness going into that period. The less experience and fitness you have, the longer you'll need to prepare effectively.

SELECT YOUR B RACE

Once you have identified your A race, it's time to decide on a few other glittering rocks: your so-called B races. These are the less-important events, which can serve as a carrot to get you through weeks of suboptimal winter training, for measuring progress, tuning up, Iron(man)ing out your wrinkles or for race-day simulation (or even some stimulation); for example, it can be an opportunity to use race-day kit and practise transitions. You should factor in a few such races, the first being a cobweb-blower that you can use to bust the rust that would have accumulated since last season or, if you are a newbie, your first foray into the triathlon world. Ideally, this season-opener would be a shorter, low-pressure race that is relatively close to home, has a fantastic name (e.g. the Beaver, Little Beaver or Speedy Beaver) and great pubs for post-race rehydration.

You can also schedule a B event five to seven weeks before your A race. The distance depends on the length of the latter, as well as your level of experience and fitness. If your A race is an Olympic distance, I would do a sprint or Olympic-distance event as a tune-up. If your A race is an Ironman, then you can consider doing an Olympic-distance event up to three weeks before or a half Ironman up to four to five weeks prior. Ideally, this race comprises some of the important aspects you'd like to simulate for your main race: terrain, climate, competition level or else a lovely technical finisher's T-shirt that you can wear with pride/use as a bike rag going into your Big Kahuna.

> 66 Don't lose heart if these races don't go according to plan. The proverbial 'ups of cock' will happen. 99

Don't lose heart if these races don't go according to plan. The proverbial 'ups of cock' will happen. That's precisely why such experiences are so valuable. They are rungs on the ladder to your ultimate prize. The important thing is to learn from them. The period of reflection following such events is incredibly important; so think carefully about how you felt mentally and physically, whether your equipment helped or hindered, what you did well, what you could have done differently or whether you actually prefer lawn bowls. This will ensure that you can build on your experiences in time for your main event.

When planning the season, you'll also want to factor in taper and post-race recovery time; the exact duration of both will depend very much on your fitness levels, experience and the distance you are focusing on. Tapering and recovery is covered in Chapters 9 and 10, but in terms of recovery times, I would suggest at least three to four days to recover from an Olympic distance, a week to ten days for a half Ironman and two to three weeks for a full Ironman. During this time, you can do some light training, such as swimming, spins on the bike and walking, but I tend to avoid running for three to four days after an Ironman due to its impactful nature.

SELECT YOUR C RACE

The last race type is the C race, which is basically a training session and one for which you don't taper or factor in recovery time. Such Cs can be single-sport (swim, bike or run) events or, for non-newbies, a sprint or Olympic-distance triathlon. For example, in 2010 I did the Amgen Tour of California Cycling Time Trial and the Bolder Boulder 10km run – the latter being masochistic fun after a 4km swim and five-hour ride the day before. You don't necessarily need to have a specific

performance (e.g. time/position) goal – although aiming to at least finish is always good – but can use such races to have some fun, be with friends and work on your weaknesses. For example, an open-water swim event where you can practise the skills you need for aquatic survival in a no-pressure environment. And you might even get a free swim cap.

CONSIDER OTHER COMMITMENTS

When planning your race schedule, you'll need to factor in all the other commitments you have, aside from triathlon. If you have a period where you won't be able to train consistently, ensure this is inserted into the calendar. That could be work, family, travel or, heaven forbid, non-triathlon social activities. Top tip: it's preferable to consult – and take into account the views of – your other half, children and pets when planning your season. You may also wish to explain that the 'Little Beaver' is actually a race before they fly into a fit of jealous rage.

Remember, the best-laid plans may not come to fruition. Things crop up, you decide you prefer sprint distance to Ironman, injuries – or saddle sores – arrive to bite you on the backside, your wife proposes and you elope to Timbuktu. Don't beat yourself – or anyone else for that matter – up if you become an acronym: namely a DNS (did not start) or DNF (did not finish). Continue to evaluate your progress, your motivation and your lifestyle, and ensure that the plans and goals you have set are still practical and desirable. If not, you may need to change and adapt the racing roadmap and head in a different direction. There are plenty of events in the calendar, and plenty more seasons in which you can fight another racing day.

One-on-One

A is for Alpe: Goal Setting with Katy Campbell

In 2014, *220 Triathlon* launched a competition with, even I if I do say so myself, an exciting and unique prize: the chance to be mentored by yours truly for a whole year. The winner was the then 37-year-old amateur runner, rower and tri-newbie Katy Campbell. Not being a fan of swimming and disliking cycling, Katy wasn't altogether sure that triathlon was for her. This changed when her close friend Laura was diagnosed with cancer. Wanting a channel to raise money for charity, and seeking a new challenge outside her comfort zone, Katy chose triathlon. I had the fantastic opportunity to work with Katy over a 12-month period starting in July 2014, taking her from self-declared tri-numpty to her triathlon finish line.

At the outset of our partnership, Katy, coach Matt Edwards and I met over a glass (only one – honest!) of wine and a curry to chew the fat about race goals, motivations, hopes, fears and that all-important training programme.

Chrissie: So, after a few weeks of deliberation it's time to set your A race goal. It should align with your ambitions, personality, schedule and lifestyle and most importantly really excite and invigorate you. The race will be the main focus of your efforts over the coming year, but also be the foundation and springboard to a subsequent world of new adventures. So what are your thoughts?

Katy: I've spoken to different people, weighed up the options, thought about what it is I really enjoy doing and ultimately what would be challenging. So even though it scares me, I want to do (and finish!) the Alpe d'Huez Long Course Triathlon.

Chrissie: It's an amazing, iconic, beautiful race. It will test and challenge you, but finishing is totally realistic. And having done the race in 2007 and 2008, I have first-hand experience of the course; but would rather you didn't catapult over a crash barrier like I did in 2007! So what are your reasons for choosing Alpe d'Huez specifically?

Katy: You mentioned it a few weeks ago, and it has been playing on my mind ever since. For all of the other events and races I have done in my life, I have been confident of success – they have been in my comfort zone. But this one is too far and too hilly and I don't know if I can do it – and that's precisely why I need to give it a go. I've previously been worried about aiming high because I've been scared of injury and scared of failure. In a way, it's also really liberating and less stressful to try something

totally new and feel so clueless about what lies ahead! I also like the fact that the race distance is unique, rather being a full Ironman – which is what everyone expects me to do.

Although I love being in the mountains, I hate cycling in them. In fact, I don't even like long bike rides! I'm also nervous about having my feet clipped in on a hill, in case I'm going so slowly that I topple over. This race will help me overcome these fears and prove to myself that I'm not as bad a cyclist as I think I am. Plus, being a July race I'll hopefully have enough time to get in shape, but it's not far enough away that I will get bored preparing for it.

Matt: Is there a tie-in with your friend Laura?

Katy: It's the desire to honour her memory that drives me every day. I met Laura in Bristol and she was from Edinburgh and also lived in France – so I have this idea of doing a 'Bristol–Edinburgh–France' racing tribute: Alpe d'Huez ticks one of those boxes.

Chrissie: Write all those motivations down and also have a visual reminder of your goal – maybe make the hairpin bends of Alpe d'Huez your screensaver? I always remember Julie Dibens putting two big posters of Mirinda Carfrae and me in her turbo room to fuel her fire. So, what will success look like?

Katy: I want to finish having done my best. It would be great not to come last, though!

Matt: Now we have the A goal in the diary we can work backwards and plan some B races that fit around this. It's really important not just to focus on the end result but also have 'stepping-stone' goals that provide focus, break up the journey and an opportunity to measure and celebrate progress. They don't have to be triathlons necessarily, although you'll need to do a few before Alpe d'Huez to get race practice. Consistency in your training will be important, but it's also great to inject variety into your life and training plan to stop you getting stale. Races that you use for training are a superb way of doing this.

Katy: I went to Bristol University so maybe the Bristol Harbourside Triathlon in June and then an event in or around Edinburgh, perhaps even one with a sea swim – something that I'm very nervous about and which I said I would never do. I'd also really like to run a marathon, but not sure it's a good idea.

Matt: Alpe d'Huez is a huge challenge and, given that you're a novice at the sport, I wouldn't set two A goals. If you really wanted to do well in a marathon, and fulfil your running potential, the training programme would look very different to that aimed at long-course triathlon. That's not to say you won't become a faster runner from the tri training but setting, and then mentally focusing on, two big goals would mean that you'd risk compromising your training for both, and end up not being able to fulfil your potential in either. I'd suggest focusing on Alpe d'Huez, with other B and C races, and look at doing a marathon in late 2015 or 2016 – when you can build on your triathlon fitness but target the training specifically for the marathon distance. Now we've finished our wine and set that A goal, it's time to stop talking and get training. Let the journey to the finish line begin! ●

CHAPTER TWO

TRAINING FOR TRIATHLON

One thing I love about triathlon is that you have to master three separate disciplines, with the real art being to successfully combine them into *one sport*. This philosophy should guide all we do: the way we must train, the equipment we use and the techniques we adopt. We are not swimmers, cyclists or runners. We are triathletes. A case in point is bike position. Some athletes sacrifice everything to be aerodynamic and look like a Tour de France time-trial specialist. In doing so they compromise comfort, and are often seen walking/staggering/DNF'ing on the run because their back/legs/entire body have seized up. There are no bragging rights for a great bike split if you fail to cross the finish line.

Over the past 40 years, 'triathlon training' has become a specialist field. There is now a wealth of fantastic, valuable information and no shortage of 'experts' on the subject; however, it has also bred such a wide variety of practices, philosophies and parlance as to sometimes confuse, baffle and confound. It needn't be so.

This chapter includes sections that will shed light on the tri-training fundamentals, developing a triathlon programme, coping with injury, fitting sport into the rest of your life and whether or not coaches and gadgets are needed to facilitate the whole process.

The ultimate aim is to cut through the terminology, lift the veil of confusion and outline the tri-training basics so you can explore the minefield in more detail if your pounding heart desires.

KEEP IT SIMPLE: CUTTING THROUGH THE COMPLEXITY

At its heart triathlon training is simple. You swim, you bike and you run. Yet, it can seem so much more complicated and complex. Advice comes from left, right and centre. There are more training philosophies than I have had bike accidents (and that, dear reader, is an embarrassingly high number). Gadgets abound. Clothing and kit options are endless. We hear of lactate threshold or VO2 max. We have hill repeats, time trials (TTs) or tempo efforts. We have compression and ice baths. The terminology and jargon can be baffling. Then we have to combine three separate disciplines rather than just practising and perfecting one. It's no wonder some people get confused, put off, concerned or frustrated.

The good news? It really isn't that difficult or complex. Take my story for example: I believe that the foundation for my success lay in experiences I had before I really knew what 'training' was: the time I spent going up and down Himalayan mountains, the cycle touring I did with my supersized panniers, hiking to 5,000m or running without a care along the Thames towpath. I didn't have a clue about compression attire or recovery shakes. I didn't know that you shouldn't carry your bike spares in a bum bag. I'd never heard of the term VO_2 max, let alone known that I was probably doing things that would ultimately benefit that so-called 'max'. Even as a neo-professional I couldn't tell you what gearing I had on my bike. Yet my body and my mind became ever stronger.

My friend and I cycling to the base camp of Mount Everest in 2005.

If it was possible to go back and analyse the physiological demands placed on my body through being in Nepal or cycle touring, it's likely that they weren't too dissimilar to a systematic training programme. We did long 'aerobic' rides and worked on strength by climbing high mountains with rucksacks on our backs. This was often done at altitude where oxygen is limited. We did rides where we would ascend short hills, and where I would repeatedly sprint after the guys, mimicking interval sessions. My mind was also free of worry about what sessions I should or shouldn't be doing; of times, of targets, of pacing and of performance. And my nutrition, well, it may not have been complex but it contained the right mix of nutrients to fuel as well as facilitate recovery.

Despite becoming more structured, holistic and focused in my approach to triathlon over time, there's no doubt that rawness, hard work, passion and initial naivety counted for so much; and still do to this day.

Yes, in training for triathlon there's a lot of information to take in, but try not to let it confound or worry. You are at your best when you are least stressed, frustrated or anxious, when you commit to keeping things simple and relish the rawness of sport, rather than losing yourself in the minutiae and undermining the most important aspect of triathlon – keeping the 'fun' in fundamentals.

RETAINING THE FUN IN FUNDAMENTALS: TRI-TRAINING ESSENTIALS

PLANNING A PROGRAMME

No matter your ability or goal, it's likely that you want to develop a training programme to enable you to get from point B (where you are right now) to point A (your A race). Ideally, this will be a programme that is tailored to you. While triathlon training is very individual, there are fortunately some generic issues you should consider, and steps you can take, when devising an effective programme. These will help you to develop your own personal plan or, if you are coached, understand what you are being set or even feed into the process of programme development.

The reason it's difficult to develop a successful individualised training programme is that there are many personal variables to take into account. These include, but are by no means limited to: your goals, your strengths and weaknesses, your lifestyle and the time you have available, as well as your genetics, physiology, location and budget.

Let's take goals, strengths and weaknesses, and time available, in turn:

Goals

Your A race goal/s will shape your training. For example, if you're focusing on an Ironman, there's no point only doing rides that are an hour long and expecting miraculously to pull a five-hour bike split out of your posterior come race day. If you're doing a bike/run duathlon, there's not a lot of point in spending hours in the pool. If your goal is simply to finish a race, the training will likely be very different to that of someone who has the intention of qualifying for the World Championship or winning their age group.

Strengths and weaknesses

Identify your strengths and weaknesses, listing a maximum of three for each discipline. The ability to consume a whole packet of biscuits on a two-hour ride is not a valid strength and nor is your inability to resist said biscuits necessarily a weakness. I am thinking more along the lines of: my strength is hill climbing on the bike and a weakness is my lack of bike-handling skills. It's also good to have objective data to support your list, as our perceptions can be inaccurate. For example, if you're struggling to complete 100m in the pool in two minutes and your goal is to do an Ironman swim in 1 hour 10 minutes, then you will, quite rightly, see swimming as a current weakness. You can then look at the possible underlying cause/s – in this case, it could be poor technique and/or incorrect training – and then find solutions. It's useful if this analysis is focused on your A race. For example, Ironman Wales is a challenging bike course, so scrutinise your ability to ride strongly on hills. You'll need a programme that addresses and minimises your weaknesses, but also enables you to maximise your strengths.

Time available

Some athletes dedicate six hours per week to training, while others do twenty-plus hours. Divide your programme into weekly blocks, with at least one full rest day every seven to ten days. Beginners or those who are coming back from injury or illness, especially, may wish to have many more. Then consider how many hours you can and importantly *want* to spend chlorinated, saddled up or pounding pavements. You can then identify the 'always available' training slots and club sessions (if you're a member of one), as well as when 'possible/nice to have/if I'm lucky' opportunities might crop up.

Fantasies are all very well, but are rarely advantageous in this context. Be realistic and consult your spouse/children/employer/clairvoyant as necessary. Remember that psychological recovery is just as important as physical recovery and that means having some semblance of a life away from triathlon. Leave room for social activities and food shopping. There are few things worse than doing a six-hour bike ride and coming home to an empty fridge or having to go straight out to a children's party when you can hardly stand.

Those who work irregular hours may find the scheduling aspect particularly challenging. Thankfully the handy Q & A at page 64 offers specific ideas for the shift-working triathlete.

Having a 'traffic light' system is a good way of structuring training if you've got a life that varies from week to week in which consistency is hard to come by. Originally designed by coaches working with junior national-level athletes, it is equally effective for those who are not full-time professionals:

RED: During exam periods or when very fatigued, do whatever training you feel like and can fit in but with no pressure.
AMBER: During school terms, ensure 2–3 key sessions are done each week and an additional high-volume session.
GREEN: During school holidays, train as much as you can, with races also scheduled. Rest when essential, but at least one day off every 7–10 days.

Although it's very individual, I believe that at a minimum you should commit at least seven hours a week to Olympic-distance training, around ten hours for a half Ironman and fourteen hours for an Ironman. There are those who have got by with less, but this needs to be factored into the goal-setting process.

Based on the above, allocate time to each discipline. For example, if you have ten hours per week to train for an Olympic triathlon, you may wish to spend three hours swimming, five hours biking and two hours running. However, if your biking needs work you may wish to dedicate more time to cycling, and less to swimming and running.

THE DISCIPLINE, VOLUME AND INTENSITY

When getting down to the nitty-gritty of scheduling sessions within a programme, you'll need to consider the sport/discipline you are doing and the frequency, duration and intensity of the sessions, as outlined below.

The discipline

Your programme will primarily include separate swim, bike and run sessions as well as the 'brick'. This is when you combine two disciplines within the same workout, one after the other, with minimal or no break in between. Generally, a brick session consists of a back-to-back bike/run, but a brick could also be a swim/bike or, for duathletes, a run/bike workout. Training might also comprise strength and conditioning sessions, as well as time for rest and recovery (as covered in Chapters 6 and 10).

Duration and frequency (aka 'volume')

Duration is the length of the session and frequency is the number of times (usually per week) that you train in each particular discipline. There is a widely held belief in triathlon that more is better; I was in this camp. I used to add up how many hours or kilometres I did, and think that the higher the number, the better I would get – until I got injured and was forced to realise that quality trumps quantity every time. Yes, we race for hours, but greater volume does not always equate to improvement and can lead to plateauing or a decline in performance. Effective training is essentially doing the best you can with the time you have available. That certainly doesn't mean taking the path of least resistance, but it does mean training 'wise'. This often means adopting a 'less can be more' and 'biggest bang for your buck' philosophy.

Intensity

I'm sure you've heard athletes say 'I swam really easily in the pool today' . . . or 'I smashed those hard, eyeballs-out efforts on the bike.' What they are describing is intensity of effort. In short, *how hard* and/or physiologically demanding a session is. As the triathlon coach and physiologist Dr Andy Kirkland once said to me, intensity occurs on a scale starting at complete rest through to 'I think I'm going to explode'. Unfortunately, different coaches or sports scientists use a variety of terms to describe different intensity levels – which often confuses even the most experienced athlete. The information below will help you navigate around this complexity, explaining the changes that occur to our bodies when we train at different intensities, and helping you understand why training at different intensities can improve your performance.

Variations in intensity

If you're an endurance-sport novice, you will initially improve by doing your sessions at roughly the same 'steady Eddy' intensity. Yes, you will be able to finish a race this way, but if your aim is to get progressively faster you will need to train *at*, *above* and *below* the intensity that you want to sustain on race day. Again, using the car analogy: you want to have a range of different gears in order to be able to

ENERGY SYSTEMS AND FUEL SOURCES

You may be familiar with the terms *aerobic* (with oxygen) and *anaerobic* (without oxygen). While both these systems are always 'switched on', we use them in different proportions depending on how hard we are working. Lower intensity exercise is more aerobic and less fatiguing. Higher intensity exercise, and when we change pace a lot, is more anaerobic and more fatiguing. Regardless of whether you're doing a sprint or Ironman, triathlon is an endurance sport where the aerobic system is dominant. However, there will be times in a race – e.g. starts, surges or coming out of corners on the bike – when the anaerobic system is used.

You may have also heard triathletes and coaches use the term VO_2 max, which I mentioned earlier. VO_2 max is the maximum amount of oxygen your muscles can take in and use during exercise (maximal oxygen uptake), and is expressed numerically: the higher the number, the more oxygen your muscles need to use.

If you think of the body as a car, the engine (your muscles) requires a supply of gasoline (fuel) and oxygen in order to be able to function. The aerobic system is fuelled by fat and carbohydrate, with protein only comprising about 5 per cent of the energy required. Carbohydrates are stored in the body as glycogen and we have about 60 to 90 minutes' worth of glycogen stored, depending in part on the intensity at which we are exercising. Our fat reserves, below the skin and in muscle, are much larger and they release more energy per gram than carbohydrate, but they release this energy more slowly. A steady supply of carbohydrate is also needed for the breakdown of fat into energy. This can come from the body's glycogen or ingested carbohydrate. Carbohydrate is more oxygen efficient than fat. Put another way, burning fat requires a lot more oxygen than burning carbohydrate.

Fat will be the predominant fuel when doing lower to moderate intensity exercise. As exercise intensity increases, there is a gradual shift from fats towards carbohydrate and, at really high intensities, fat simply cannot provide enough energy. If the muscle glycogen stores are also depleted, only low intensity exercise is then possible. However, as discussed in Chapter 7, if we get our nutrition right, then this should not happen.

Some scientists suggest that these alterations to how our body works occur at clear *threshold points* but, for most of us, the changes are far subtler. Nevertheless, the term 'threshold' is often heard in triathlon circles and so it's worth knowing its meaning in the training context.

The purpose of triathlon training is to increase the capacity of your 'engine', i.e. to deliver more oxygen to power your hard-working muscles, as well as to improve your efficiency, i.e. so that each contraction of your muscles requires less fuel.

perform to your potential. In a nutshell, by incorporating varied intensity training into your programme, you stand a much better chance of knocking seconds, minutes and even hours off your PB.

> **I frequently used perceived effort to gauge how hard I was working, with 1 being at rest and 10 being 'eyeballs popping out, balls to the wall, I want to vomit'.**

METHODS OF MEASURING INTENSITY

Many triathletes go too hard in easy sessions or during rest intervals and too easy in hard sessions, and wonder why they don't see any improvement come race day. So how do you actually measure intensity to ensure you are getting the maximum benefit from your training? There are several ways including: perceived effort, pace/speed, heart rate and power. These are considered in turn below.

Perceived effort

Being able to perceive and control effort accurately is one of the most important but sadly neglected skills in triathlon. To develop this skill requires conscious practice. I frequently used perceived effort to gauge how hard I was working, with 1 being at rest and 10 being 'eyeballs popping out, balls to the wall, I want to vomit'. A Swedish scientist called Professor Gunnar Borg invented a slightly different scale with no mention of eyeballs. It's called the Rating of Perceived Exertion (RPE) or the Borg Scale and is often used in scientific and triathlon training literature. The scale goes from 6 to 20, with 6 being no exertion and 20 being maximum effort. The seemingly strange range of 6–20 follows the general heart rate of a healthy young adult: the Borg number multiplied by 10 matches the heart rate. For instance, a perceived exertion of 12 would be expected to coincide with a heart rate of roughly 120 beats per minute.

THE BORG RATING OF PERCEIVED EXERTION (RPE) SCALE

RATING	PERCEIVED EXERTION
6	Sedentary – no exertion
7–8	Very, very light
9–10	Very light
11–12	Light
13–14	Somewhat hard
15–16	Hard
17–18	Very hard
19	Extremely hard
20	Maximum exertion

Pace/speed

A combination of perceived effort and pace was used to guide and measure my sessions. Pace is normally expressed as a combination of distance and time; such as 3 minutes 55 seconds per km (when running) or 1 minute 30 seconds per 100m (in the pool). A clock at the side of the pool (or a simple wristwatch), a bike computer and a GPS watch can be used to calculate pace. If you are running on a track or somewhere with distance markers, you can simply use a regular watch.

To use pace effectively to guide my training, my coaches needed to know my approximate race pace. This was based on certain target sessions as well as previous race performances. For example, if my 3.8km Ironman swim split was 52 minutes, my race pace would be 1 minute 22 per 100m. Hence, when Dave told me to 'swim at Ironman pace' during a training session, I knew exactly what he meant. Of course, pace varies based on the race duration (as considered on page 256). For example, in an Olympic-distance event I would be able to sustain 1 minute 19 per 100m for the duration of the 1.5km. My programme was, however, focused on my A goal of Ironman.

Note, too, that pace can vary according to conditions and hence isn't always the best barometer for intensity. For example, swimming against the current in choppy open water may slow you down to the speed of a sea snail, despite you working at race intensity. Similarly, if you wish to maintain a specific pace when running up a hill, your exercise intensity will obviously increase. Nonetheless, in a controlled environment such as a swimming pool, running track, flat road/trail or when on a treadmill or turbo, pace is more useful as a measure.

Predicting your race pace comes with experience so, if you're a beginner, you may initially find it difficult to know what your race pace should be. That said, a lot can be done in training to develop understanding and the guidance that follows should help.

Heart rate

Heart rate can correlate well to exercise intensity; in short, as you work harder your heart rate goes up. Hence, by measuring your heart rate during training you can have a clearer idea about the intensity at which you are working. However, as the Q & A at page 68 makes clear, there are limitations, as factors like external temperature, anxiety, caffeine, altitude, fatigue and levels of hydration can also influence your heart rate. Keep in mind, too, that the heart-rate response to changing intensity is not immediate – the so-called cardiac lag means it takes several minutes at the start of exercise for your heart rate to match any change in effort.

Power

Some athletes use power meters on the bike – devices that measure the force (in watts) being applied to the pedals. See page 70 for the pros and cons of using power as a measure of how hard you're working.

TRIATHLON TRAINING ZONES

'This is all very well,' you may be saying, 'but how do you actually decide what intensity to train at and for how long and how often, and hence develop a programme based around this?' What follows is the specific philosophy and approach that my coach Dave Scott used to formulate my training programmes.

When exercising at different intensities you place varying demands on your body, and your body responds in different ways. These variations can be grouped into workloads or, as Dave calls them, *training zones*. Dave identifies the following six main types of training zone, in ascending order of intensity:

> Recovery

> Cruise

> Aerobic

> Lactate threshold (LT)

> VO$_2$ max

> Anaerobic capacity

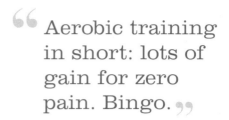

Aerobic training in short: lots of gain for zero pain. Bingo.

It's worth reiterating that, although Dave calls it 'lactate threshold', this is in fact a zone, rather than a clear transition point or switch as the term 'threshold' might initially imply.

We will now take a closer look at each of the training zones, with Dave contributing examples from my programme to add context and a little colour.

Recovery

This is the lowest intensity zone. Warm-ups and cool-downs should be done in this zone, as can very easy, active recovery sessions; for example, those following a big race or in the off-season (see page 300). This work would be the equivalent to 7–8 on the Borg Scale.

Cruise

The workload in this zone is light to moderate, undertaken at a steady pace and without any discomfort. Ideally, it should follow days when you have done a long session or more intense workout, and also be used as recovery between hard intervals. This would equate to 9–10 on the Borg Scale.

Aerobic

Aerobic training is moderate intensity exercise that should feel relatively comfortable and not too taxing. It would measure about 11–12 on the Borg Scale. Aerobic training helps to develop efficient muscles, strengthens tendons and bones, teaches your body to spare glycogen and use fat as a fuel, and facilitates recovery from more taxing efforts. In short: lots of gain for zero pain. Bingo.

Insight

DAVE SCOTT on aerobic training

Aerobic training should comprise around 70 per cent of the total workout time for the bike and run and approximately 50 per cent for the swim. The training intensity can be higher for the swim because the water cools the body and allows the athlete to recover more quickly. Chrissie did a few sessions entirely at an aerobic intensity; however, it was more commonly combined with higher intensity workloads. For example, she would do a set of VO_2-max hill repeats on the bike, and then follow this with a 30-minute aerobic intensity time trial on flat or rolling terrain – doing this aerobic work with hill-fatigued legs definitely gives bang for buck! ●

Lactate threshold

Your heart is pounding, your legs are starting to feel wobbly, you're breathing deeply and you start to lose the ability to talk. These uncomfortable symptoms mark the transition to the next zone. Working at an intensity at or slightly below the lactate threshold can help improve your resistance to fatigue, increase your race pace and endurance and enable you to recover more quickly from short bursts of speed.

Training in this zone should feel comfortably hard, and is sometimes called 'tempo' (especially in the running context). Some coaches like to use the 'talk test': if you can say 'supercalifrajalisticexpialidocious' and are not hyperventilating, you are probably at, or below, this threshold. Threshold work would be around 15–16 on the Borg Scale, and just below would be about 13–14. It is not as demanding as the higher intensity zones, and hence the recovery from such workouts is much quicker.

Lactate-threshold work can be done as a single block or divided into shorter segments, with a rest interval in between. By separating a block into shorter segments, you can maintain a higher intensity throughout the workout. The length of time the intensity can be sustained for is very individual, and also depends on the discipline. In terms of swimming, if you're a beginner you may be able to do a block that totals 10–15 minutes and, at the other end of the spectrum, pros can do 45–50 minutes. For a beginner on the bike it might total 20 minutes, but up to 90 minutes for top-level athletes. On the run, a beginner might do 15–20 minutes at lactate threshold and the more advanced or professional athlete 60–75 minutes.

VO$_2$ max (aerobic capacity)

Nearing the upper end is the zone called maximal oxygen uptake (or VO$_2$ max). VO$_2$-max training aims to develop the body's ability to consume oxygen and is done by stressing the oxygen delivery and processing system to its limit – in short, you develop your aerobic capacity. VO$_2$-max training comes in the form of high intensity, rapid breathing, high heart-rate work followed by a rest interval. The effort should be hard but not 'all out' otherwise you would fatigue too quickly and not be able to complete the whole session. The RPE would be around 17–18 on the Borg Scale.

The set of high intensity intervals should total between 12 and 24 minutes, with each hard effort lasting from 2 minutes up to about 7 minutes, repeated 3–8 times. For example, on the run, if you are a beginner to this type of training, you could do

DAVE SCOTT on lactate-threshold training

On a Thursday afternoon, Chrissie would do a two-hour ride, with a 60–90-minute segment at lactate threshold intensity. At the end of her longer Saturday ride, she would do 90 minutes at that intensity, but it would be broken down into blocks: for example, 1 × 30 minutes, 2 × 20 minutes, 2 × 10 minutes with a 5-minute rest interval, at cruise intensity, between each effort. An example of a lactate-threshold session that Chrissie might do in the pool would be 8 × 250m with a send-off/leave time of 3 minutes 30 seconds for each (meaning she would leave the wall every 3 minutes 30 seconds), which would allow her about 12 seconds of full rest between each one if she swam at a threshold pace of 1 minute 19 seconds per 100m.

I would also prescribe mixed threshold work, with segments of a session at threshold and just below that threshold. It might be easier to explain this in terms of pace:

Level 1: 4.10–4.20km/h

Level 2: 4.05–4.09km/h

Level 3: 4.04–3.56km/h (Chrissie's threshold pace)

Some example sessions, with a total of 27–30 minutes of LT zone work, might be:

> 10 minutes at Level 1, 10 minutes at Level 2 and 10 minutes at Level 3, done continuously and without a rest interval.

> 9 × 3 minutes broken down into 3 × 3 minutes at each level, with 20 seconds recovery between each

> 9 × 3 minutes broken down into 3 minutes at Level 1, 3 minutes at Level 3 and 3 minutes at Level 2, with 20 seconds recovery between each. ●

DAVE SCOTT on VO_2-max training

I gave Chrissie one VO_2-max workout per week per discipline. She sometimes did VO_2-max sessions in the swim and on the bike, or swim and run on the same day, but never a VO_2-max run and a bike session on the same day as this would overstress the body. Let's take a swim set as an example: she would warm up and then do 4 × 75m with an increasing amount of rest between each one, but the aim was to always hit the same pace of about 58 seconds per 75m, which I knew to be equivalent to her VO_2-max intensity. She would then swim 225m and retain that same pace. This was followed by a 4–5-minute cruise. The block would be repeated four times. ●

4 × 3 minutes with a rest interval of around 3–5 minutes (at recovery intensity) in between each effort. It is important that you can maintain the same pace for every hard effort, and have a near complete recovery before the next.

Anaerobic capacity/speed work

When you are working so hard that the aerobic system cannot provide the energy required, the anaerobic system has to leap into action. Although triathlons are aerobic events, there are gains to be had from incorporating anaerobic work into your programme. It helps promote overall speed and power, enabling you to improve resistance to fatigue and your body's ability to use oxygen more effectively. Doing high intensity work can also help you train for instances when bursts of speed may be required. This is especially relevant to professional and more experienced athletes, who may need to sprint at the start of the swim, accelerate after a turn buoy or out of corners, or even up the pace as they enter the finish chute.

Exercising in the anaerobic capacity zone comprises hard efforts, measuring around 19 on the Borg Scale, followed by a longer rest interval. Each hard effort should be between 30 seconds and about 2 minutes long, for between 6 and 10 minutes in total. I would suggest a 1 to 2 or even 1 to 3 work/rest ratio, e.g. if you do 1 minute of hard effort, the rest interval would be 2 minutes (1:2) or 3 minutes (1:3).

A WORD ON INTERVALS

Intervals can be structured in blocks of time or distance, for example 4 × 1 minute or 5 × 1km repeats, or they can be less formulaic. This is sometimes known as 'fartlek'. Rather than being something that you get when you've consumed excessive fibre, it's a Swedish term for 'speedplay'. Used mainly in the running context, it simply means a type of training in which the terrain, intensity and pace are continually varied. After a warm-up, you essentially play with speed by running at moderate to high intensity for a time/distance of your choice and then cruise until you're ready to go again. I usually do such workouts without wearing a watch and select markers such as trees, buildings or lampposts as my interval finish line. For example, I might run hard for three lampposts and run easy for two, and then run hard for two and easy for one. It can also be done on the bike and in the swim, and is a fun way of doing intervals without the structure and pressure.

DAVE SCOTT on anaerobic capacity training

This was a very important part of Chrissie's training. It can be fatiguing, though, especially in the running context, and so we tended to be a little more conservative in terms of the anaerobic run volume she did.

One example of an anaerobic run set was as follows: she would warm up at cruise intensity, then do 2 × 90 seconds, 3 × 30 seconds, 2 × 75 seconds, 3 × 30 seconds, 2 × 60 seconds – with the rest interval being long enough to enable her to perform near to maximal effort for the whole set. ●

RACE PACE/INTENSITY WORK

Chapter 9 explores the issue of pacing in a race in more detail. However, if you, like me, want to use pace to guide and measure your training, this means knowing, and then doing sessions, *at, above and below your predicted race pace*. In addition to the physiological benefits, doing workouts – or segments of workouts – at race pace enables you to discern what this actually *feels like* and can act as a huge confidence builder.

So how do race-pace sessions work in practice? For example, with Dave I did some sessions at race pace, such as those 90-minute time trials on the bike. However, he might also split up a longer race-pace block into segments. For example, in preparation for Challenge Roth and the Ironman World Championship in 2011, I would hit the running track and do the following set at my target Ironman race pace of around 4 mins/km:

2 × 400m + 1,200m + 2 × 600m + 1,200m + 2 × 400m (with 200m jog recovery)

I also did a lot of what he termed 'swing pace' or mixed intensity. For example, a run session where I would do a kilometre at a pace 25 seconds faster than race pace (3:35 mins/km), and then 500m at a pace 25 seconds slower than race pace (4:25 mins/km), and repeat this 6–8 times. He would also get me to do my long runs with some faster, shorter efforts at the beginning, followed by three or four blocks of 20 minutes at 4 mins/km with a 5-minute cruise rest interval. In doing this I was also able to gain intuitive skills at measuring RPE and sense exactly what the happy medium (race pace and intensity) felt like.

A SUMMARY OF THE DIFFERENT TRAINING ZONES

WORKLOAD/ ZONE	ENERGY SYSTEM AND FUEL SOURCE	DESCRIPTION AND APPLICATION	RPE
Recovery	Aerobic 70 per cent fat, 30 per cent carbohydrate	• Exercise should feel very easy • Warm-ups and cool-downs, very easy recovery sessions and post-race exercise	7–8
Cruise	Aerobic 60 per cent fat, 40 per cent carbohydrate	• Light to moderate intensity exercise • Feel very controlled, relatively easy and without discomfort • Follows days when you have done a long session or more intense workout or used as recovery between hard intervals	9–10

Aerobic	Aerobic
	
	50 per cent fat, 50 per cent carbohydrate
		• Moderate intensity
		• Feel controlled and not excessively taxing
		• Only starts to feel hard if
		  - you've been training for over three hours or so
		  - the weather is hot
		  - you've not been fuelling effectively
		• Top end of this zone is Ironman pace
		• Comprises 70 per cent of your total training volume (for bike and run) and 50 per cent for the swim
			11–12

WORKLOAD/ ZONE	ENERGY SYSTEM AND FUEL SOURCE	DESCRIPTION AND APPLICATION	RPE
Lactate threshold (LT)	Aerobic and anaerobic glycolysis 40 per cent fat, 60 per cent carbohydrate to 10 per cent fat, 90 per cent carbohydrate	• Positive result to the 'talk test' • Lower end is usually consistent with half Ironman intensity and feels comfortably hard • Top end is similar to the intensity at which you would do a sprint triathlon	Threshold 15–16 (just below this would be 13–14)

VO_2 max	Anaerobic glycolysis
	
	> 90 per cent carbohydrate
	
	Fat oxidisation is impaired
		• Unless you're racing at ITU level or on very hilly courses you'll rarely enter this domain when you race
		• It needs to be done sparingly as you don't want your muscles to become too accustomed to the process of anaerobic glycolysis because . . .
		  - It may compromise your ability to use aerobic pathways during exercise and will not help your race performance
		  - It's very fatiguing and may limit your ability to train the next day
		• Negative result to the talk test (i.e. if you can say a full sentence, then you're not in this zone)
			17–18

Anaerobic capacity	Anaerobic glycolysis Mostly carbohydrate, fat oxidisation is severely impaired	• Hard efforts (of 30 seconds to 2 minutes), followed by a longer rest interval • An accumulation of lactic acid is expected • As above, use sparingly, especially when running	19

WARM-UPS AND COOL-DOWNS

Given that it takes 5–10 minutes for the aerobic system to start functioning and the blood to start flowing, all sessions should include warm-ups of around that length, ideally in the same discipline as the upcoming session, and at recovery intensity. For example, if it's a run session, walk briskly or jog slowly; if cycling do a slow spin; or swim slowly before embarking on harder swim efforts. The same goes for cool-downs, which should be roughly the same duration, and which start the recovery process.

ADJUSTING FOR ABILITY AND EXPERIENCE

Triathlon novices, especially those without an endurance-sport background, should focus initially on swimming, biking and running consistently (i.e. maintaining the frequency of sessions) – this alone will lead to improvements. That means trying to fit in two or even three sessions for each discipline every week, if possible. The intensity should not be too high as it may overload and fatigue your body, from which you will need time to recover. After 6–12 months, you may wish to progress to harder and more specific sessions. That's not to say that, as a novice, you can't sometimes push yourself, but training at a comfortable and moderate effort level initially will enable you to develop the base endurance, skills and technique necessary to advance.

In addition to changing the frequency of sessions, specific sessions can also be modified to suit your ability and experience. This can be done by adjusting:

> the distance or duration of the entire session or set of intervals;

> the segment length(s) within the set;

> the rest interval;

> any combination of the above.

If you feel that you are fatiguing and cannot hold a desired RPE – or pace, power or heart rate if you are using those measurements – then you should alter one/some of the aforementioned variables so that the desired intensity can be maintained. If not, the purpose of the session is lost.

PUTTING IT ALL TOGETHER: SOME KEY PRINCIPLES

The different training zones can be incorporated into a training programme bearing in mind the following tri-training principles and practices:

1. Interconnectivity: Essentially the impact that given training sessions, both those of the same discipline (i.e. swim, bike or run) and of different disciplines, have on the others within your programme. The correct scheduling of these sessions maximises the benefit that can be accrued from the different sessions you do.

2. Balance: Linked to the first point, interconnectivity requires that the programme be carefully balanced to get the appropriate mix of the different training zones.

3. Specificity: Every session should have a purpose, whether that's to recover from a previous session or to raise the heart rate close to its maximum.

4. Integration: As we have seen, different training zones can be incorporated into one session (a mixed intensity session). For example, you could do a set of hard VO_2-max intervals, followed by a longer period of aerobic zone work.

5. Variety: A programme should incorporate variety – for example, in the types of session, the training environment or the people with whom you train – in order to provide different stimuli and sustain interest and motivation (see page 86 for more details).

6. Moving feast: Linked to the above point, training is an iterative process that must evolve over time. As the old adage goes, 'If you do what you've always done, you'll always get what you've always got.' When I first started working with Dave, I was reluctant to abandon the training programme I had previously followed with my first coach, Brett Sutton. However, as you will see in the coaching section (page 73), to improve I had to accept that my training needed to change subtly. This also meant communicating with Dave on a regular basis so that he could monitor my progress and adjust the programme accordingly.

7. Consistency: Given the specific purpose of, and interconnectivity between, each session, retaining consistency is important; so try your best to follow your programme as set.

8. Flexibility: Accept the need to be flexible and change your plan as the situation demands. Consistency with flexibility. Isn't this paradoxical? Not really. Triathlon is just one part of a much fuller life. You have work, family and social commitments, you may get ill or injured, the swimming pool could be closed for refurbishment or a dog might bury your bike shoe (just ask my husband Tom, who spent hours searching for his shoe and missed a bike session, only to discover that it had been buried by a friend's crafty canine). Things crop up and we must all be prepared to adapt.

PLANNING ACROSS THE SEASON

You may have heard triathletes and coaches mention the term 'periodisation'. This is essentially the process of dividing an annual programme into various stages, each having very specific training objectives. It's difficult to provide generic advice on how to best periodise your training, given the very specific nature of our goals, lifestyles and abilities and the fact that, as we just saw, things crop up and plans often have to change. However, a few pointers are as follows:

Count backwards from your A race, schedule some B and C races beforehand (see page 31), and then break the season into 4–6 week blocks. Dave called these microcycles. In each of these blocks or microcycles, you should set process goals: things you want to achieve in the period. For one block, you could have goals such as:

> complete a main set in the pool of 10 × 100m with a 2-minute send-off;

> progress my long run from 60 minutes to 90 minutes;

> compete in my first 25-mile time trial.

All these goals should build towards and complement your A race. Planning two or three microcycles rather than a whole season in advance gives you plenty of 'wiggle room' but still keeps you moving forward. Having different goals in each block will give your body and mind diverse stimuli, which accounts for two of the most important principles of training: variety and iteration.

In terms of training zones, I believe that intermediate and advanced athletes should incorporate some higher intensity work all year round (aside from the off-season, of course). However, as just considered, the difficulty of the sessions should be adjusted depending on the stage of the season.

There should be plenty of sustained race-pace work close to your A race and a period of recovery (taper) to ensure you are fresh on race day. See Chapter 9 for more details.

Planning this way, while not rocket science, allows you to build a programme that is specific to your needs, can be easily adapted and will keep you focused to perform at your best when it matters.

I hope that the above has provided a starter-for-ten in terms of understanding the tri-training fundamentals. It cannot answer every question you may have, but should act as a springboard to empower you to develop your own programme or, if you are coached, better understand the programme you have been set.

I'll close with a little reminder: a programme is a guide – it's not set in stone. Aim to do at least 80 per cent of your planned sessions, but accept that the schedule is also malleable. The world is not going to stop revolving and your race preparation isn't going to fall apart if you have to miss or revise a session. Retain perspective and remember that you can only ever do the best you can in the context of your life.

A TYPICAL TRAINING PROGRAMME

On the next page is an example of my typical weekly training programme, as prescribed by Dave. It dates from August 2011 as I prepared for Timberman 70.3 and the World Ironman Championship. Please bear in mind that my training was tailored to me – I was a professional athlete, with a specific background and physiology, an extensive support network, individual goals and 24 hours a day to devote to triathlon. This is included purely as an insight into my training, rather than something that you should try to emulate or copy. In addition, I've included one of Katy Campbell's weekly programmes from a month before her A race.

MY IRONMAN TRAINING PROGRAMME – AN EXAMPLE WEEK

	MORNING	MIDDAY	AFTERNOON
Monday	**Swim: 4.5km** 1.5km total lactate threshold zone work, 500m drills and short VO$_2$-max repeats		**Bike: 3 hour** 8 × 3 minutes at lactate threshold (RI* 2 minutes) and 12 × 6 minutes at sub lactate threshold (RI 30 seconds)
Tuesday	**Run: 1 hr 15** VO$_2$-max session on treadmill. Includes pick-ups of 6 × 30–60 seconds plus of 6 × 3 minutes at VO$_2$ max (RI 2 minutes) at varying inclines and a longer 15-minute segment just below threshold	**Swim: 5km** 2–3km of threshold zone work with 500m–1km aerobic or cruise with paddles, pull buoy and band to finish	**Run: 40 minutes** Cruise on gravel trails Strength and conditioning (60 minutes)
Wednesday	**Swim: 3km** Includes 1km of lactate threshold efforts (in shorter segments of 75–150m)	**Bike/Run Brick** **Bike: 3 hours** Set 1 (hill repeats): 4 × 5 minutes climb, very hard effort with descent as RI Set 2: 30 minutes at 42km/h (broken into 6 minutes, 5 minutes, 4 minutes, 3 minutes, 2 minutes, 10 × 1 minute with 60–90 seconds RI) Set 3: 8 × 6 minutes at 36–37km/h **Run: 15km** Build for 3km; 10km alternating 1km at 3:35 mins/km pace and 1km at 4:05–4:10 mins/km. No RI. 2km cruise to finish.	
Thursday	**Bike: 2 hours** 60 minutes of hard 5–10-minute hill repeats and 20 minutes TT to finish	**Swim: 5km** Similar to Tuesday swim	**Bike: 2 hours** Includes 60–90 minutes of TT, average 40–41km/h
Friday	**Run** Session on flats and hills. 2 minutes on flats (3:35 mins/km for first minute and 3:45 mins/km for second minute) straight into 4-minute hill, holding same effort as the final minute on the flat. Jog downhill. Repeat 8 times.	**Swim: 4km** Recovery	**Strength and conditioning: 60 minutes**

	MORNING	AFTERNOON
Saturday	Swim: 4.5km Includes 2.5km of threshold and VO_2-max work and 1km aerobic with paddles, pull buoy band to finish	Bike: 4.5–5 hours Includes 70 minutes at Ironman race intensity, 45 minutes' threshold-intensity climb and 40 minutes' TT to finish
Sunday	Run: 28–32km Includes 4 × 2km at 3:55 mins/km, 2km at 4:20 mins/km and 6 × 5 minutes at 3:40–3:50 mins/km with 2 minutes RI	Strength and conditioning: 60 minutes

KATY CAMPBELL'S PROGRAMME – A MONTH BEFORE HER A RACE

	MORNING	AFTERNOON
Monday	Rest day	
Tuesday	Bike: 18km (approx. 45 minutes) commute to work at cruise intensity	Bike: 90 minutes with 30-minute cruise warm-up, 60-minute TT at lactate threshold effort
Wednesday	Swim: Pyramid swim set 300, 200, 100, 50, 25, 25, 50, 100, 200, 300m. RI 20 seconds. Increase pace as distance instances, building from cruise to VO_2-max effort on 25m (teaching good pace judgement)	
Thursday	Brick: 50km bike (cruise 20km and 10km at race intensity)/5km run (5km at 4:45 mins/km pace)	
Friday	Active recovery: 30 minute bike or swim	
Saturday	Swim: 3km open water	Bike: 120km steady effort in race kit
Sunday	Run: 23km (include off-road). Slowly build to halfway, then 4 × 5 minutes at 4:35 mins/km (1 min RI) and cruise to finish	

Shifting to Tri and Juggling Balls – Fitting Triathlon into Your Life

Q 'I'm a children's nurse and work a mixture of 12-hour night and day shifts in a random pattern. This makes setting and following a structured diet and exercise plan difficult. What suggestions do you have to get around this problem and help me train myself into Ironman shape?'

SIMON WEAVER

A Your need to balance tri training with your career, family, house upkeep and other obligations is common the triathlon world over: not least because of the time- and energy-intensive nature of our sport. As an amateur, I was a pro juggler. I trained for about 20–22 hours a week, had a full-time job, and squeezed in social and family time too. Granted, I didn't have a child at that point – which adds another ball to the mix. However, the thousands of age groupers who cross Ironman finish lines prove that combining a variety of activities is possible, with careful planning, time management, organisation and flexibility. Indeed, it's that which I always find so inspirational.

Before we go on to look at the practical tips for effectively fitting triathlon into your busy and unstructured life, let's consider the importance of *perception*. Triathlon should be an activity that, on balance, generates positive rather than negative emotions. There will always be times when we get stressed with what life throws at us or frustrated that we can't do something as planned, but our hobby should never be the thing that causes us anguish. If it is, then maybe it's time to change either our approach or our chosen sport.

Remember that you're not (yet!) a pro, so you can't expect to train/race like one. Instead of worrying about what you can't do, focus on what you *can* do. You may see your shift work as being unstructured and detrimental. Others would relish the opportunity to train at different times of the day, and also enjoy the variety that such a life brings. It's about changing the lens through which we view things to ensure we are 'cup half full'.

A last word on perception: try not to draw comparisons with others. There will always be those who do more (or at least claim to). This is your life, and as long as you are living it to the full, that's all that matters.

In terms of practical advice: prioritisation, time management and organisation are paramount. Take a yearly, monthly and weekly approach to planning, ensuring that the non-negotiable activities and obligations are factored in at the outset. In terms of triathlon, the advice in this guide can help you organise your season, choose your A race and better understand the benefit of different training sessions that can assist you in the planning and prioritisation process. This will enable you to create some structure that fits around your shift work, lifestyle, physiology and goal amid what seems to be an unstructured existence.

> " Make hay while the sun shines (or doesn't, as the case may be). If you have time to train, use it. Don't waste time faffing, ironing your T-shirt or deliberating about what gel to eat. "

For example, look at your typical week and carve out slots that you can certainly allocate to training, and then look at secondary times that may provide additional training opportunities. Determine your key sessions (based on your strengths and weaknesses), which you should always try to complete, and then less essential, supporting workouts. Place the key sessions in the 'always open' time slots, and then fit the supporting workouts in if you can. It sounds simple, but that way you have a better chance of completing the specific and foundation sessions, and hence retaining some consistency and progression. Of course, it will be important to adapt your schedule when needed. At times, you may have to abbreviate and shorten sets or sessions, or drop one altogether. Frustration serves no purpose here. Just accept this as your reality, and move on.

Although I can't tell you how many hours a week you should personally train for an Ironman, remember that quality trumps quantity every time. Often a 40-minute run with high intensity efforts can be more beneficial than a long steady slog. In this sense a turbo trainer is invaluable. No free-wheeling means that the time you need to invest is much less than on the road and equals serious 'bang for your buck'. Set it up the night before so you can wake up and jump straight on.

Q&A

Make hay while the sun shines (or doesn't, as the case may be). If you have time to train, use it. Don't waste time faffing, ironing your T-shirt or deliberating about what gel to eat.

Multitasking is also useful – for example, running or biking your commute. A good set of lights can make nocturnal journeys possible. These commuting cycles and runs can be structured sessions (intervals, hills, sprints, tempo) if the road conditions and traffic allow. Or perhaps there is a swimming pool en route where you can stop, do a session and then head to work.

It sounds like you are on your feet for much of the day, and are likely to be tired from working varied shifts, including nights. It will be paramount that you prioritise getting enough rest, and not trying to fill every non-work minute with training and risk stressing your body further. Of course, you can use your lunch break to squeeze in a run or strength and conditioning session, or even do some squats while waiting for the kettle to boil. However, if you get a break during the day, think about also using it to get some rest – your triathlon performance and overall health will be all the better for it.

On the subject of rest and recovery, you could wear compression attire under your nurse's uniform – if permitted. And don't forget the importance of nutrition for

effective training and recovery. If time is short, try to prepare large batches of food that you can freeze if necessary. Also, have to hand easily transportable, nutritious grub – muesli bars, smoothies, bananas, rice cakes with peanut butter, sweet potatoes in foil – that you can eat on the 'fly' (see recipes on page 193). Perhaps you can also store food at work so you don't always have to go to a shop, café or restaurant to buy your next meal.

Many people prefer training with others for performance/social/motivation reasons, but I usually train alone (see page 86 for more on this). This means that I don't have to plan around others, never let anyone down and prioritise my own goals. It's not always as enjoyable, but it does mean that training is 100 per cent focused on my own needs and schedule.

If you have a partner/children, you could make sessions 'family time'. Three-time Ironman World Champion Craig Alexander does a long run with his family biking beside him. Such an approach ensures they are fully involved in the journey and the pursuit of a shared goal. If you have a small child, consider buying or borrowing a running buggy or bike seat so that they can come along for the ride. And it's not only family: talking openly with work colleagues about your Ironman goals can make them a little more understanding and accommodating. Maybe there is scope to swap shifts occasionally if you have a tolerant boss or workmate? Even better, maybe you could persuade them to also do a triathlon so that they can share the journey, and increase the level of workplace empathy with your training and racing plans.

Ultimately, remember that doing triathlon is your choice; it is your hobby and one that should bring joy rather than stress or anxiety. Juggling balls effectively is one part of the challenge, but when you do manage it, the achievement is so much more satisfying. So, focus on what you can do; controlling the controllables, making the best of any situation and ultimately always trying to stay positive.

Gadgets and Gizmos –
Measuring Performance

Q 'I am currently training for my first Ironman and want to know if I should train using a heart-rate monitor or something else. Everyone I speak to has a different opinion and I'm getting confused by all the technology options.'

ROB MARTIN

A I'm not surprised you're baffled. We're bombarded with an array of training philosophies and gadgets: the 'must have' silver bullets that claim to revolutionise our performance. Nearly every piece of data imaginable can be tracked, recorded and analysed using heart-rate monitors, power meters, GPSs, lap and cadence counters and more. With such a smorgasbord of technological options it can be incredibly confusing and, if you choose to trial or use such gizmos, it can hit the wallet hard, too.

Choosing a training philosophy and supporting gadgets is highly individual. I'm generally a 'back to basics' person: I used to bike in Nepal with nothing but my breath to tell me whether I was working hard. I cycle-toured in Argentina, with 30kg of kit in my panniers; pushing, pulling and sweating over rocks, glaciers and rivers. There wasn't a computer in sight, yet it made me as strong as an ox. I won my first Ironman on a road bike with regular wheels, unaware that I was supposed to be sporting an aero-helmet, heart-rate monitor or power meter. As a professional, I did use pace to guide my swim (the clock at the side of the pool) and run (GPS watch, track or treadmill) training – but my general motto is 'keep it simple'. Others disagree and worship data deities. I think the answer lies in-between being technologically naked and a slave to every gadget.

Ultimately. we should assess each technological option based on whether they help, hinder or have zero impact. And even if helpful, do the financial costs outweigh the benefits? Consider some of the pros and cons of the most common measurable markers.

Heart rate

Heart-rate monitors measure . . . yes, you've guessed it . . . your heart rate and therefore purport to gauge the intensity of effort (measuring intensity is covered in the training fundamentals section on page 42). This is commonly done through a transmitter housed in a chest strap, which then sends an electromagnetic signal to a receiver (such as a watch or phone) that displays the heart rate, or a wristwatch with an inbuilt monitor that measures the radial pulse. Not all monitors are made equal, as some are much more accurate than others. In addition, simple versions may only display your current heart rate whereas more elaborate monitors can record time, calculate the average and maximum heart rate for a given period, and even sound an alarm if you reach or exceed a predetermined target heart-rate zone.

First, let's consider the pros. Beginners, especially, may find it difficult to differentiate between easy/steady/hard/all-out effort, and different heart-rate zones can assist athletes in exploring these different intensities and exerting more control over their effort level. Such monitors can also provide positive reinforcement and motivation as you have a tangible number that indicates you're ticking the 'intensity box'. You can set targets for how quickly your heart rate recovers after harder efforts, which can be an indicator of fitness, and also see if you can hit the same or faster times but at a lower heart rate. Coaches also like such tools because they provide quantifiable feedback and help hold you accountable.

And the cons? Wear a heart-rate monitor on a rollercoaster and you'll see that the rate will climb near its max. Are you working flat out? No, it's just that your sympathetic nervous system is highly stimulated, and the same goes for a race when the adrenalin is running higher than normal . . . meaning that heart rate may not always be the best indicator of how hard you are working. In addition, it is also affected by other external factors, such as diet (especially caffeine), stress, clothing, (de)hydration, weather, altitude and more. Also, such monitors use formulas to calculate zones, but they tend to be generic and lack individual specificity. Further, there is a cardiac lag (the delay as your heart rate increases and decreases relative to effort), meaning the numbers may not always immediately reflect what your heart is actually doing at that specific point in time. This has a bearing specifically during sessions with dramatic, short fluctuations in intensity.

Setting predetermined heart-rate targets could also lead to either conservatism or over-exertion. This may be beneficial, as previously mentioned, but can also place unnecessary limits on your performance. This is because you're a slave to

the number, rather than being able to intuitively read your body and respond to its signals. As with other gadgets, you might experience an emotional slump if the digit you see isn't what you would have wanted. Last, chest straps may not always be that comfortable, especially in hot conditions.

Power

Many pro athletes now use power meters to help their cycle training. Such gadgets essentially measure the force – or wattage – being applied to the pedals. I never used a power meter (or a heart-rate monitor, for that matter), preferring perceived effort (see the training fundamentals section on page 42 for more details) as a gauge of how hard I was working, but there's no denying that using a power meter has its advantages. It can allow the cyclist to control their riding intensity more effectively, and the data can be downloaded and shared with a coach, enabling a more objective review of the session or race. Be warned, though: such devices can cost as much as the bike itself and you would need to understand how to use it and interpret the data, or have a coach who can. In addition, as with heart rate, the risk is that you

may become a slave to the gadget, and become dejected and discouraged if you don't like the number that's in front of you. Finally, although power is an absolute measure of performance, it does not tell you much about impact of exercise on the body. Heart rate gives an indication of that impact, but doesn't give an absolute measure of performance . . . therefore combining both can be useful.

Cadence

Cadence (or revolutions per minute: rpm) can be measured as swim stroke rate, cycling rpm and run stride rate (steps per minute). Although there are rough ranges to aim for, ultimately our natural cadence is very individual, and is as much about what feels right and is sustainable over the given race distance. Swim, bike and running at different cadences will result in different physiological adaptations. For triathlon swimming, long strokes are not necessarily suitable in open water (given the disruption from waves/turbulence) so aim for shorter strokes, with a strong fast catch and forceful finish at your hip (see Chapter 3). On the bike, the consensus is that triathletes should aim for a cycling race cadence of 80–95rpm, although I personally felt more comfortable at a lower cadence of around 75–80. I would also do training sessions where my rpm was either lower or higher than this to build strength and improve pedalling technique. On the run, increasing stride rate can improve running efficiency and speed.

There's no need for gadgets to measure cadence – just an ability to count. However, it's only useful if you combine it with another indicator, such as power, heart rate or pace. That way you'll have a better indication of the impact of cadence on output and performance. Many bike computers combine cadence counters with pace and power to help with this.

Pace

Pace, or speed, is the time it takes to cover a given distance. A pace clock at the side of the pool (or a simple wristwatch), a bike computer and a GPS watch can all indicate the speed at which you are swimming, cycling or running. The latter two gadgets give a reading in real time, although there may be a slight time-lag on a GPS watch. Keeping it simpler still: if you know the distance and have a simple wristwatch and an aptitude for maths, you can calculate your pace. Pace has its limitations in that it can vary according to conditions – for example, your speed decreases if you are biking or running up a hill or swimming in rough open water. Likewise, with a tailwind you may feel like you're emulating two-time Olympic gold

 medallist Alistair Brownlee but may not actually be working as hard as you think. As mentioned on page 48, in a controlled environment such as a swimming pool, running track, flat road/trail or when training on a treadmill or a turbo, monitoring pace becomes more useful. The 'Retaining the fun in fundamentals' section of this chapter covers pace in more detail, and when and how to use it in training.

There is a place for technology, but ultimately over-reliance on any data and gadgets can be physically and psychologically problematic and, in my view, nothing replaces the use of feel. Listening to your body's signals is a crucial part of being a successful athlete; it then becomes a matter of picking tools to help amplify these messages and avoiding those that may dull/suppress them.

If you do decide to use a gadget to measure some/all of these variables, I would suggest doing some training without any toys and then some sessions where you use them but don't actually look at the numbers during the session, and instead use feel to guide your effort. You could then download the data afterwards and see how close your perception of effort was to the numerical reality. This will help to develop your sense for what a given heart rate, wattage, cadence or pace actually *feels* like. Generally, the more experienced you are, the better you become at this.

Training and racing is about coping with highs and lows: you against the elements, your ability to respond to the voices in your head and react to the unknown. No single gadget can do this. No lab tests or glitzy monitors can tell you to keep pushing when you want to quit. Yes, it takes practice and effort – but it is also incredibly liberating to rely on perceived exertion, to trust in that intuitive 'brain–body' connection and ability to self-regulate rather than blindly worship a gadget/number. While those who love technology and numbers may disagree, I also believe that going gadget-free helps sport retain an appealing rawness and helps to free your mind from clutter.

With experience, I found that I became much more in tune with my body. I didn't need a monitor to indicate that I was working hard, to give me a technological pat on the back or to tell me to back off or to speed up. I still don't. I just know, because I've invested time training the most valuable (and cheapest!) computer of all – the mind. ●

HELPING HANDS: THE COACHING CONUNDRUM

You've had a drunken Guinness-fuelled bet with a friend and accidentally signed up for an Ironman. You've got ten months to train. The problem is that, up to a few inebriated nights ago, you thought an Ironman was a bloke with a penchant for wrinkle-free shirts. Now you know differently, and your mind is flooded with questions. How do I maximise my chances of success? How do I improve? What race/s should I do? How can I balance training with work, family and other life commitments so that I don't end up divorced and unemployed? Why do I drink Guinness?

Brett Sutton offering me his words of wisdom.

Whether you're the intoxicated novice or an elite athlete, every triathlete considers these conundrums at one time or another. Another million-dollar one is whether or not to be coached, and if so, how to find one who can turn you from zero to hero.

Coaches come in all shapes and sizes: your local triathlon club coach who's often unpaid; an internet-based coach who provides an online or emailed programme; someone you work with face-to-face and one-on-one on a regular, often daily, basis; those that focus on one of the three disciplines; or a coach who you may encounter once, for example at a workshop or during a training camp.

I've been fortunate to work with some fantastic coaches throughout my life, from the swimming club coaches of my youth, to my first running coach – the legendary, late Frank Horwill – to those I've worked with as a triathlete. As a professional athlete, I had three coaches. My journey began with Brett Sutton in 2007 – a partnership that ended following my Ironman World Championship victory in 2008. I then worked briefly with multiple ITU World Champion, Simon Lessing, and spent the last two and a half years of my career with Dave Scott.

A coach–athlete relationship is a partnership, and one that can make or break your triathlon journey. So, what are the pros and cons of being coached and, if you decide to get a coach, how do you go about finding one who will ensure that you fly rather than flop?

ADVANTAGES OF BEING COACHED

So why did I decide to work with a coach for much of my career?

Knowledge gap

I had the will, determination and work ethic, but I lacked the knowledge, experience and understanding needed to plan my training, and other aspects of my life, to ensure I could fulfil my potential. My coaches filled this triathlon knowledge gap. That included providing guidance in terms of the volume and intensity of the swim, bike and run sessions but also on my technique, and other aspects of training such as nutrition and strength and conditioning. Some imparted this advice and support in a democratic fashion, involving me in decision-making (Dave), whereas others favoured the more autocratic approach (Brett and Simon). And it's not just training. Coaches can help plan your race schedule – or, in Brett's case, set your schedule for you – and provide tactical and strategic input based on your own particular strengths and weaknesses.

> " I had the will, determination and work ethic, but I lacked the knowledge, experience and understanding needed to plan my training. "

Targeted, tailored advice

Generic programmes can be of use, especially if you are starting on your triathlon journey or have the experience to adapt them to suit your needs, but to ensure you can reach your absolute potential a bespoke approach is so important: one in which the coach can factor in your background, goals, strengths and weaknesses, lifestyle and personality. For me, this individualised approach was essential to my success.

Iterative approach

If left to my own devices I probably would have regurgitated the same old sessions over and over again – especially if they had proven successful in the past. A coach can take the longer-term perspective and see your programme as a dynamic, evolving feast; ensuring consistency but nuancing the training over time so that you don't plateau or regress.

Time efficiency

Time is valuable and I didn't want to spend hours clutching at straws and doing poor-quality, possibly deleterious, workouts or races. I wanted to improve and I wanted it to happen as quickly and efficiently as possible. When I joined Brett's squad in 2007, I remember telling him: 'My savings will only last 12 months, and after that I'll need to go back to work.' He replied simply: 'We make every hour of every day count.'

Take the strain

A good coach takes the decision-making away. While this sounds disempowering, in the earlier stages of my career it was vital. I tended (and still tend!) to be an over-analytical worrier, and constantly question everything. Brett called this 'paralysis through analysis'. Once trust is established, a coach can assuage, or eliminate, this fretting and fussing. Personally, I felt freed by not having to make uninformed guesses about what I should be doing and where I should be racing; instead, relying on the coach's judgement and expertise to make the right decisions for me and liberating me mentally to concentrate on the hard work.

Matt Edwards casting an expert eye over Katy Campbell's swim stroke.

> **My coaches understood me as a person and not just as an athlete. They had an ability to read me, to know how I think and to coach me accordingly.**

Bigger picture perspective

A coach can also see the bigger picture, over the short and longer term. Many of us have a tendency to get caught up in the minutiae and worry about a missed session or if our performance in a workout or race falls short of expectations. Coaches, as well as friends and family, can help keep our feet on the ground and ensure we see such blips, and triathlon generally, as part of a much bigger picture.

Motivation and support

Some athletes require extrinsic motivation from external accountability. Knowing you have to feed back to 'the boss' means that you may be far less likely to skip or modify a session. You can also be buoyed by their praise when things go well. I undoubtedly felt a buzz when reporting back to Brett or Dave after a tough but successful workout. That said, Brett was somewhat more reluctant than Dave to dish out compliments – after my first Ironman World Championship win in 2007 he simply said 'Good job, kid.' Whether effusive or not, my coaches' feedback gave me an added spring in my step. There were also specific occasions – when I was injured, for example – when I really valued the unwavering support and encouragement that a coach gave. Take the World Championship in 2011: I know that Dave questioned whether I could even get to the start line, but he never once conveyed his fears, instead convincing me that I could and would finish the race despite the bad bike crash that had left me with open wounds all over the left side of my body. A coach can be like a rock. Steady and secure; instilling in you the confidence, self-belief and fortitude necessary.

Reining in

That said, I often needed more restraint: I needed reining in. As a committed masochist, more was always better and I didn't lack the drive to put that philosophy into practice. My coaches taught me that quality trumps quantity every time: less was, and is, often more. Especially if it's Guinness. Motivation with management was key. In fact, the most valuable counsel Dave gave was at the Ironman World Championship in 2010. As explained in Chapter 9, I had been feeling ill and was unsure whether or not to start. In the end, it was Dave who convinced me that the best decision was the hardest – to DNS. Of course, he was right.

Holistic approach

My coaches understood me as a person and not just as an athlete. They had an ability to read me, to know how I think and to coach me accordingly. In many respects, they were also sports psychologists; training my mind as well as my body – sometimes without me even knowing it. Brett used to scream and shout at me in front of the other athletes, on occasion inducing tears, or even taking steps to pit the other athletes against me. This would either crush me or fuel my fire. It did the latter, and he was deliberately carving me into a warrior. Dave adopted an altogether different, and much softer and subtler, strategy that was no less effective.

This is not to say that coaches are the font of all knowledge. Yes, some coaches are one-stop shops (or at least claim to be) but there is always the option of consulting specialists in other important areas such as strength and conditioning, physiotherapy, bike fit, sports psychology and nutrition. For example, Asker Jeukendrup was my go-to person on sports nutrition and, latterly, Mike Taylor has been my bike-fit guru. I was less inclined to ask Dave for fashion advice, given his fondness for skimpy shorts and handlebar moustaches.

SELF-COACHING

So, conversely, what are the benefits of being self-coached? Here are just a few:

> No one understands yourself better than you do. Hence, provided you have the skills to do so, you can individualise your programme.

> You can apply your own philosophies and practices without having to follow someone else's, especially if you have a wealth of triathlon experience in the bank.

> You may learn to listen to your body more effectively.

> You can become a student of the sport. By reading around a subject, learning from others and adopting a process of trial and error you inform and educate yourself about all things triathlon-related. This deeper understanding of why things work (or don't!) can be incredibly empowering.

> It's free, meaning you can spend more on equipment, race entries or . . . on occasion, your spouse's birthday present.

> You can be your own best motivator: an incredibly valuable gift, when training or racing.

> It can be extremely gratifying to know that you have guided yourself to that finish line and are able to take full credit for your own success.

Just look at the athletes from the 1980s and 1990s, such as Dave Scott, Mark Allen, Paula Newby-Fraser and Scott Tinley. There wasn't the plethora of specialist triathlon coaches that exist today and so those athletes largely found out for themselves what worked and what didn't. They were at the vanguard and their innovative philosophies and approaches still inform triathlon training today.

Even if you can't afford, don't want or don't have access to a personal coach, I would always suggest speaking to athletes and coaches who have been in the sport for a number of years to pick their brains and learn from their experiences, as well as devouring guides such as this of course! When coupled with some experimentation, this will enable you to develop your own bank of knowledge that will evolve and grow as your triathlon journey progresses.

CHOOSING A COACH

If you've decided to be coached, how do you go about choosing one? It's like dating. Unless your wife or husband sets your programme (and hopefully saves you a few pennies in the process), you'll need to do some research to find Mr or Mrs Right, and also put in the leg- (and arm-) work afterwards to make the partnership productive.

I would talk to other athletes; word-of-mouth and personal endorsements count for a lot; magazines also provide contacts (*Horse and Hound* may not be the best place to look, though); scour internet forums, blogs and podcasts for coaches who tend to post (it's useful if you actually like what they say); ask your national governing body (i.e. British Triathlon) for a list of coaches or else do a web search, cross your fingers and hope for the best. Then have a list of non-negotiables in terms of what you are looking for (e.g. philosophy, personality, qualifications, location, cost).

Triathlon is awash with good coaches, as well as those who should come with a huge health warning. The most important thing to remember is that, just as every athlete is an individual, no two coaches are the same. Even if they follow similar schools of thought, they will bring different levels of experience, style, backgrounds and personalities. It's not one size fits all, otherwise there would be a lot of triathlon coaches out of business. Things you should ponder – and may wish to raise, and discuss with, prospective coaches – could be:

Type of coach (expertise and methods)

> The style of coaching that suits you. This could be a club coach who you see regularly, but only as part of a group; a private, personal coach that you see face-to-face; or an online coach who sends programmes electronically.

> On what aspects of triathlon you need guidance. For example, do you simply want a swim coach to look over your technique or someone to help improve your run form, or do you want a comprehensive training programme that is specifically tailored to you?

> The coach's level of experience at the distance you are racing. For example, there are those who specialise in short course and those who focus on Ironman.

> What level of athlete, from beginner to professional, they prefer to work with.

> Whether you want advice on other aspects of training, such as nutrition and strength and conditioning and, if so, if the coach can to provide this.

Coaching philosophy and style

> There are coaches who are more autocratic and others who are consultative and collaborative, so think about your personality and to which style you might best respond.

> If you want a comprehensive training programme, it's important to know how the coach will tailor it, if at all, to suit your needs, goals, lifestyle, background and ability.

> If they like using technology or prefer to use perceived effort, or a combination of both. For example, would they want you to work with a power meter or heart-rate monitor to give them quantifiable measures of performance and progress?

Cost

> Costs can vary considerably, so consider what represents good value for money given your budget. (Don't be fooled into thinking that cost correlates to coaching quality; there are plenty of coaching cowboys/girls who cost a small fortune yet you and your bank balance are no stronger for it.)

> Whether you need to pay weekly or monthly.

Practical issues

> The frequency with which you will see/speak to/email your coach.

> Whether any time differences might make phone, email or carrier-pigeon communication difficult.

> If required, whether they will attend your races.

> The number of athletes on their roster, and how much time they will devote to you personally.

Personality traits

> What characteristics they demonstrate, e.g. passion, enthusiasm, calmness, empathy, compassion, openness to new ideas and life-long learning. Do you want an effusive, enthusiastic coach, or do you want to join the somewhat unyielding Brett Sutton-style school of tough love?

> Your gut feeling about the coach, professionally and personally, and whether you like and warm to them.

> How they conduct themselves when communicating with you, in blogs and on social media. For example, is it with professionalism and integrity?

Experience and qualifications

> Who they have coached and at what level.

> Their reputation (professionally and personally).

> How long they have been coaching for.

> Whether they have specific qualifications from an approved body. (Note, though, coaches can have a qualification but may not have the depth of hands-on experience and not all great coaches have a pocketful of qualifications.)

I must point out that this is a two-way relationship; with any partnership comes obligations and you owe it to your coach, and yourself, to follow the programme as best you can, to trust in him/her and to feed back honestly and regularly.

Remember, too, that coach selection is not irrevocable. There's no shame in separation and divorce. As people and athletes, we all evolve. Sometimes we can grow together, and other times the relationship runs its course and both parties should be mature enough to move on, carrying the lessons learned. Of course,

improvements can take a while to be realised, and change doesn't happen overnight, but if you get a sense that the relationship isn't working, or will not work, then it's important to find someone who can tick your personal boxes. This was the case with Simon and me. He was a phenomenal athlete and has been a successful coach to some, but he and I didn't 'fit' either professionally or personally. We parted after only a few months, with no hard feelings and lessons banked on both sides.

In summary, I was the athlete I was because of the coaches with whom I have partnered. My victories are also theirs, and if you do choose to work with a coach I hope the relationship will also be paved with gold medals and you're bestowed with the nonchalant platitude: 'Good job, kid.'

PROS AND CONS OF DIFFERENT TYPES OF COACH

TYPE OF COACH	PRO	CON
Face-to-face club coach	• Usually free (aside from club membership fees) • Can provide immediate advice and listen to feedback • Usually willing to provide ad hoc advice outside of club sessions • Often travel to (local) races with the club • Group sessions provide friendship, fun and potential training partners outside of club sessions	• Sessions are not tailored specifically to individual athletes • Athletes may not get as used to training alone or learn to motivate themselves • Less flexibility with training, as club/group sessions take place at certain times and locations • Group environment can foster overly competitive behaviour, which may lead to over-training and injury
Personal, private face-to-face coach	• Provides a tailored, individualised training programme and advice • Can react to situations quickly and adapt programme based on what they see and hear • Can often provide advice and support on other aspects of training (e.g. race selection, race strategy, nutrition, strength and conditioning)	• Can be costly • Requires a time commitment given the more in-depth nature of the relationship • Smaller pool to choose from, as the coach and athlete need to be located in the same place • As the programme is tailored, the athlete may end up training alone (missing out on the motivation and socialisation that comes from training with others)

> **I was the athlete I was because of the coaches with whom I have partnered. My victories are also theirs.**

With Dave Scott and former *220 Triathlon* editor James Witts at the *220 Triathlon* Awards, 2010.

TYPE OF COACH	PRO	CON
Online coach	• Reliable format for accessing training programme and providing feedback • Can provide an individualised programme tailored to the athlete • Flexibility with regards to the location, as the coach and athlete can be based anywhere	• Effective communication is vital • Difficult to assess and advise on technique remotely • Difficult truly to 'read' an athlete and build a deep relationship via the phone or email • Potential for delayed feedback • Lack of direct observation may mean that problems (and positives) are not easily picked up • As above, training alone (if following an individualised programme) may not always be beneficial
Discipline specific	• The athlete can focus on one area, especially a weaker discipline; receiving deeper knowledge and insight • Often cheaper than a triathlon coach	• Not all discipline-specific coaches understand triathlon, and fail to take into account the athlete's other training and the impact that one discipline has on the others
One-off workshops or training camps	• No long-term commitment or cost	• Unlikely to provide individualised advice • Not ongoing, and so there's a risk of forgetting what has been taught

Insight

DAVE SCOTT on coaching me

At the start of 2009, Chrissie was working with Simon Lessing, but over the spring decided to come down to my swim sessions in Boulder. It's an unpretentious environment, with amateurs and pros swimming together, and she fitted right in. I started giving her some swim-stroke guidance, for example: 'relax your hands, your head's too high, you're flipping your wrists . . .' She liked the feedback, as it gave her something tangible she could work on and she began to see improvements.

She confided that she wasn't altogether happy with the relationship with Simon, and asked if I would comment on her training plan. Our relationship evolved gradually and my involvement in her training deepened, especially after Challenge Roth in 2009

when she and Simon parted ways. I've also had similar coach/athlete situations; you reach a point and things just don't flow.

Chrissie always wanted to understand why she was doing things and I like to hear the opinions of my athletes, rather than being overly bossy. She was obviously doing a lot of things right, so I'd ask her what she thought she was doing well, what she enjoyed, what she thought she could improve on and also what races she ideally wanted to do. Based on those discussions I developed a plan for her, based on 4–6-week microcycles that fitted around the race schedule that we had agreed upon. The training was iterative – with each cycle building on what we had done in the last.

I also needed to take the time to truly understand Chrissie and what made her tick. That was the challenge. Any coach needs to know their athletes, and tailor their approach and the training. For example, she had a tendency to always overdo things; it was my job to hold her back as much as it was to push her that bit further. As an athlete, I was the same, which is maybe why I understood her so well.

We did collide a few times, though. She was World Champion and was improving, but still had a hard time fully trusting me and sometimes wanted to modify sessions. I didn't agree on the changes she wanted to make and it actually got to a point where I didn't know if the partnership could work for me. I told her this, and I think it shocked her: this was probably the moment where she fully bought into what we were trying to do. Trust really does have to be there on both sides for a coach/athlete relationship to be successful.

It was vital that I got to grips with her strengths and weaknesses. For example, physiologically she was really asymmetrical – her right side was pretty weak. So she was always lopsided on the bike, she had a lot of torque in her spine and her right knee also collapsed inwards. She ran like a boxing chicken with one arm rocking across her body and swinging too far back. Through some technique work and strength and conditioning, she was able to rectify some of this and become more biomechanically efficient.

Training-wise, I felt she had a tendency to stay in her comfort zone and do all her sessions at roughly the same pace. That was OK for a while, but soon she would plateau. We integrated more higher intensity work, and mixed threshold training too (see 'Retaining the fun in fundamentals' in this chapter for more details).

I didn't want her to lose her swim or bike strength, but I wanted her to think of the run as really being her asset. It was her weapon. I wanted her to have the physical ability, but also the confidence in her

> 66 I knew that when the going got tough she had the mental fortitude to overcome anything that a race might throw at her. This is vital as anything can happen. 99

running ability to truly shine. So a lot of sessions – for example, the brick where she did 10–12km worth of threshold run intervals after a hard bike – were designed to build and cement that psychological pillar of self-belief.

That said, I knew that when the going got tough she had the mental fortitude to overcome anything that a race might throw at her. This is vital as anything can happen: it's not like bowling; there are so many variables and factors that come into play, some of which you just can't predict or plan for. Yes, she was strong physically, but she won her races on the strength of her psychology as well as the physiology.

The relationship worked, in part, because I'm so brutally honest. She liked that straightforward candour and maybe it would sometimes catch her off-guard but I always told her what I thought. Sometimes she may not have liked or appreciated the message, but nevertheless she didn't want me to code anything; she liked straight talking. I got the same from her – she never held back with telling me how she felt, and that approach worked for me. Although she frustrated me occasionally, it really was a great partnership and I'm really proud of what Chrissie and I achieved together. ●

To Go it Alone? Group Training Discussions with Katy Campbell

As triathletes, we have the option of training alone or with others – whether that be one training partner or a group. Some of the advantages of training alone can be that it allows you to:

> follow your own plan, and not compromise your training;

> not rely on other people to plan/schedule your sessions;

> develop mental toughness;

> become attuned to the race environment where you compete on your own;

> have the opportunity to think and focus, away from noise, disturbance and chatter.

However, conversely there are advantages to training with others:

> motivation, support and encouragement;

> you can receive (and give) help and advice;

> others can provide an overview of your form and technique;

> safety and security;

> camaraderie and friendship.

A novice, Katy didn't know many other triathletes in her hometown of Exeter. She wanted to meet some but was worried about what people would think of her, concerned about appearing ignorant and nervous about training with others in case she couldn't keep up.

I'm sure this sounds familiar to many readers; after all, we were all beginners once and probably felt a little apprehensive and daunted by this new sport. However, these fears can be overcome and, when they are, a whole world opens up, including the opportunity to widen our circle of friends. I look back at my own experience since starting triathlon and I am so grateful to have met so many wonderful people, from all over the world, and developed friendships that endure even though I have hung up my tri-kit. In fact, I even met my husband though the sport. Now that's what you call a win-win!

Katy tended to cycle alone or with her hubby, Ed. This meant that she wasn't especially confident in a group-riding situation and didn't know who to turn to for advice about bike handling and hill climbing. She was also a novice swimmer and struggled for motivation when training alone in the pool, as well as needing regular guidance on her swim technique. A more experienced runner, Katy had joined the local running club a few years previously and felt confident in her ability to train for this discipline, either alone or with members of the club.

Taking all of this into consideration, I suggested she join her local tri club in Exeter. This would enable her to find training partners for the swim and bike, make new friends, learn from more experienced athletes and access the free coaching. I spoke from experience. As a novice, I joined and raced for the Birmingham Running and Triathlon (BRAT) Club.

> **We were all beginners once and probably felt a little apprehensive and daunted by this new sport.**

This club provided me with a cocoon of support that was absolutely invaluable, even as a professional athlete. Its members lent me equipment, cheered for me in races, encouraged me to become a professional athlete and organised parties to congratulate me as Age Group and then Ironman World Champion. Of course, the process is reciprocal and once a member you can also encourage newcomers to join in the fun and help them on their journey.

Me with some of my BRAT Club teammates.

There are hundreds of tri clubs in the UK, from those with a few members to those nearing a thousand. No matter the size, they usually have coaching and sessions to suit all ages and abilities and greet new members with glee. Exeter Triathlon Club was no different and welcomed Katy with open arms. In fact, at Alpe d'Huez Long Course Triathlon a year later, it was the Exeter tri-club members who Katy chose to meet up with before the race and the people she high-fived during the run.

If you don't want to or can't join a tri club, there are still opportunities to meet people and potential training buddies: at races, at work, in single discipline (e.g. swimming, cycling or running) clubs, while out training, on online forums, through existing friends . . . in lonely hearts columns. Triathlon is a sport that is growing like wildfire, and there's no shortage of people out there ready and waiting to do a group training session and/or provide advice, encouragement and support. For example, while walking on a beach Katy had a chance meeting with a few people who were doing an open-water swim and they subsequently became her open-water buddies; she found new running partners at the local parkrun; and chose to do some of her bike sessions with one of her non-triathlete, rowing friends, Becca.

Although group training is really beneficial, I stressed to Katy the importance of following her own programme, and not compromising her plan for the sake of training with others; as well as learning to love (or at least endure!) her own company, deal with problems (such as flat tyres) by herself and cope with those inner training demons without relying on others for motivation. That meant also doing some of her training sessions alone. That wasn't to say she couldn't meet up with others for a post-training pizza or pint of beer though. After all, this is a journey, and it is the friendships we cultivate and the shared experiences we have that truly make it one to remember. ●

The Great Healer – Coping with Injury

Q 'I recently fractured my ankle. I know the most important thing is to heal that bone, then rehab the muscles around it to the point I can run again. I know you suffered injuries going into your last World Championship in Kona. How do you keep positive during your healing process?'

SANDY JACKSON

A I'm really sorry to hear about your ankle. As athletes, we are pushing our bodies and unfortunately will all encounter injury at some point along our sporting journey – it's something that we must expect and accept. The important thing is to minimise the risks of them occurring and, if they do, deal with them correctly.

The psychological impact of being injured can be just as debilitating as broken bones, and so healing means addressing both the physical and emotional aspects. While I urge you to consult a sports doctor for individualised advice on your specific injury, my experience in this area means that I can nevertheless guide you along the path of positivity and offer some practical tips for getting you back to full fitness.

Staying positive despite my broken bones, in January 2010.

A brief meltdown

By all means, have a brief 'toys out of the pram' tantrum and spend a few days wallowing on the sofa watching *Pretty Woman* for the hundredth time, but then look forward and choose the path of positive action.

If applicable, take responsibility

Could you have prevented it? If yes, learn from that and try not to make the same mistakes again. For example, choosing to ride outside on 2 January 2010 with ice

on the ground was not the best decision I have ever made. Reminiscent of Humpty Dumpty, I crashed. Rather than engaging my brain, I engaged my arm and my two friends landed on top of me with a resounding crunch. A passing driver took me to a local pub (I resisted using whisky to numb the pain) and thereafter the hospital where they diagnosed impressive fractures in my radius, two metacarpals and fingers. I had my arm in a cast for six weeks. This gave me the time to reflect, and realise that the accident had arisen because I failed to make the correct decision about my training – a lesson I banked and learned from. However, if forces have intervened beyond your control, rather than carrying bitterness or blame try to accept that sometimes bad luck does strike. You can't turn back the clock, you can only deal with the situation as it stands.

Understand your injury and treatment

Take control by learning about your ankle injury, preparing yourself for the road ahead and alleviating the frustration, confusion and fear that come from the unknown. This means seeking expert medical help, getting a clear diagnosis and prognosis, discussing various treatment methods, possible complications, duration of recovery and rehabilitation. Ask questions and inform yourself. Are there techniques or therapies that expedite healing? What foods should you consume? Internet searches can be useful, but excessive or even contradictory information can confuse, and so try to focus your research and only use trusted sources.

Lean on, and be inspired by, others

Often, we want to appear invincible and self-reliant. However, just as it's much more enjoyable to share good times, you also need to lean on others for support when the going gets tough. Surround yourself with positive, cup-half-full people and don't be afraid to ask for practical help (for me this was washing my hair, doing up my bra, opening a jar of Marmite) and emotional support. This might also mean seeking inspiration from others. For example, while injured I watched videos, read books and spoke to those who faced, and overcame, adversity. Their strength and courage motivated me, ensuring I retained perspective and belief in the power of the human body and mind to heal.

Adapt and do what you can

Focus on what is possible. You're not helpless. You're in control. Dealing with this simply requires adaptation and adjustment. Replace 'If I hadn't broken my ankle I could

have done this or that' with 'Even if, or because, I'm injured it means I can do X, Y, Z.' You can still set – and progress towards – measurable, achievable goals. In addition to seeking advice from medical professionals regarding what you are able to do, you could also speak to para-tri athletes who haven't got use of their legs and find out what they do to train – and then see if you can emulate them. There's also the option of doing land-based swim-stroke work or upper body strength exercises (see page 160 for more details), and training your mind through visualisation and relaxation. Gyms sometimes have hand-cycle machines or you could even try something totally new, like wheelchair basketball. When I broke my ribs later in 2010 (yes, 2010 was a challenging year!) I replicated all my run sessions on the cross-trainer, and won Ironman 70.3 Kansas four weeks later with my fastest half marathon. Concentrate on what you can do.

Alternatively, perhaps you could spend time giving something back to the sport; for example, helping out at your local tri club, volunteering at an event or mentoring a novice triathlete. Or perhaps set a non-triathlon goal, such as learning a new language, taking an art class or simply spending more time with family and friends. You're more than just a triathlete. Your sense of self and self-worth shouldn't be tied to ticking the training logbook, so use this as a window of opportunity to do something you may not have otherwise made time to do.

Remain positive

Of course, any injury is a short-term setback in the pursuit of specific sporting goals, but there's light at the end of the tunnel, which you must focus on – even when it might seem dim or extinguished altogether. If it helps, remember that I broke my arm in 2010 and five months later won Challenge Roth.

Be patient

A final word: when your ankle heals, don't rush back. Rehabilitate slowly and effectively, with sporting longevity and your overall health in mind. A few months may feel like an interminable period of time, but when you reminisce a few years from now – fully fit and with multiple finishes under your race belt – it will be a small speck on your triathlon landscape.

In the words of Kareem Abdul-Jabbar, one of the greatest basketball stars of all time, 'Don't ever forget that you play with your soul as well as your body.' Your ankle may be fractured but I truly believe that these injuries, accidents or problems can make body and soul stronger, more adaptable and increasingly resilient, as long as we learn the lessons they have taught us. Good luck and heal well! ●

CHAPTER THREE

SWIM

Swimming, whether in a pool, lake, canal or ocean, is one of life's most uplifting, liberating, fun and often tranquil activities. Yes, it can be a hard sport to master, especially if you are taking to it a bit later in life; yet no matter your initial ability you can develop the skills and speed needed truly to embrace and enjoy it. Just take my mentee, Katy Campbell, for example: two of her biggest fears were attending the tri-club swim sessions and swimming in open water. With a little encouragement, she overcame the first hurdle, soon relishing the opportunity to train with like-minded people and benefit from the coaching and support that such an environment offered. Within a few months, she was jumping in the ocean close to her home in Devon without batting a goggled eyelid and, over the course of the year I spent mentoring her, successfully finished a number of triathlons, all of which included open-water swims.

You may decide only to swim in a pool in both training and racing. That's perfectly fine; however, I find open-water swimming to be the ultimate endurance adventure. It is you against the elements . . . and a few hundred other people . . . immersing yourself, literally, in the natural world. Open-water swimming enables you to dig deep, test your limits, tackle your fears and experience an environment that most non-triathletes never will.

Whether you're in search of technique or training advice, this chapter will help you develop the aquatic ability you need to embrace and enjoy taking to the water. It's largely focused on open water, as that's where the majority of triathlon swims take place, but includes tips and ideas for how to practise and perform in your local chlorinated puddle, too. The watery world truly is your oyster and with perseverance and guidance you can find your pearl.

FINDING YOUR PEARL: SWIM TRAINING FUNDAMENTALS

EQUIPMENT

Swimsuit

Mainly for training. Some athletes, male and female, choose to race in swimsuits although it can be slightly painful on the undercarriage. It's worth investing in a swimsuit made out of long-lasting, endurance fabric to prevent premature wear and unsightly bum cracks. Rinse your suit with warm water after each swim.

Goggles

They should be tight enough not to leak, but not cause pain around your eye sockets. Spit is the best anti-fogging agent around and it's free. Always make sure to inspect your goggles in the days before a race (sun, chlorine and moisture can cause wear and tear, so keep your goggles dry and protected when not in use). When packing pre-race (see Annex: Race-day Checklist) I always included two goggle options: a tinted pair for sunny conditions and a clear pair for darker, overcast days. If you have a ponytail, tie it at the nape of your neck (so the goggle strap is above the ponytail bulge – as well as below your helmet when you are on the bike).

Swim cap

Silicon caps are more expensive but more durable than latex, and hence great for training. You will usually be given a specific, colour-coded cap to wear in a race. If possible, try it on the day before, carefully stretching it if it feels too tight. You might consider having your goggle strap under your cap, which can help prevent your goggles being removed/dislodged in the swim. You could wear two caps if the water is cold, or even invest in a neoprene version that secures under the chin.

Pull buoy

Pull buoys are egg-timer-shaped floats that you put between your upper thighs in training, keeping your hips elevated but allowing your feet to drag. They come in a range of sizes and buoyancies.

Band

A piece of circular rubber tubing (an old mountain-bike inner tube works well) that, when placed around your ankles, hinders your ability to kick and focuses attention and effort on the upper body position and stroke. When swimming with a band it's important to keep your head and neck in a neutral position, bringing your hips and feet as high as you can.

Paddles

Rectangular or oval pieces of plastic that attach to the palms of your hands. They come in various sizes – choice being dependent on hand size, swim stroke and level of experience. We used them in Dave's swim sessions to increase the muscular load and hence build strength, as well as enhancing stroke technique (specifically it encourages subtle wrist flexion, a high elbow, forearm pressure and hyperextension of the wrist at the end of the stroke). It's best to use paddles under the watchful eye of a good coach to ensure correct use.

Kickboard

A rectangular piece of foam that you hold with outstretched arms to encourage effective kicking.

Flippers/fins

Can help improve ankle flexibility and kicking technique (e.g. kicking from the hip with limited knee bend), as well as allowing you to focus on the catch by creating additional propulsion and encouraging a better body position. They come in varying lengths; longer fins are more flexible and create more propulsion at a slower tempo and shorter fins are better for a faster, rapid kicking motion.

Wetsuit

Wetsuits (or wetties) are made of neoprene, a flexible and soft material that allows a very thin layer of water between your skin and the suit. This water heats up and the insulation keeps you warm. Wetsuits should fit snugly to prevent cold water constantly flushing through. In addition to warmth, wetsuits provide buoyancy, assist in better form and technique, reduce drag and help protect against sharp objects, including flailing limbs. Swimmers will be faster in a wetsuit than without, and race-day water temperature will dictate whether or not you are allowed to wear a wetsuit in a race (races permitting neoprene are called 'wetsuit-legal'). To complicate matters these rules differ depending on the race organiser/governing body, e.g. the ITU, British Triathlon Federation, Ironman/WTC. If the water measures above the wetsuit temperature cut-off, competitors can choose to wear: 1) only their race kit; 2) a so-called 'speed-suit' over the top of their race kit (check the race-specific rules regarding the use of these suits); or 3) a swimsuit. If you choose to wear your race kit, remember that any pockets will fill with water and slow you down. Practise swimming in your wetsuit in training, either in a pool (take care not to overheat) or in open water. See overleaf for more information about choosing a wetsuit and then successfully donning the neoprene.

All smiles with Olympic medallists, Alistair and Jonny Brownlee.

Silicon earplugs

Very useful if you suffer from ear infections and/or if the water is cold.

Vaseline and/or body glide

Chafing occurs either where areas of your body rub together, such as the underarm or between the legs, around the neck/armpits while wearing a wetsuit or underneath the timing-chip strap. It is often worse in the sea where salt creates extra friction. Vaseline is an easy solution, though petroleum jelly can cause neoprene to deteriorate over time. If you do use Vaseline, then applying it with a rubber glove is a good idea (oily hands affect the catch in the swim). There are also some good wetsuit-friendly lubricants on the market, many of which come in a convenient roll-on stick, and some athletes opt for cooking oil spray.

Throwaway shoes

Cheap, throwaway slippers/flip flops can be worn before the race, including when walking down to the swim start. These help to prevent you from getting cold feet (literally) and cuts from sharp objects.

CHOOSING A WETSUIT

Fit

> Trying before buying is crucial when first purchasing a wetsuit and/or if your body shape has changed significantly. Remember that not all manufacturers use the same sizing: a medium in one brand may be totally different to a medium in another. There are women-specific suits, although I know of many women who actually prefer men's suits due to their body type.

> Triathlon wetsuits are different from surf wetsuits, so if you are buying a wettie make sure it's the former. If you only have a surf wetsuit, and can't afford a new one, don't worry – some neoprene is usually better than none provided you can still swim in it.

> Neoprene loosens with wear and relaxes in water, so ensure a snug fit when you initially try it on, as this is the tightest it will ever be. A properly fitting wetsuit will make contact over most of the area it covers, leaving as little space as possible between it and your skin. Special coatings are found on almost all tri wetsuits, reducing friction and hence increasing speed through the water.

> Thicker material is generally used in the chest, stomach and legs to help with buoyancy. The thinner and generally more flexible material should be around your shoulders and arms to allow for freer, unrestricted movement. Make sure you have a good arm reach.

> The neck shouldn't be too high or feel constrictive, although there should be a good seal to prevent the wetsuit 'flooding' with water (the same goes for the wrists).

Price

> Suits range from around £100 for entry level through to £850 at the top end. It's not necessary to spend a fortune: just make sure it fits.

> If you're on a budget it's worth looking for end-of-season or end-of-range bargains, considering an ex-hire suit or hiring one for a race or a whole season.

Sleeved or sleeveless

> Wetsuits can come with arms (sleeved) or without (sleeveless). All things considered, I would always opt for a sleeved wetsuit, as would most professionals, but ultimately it's personal preference. When choosing, you may want to bear the following in mind:

- For some, a sleeved wetsuit may feel too restrictive around the arms/shoulders. e.g. those with really big arms may find it somewhat harder to find a sleeved wetsuit to fit, but if you shop around there should be a sleeved wettie to . . . suit nearly everyone. Note that, although a sleeveless wetsuit may provide more mobility, it can be hard to get a good seal around the armpit and shoulder and hence there's an increased risk of water entering the suit, increasing drag, chafing and exposure to cold water.

- A sleeveless version is slightly cooler and, some triathletes believe, minimises the risk of them overheating in warmer (but still wetsuit-legal) waters. Overheating on the swim is less of an issue in cold and temperate climes and so a sleeved wetsuit will always provide more warmth.

- A swimmer will usually be faster in a full, sleeved wetsuit as long as it fits properly.

GETTING INTO YOUR WETSUIT

While you may all have your own special way of donning the neoprene, here's my tried and tested method:

1. Long nails can rip through wetsuit rubber. Cut/bite your nails or wear thin gloves when putting the suit on.

2. Prepare the suit by unzipping and rolling it inside out down to half a leg. Put your foot in a thin plastic bag and then slip it into the leg pulling the suit up as you go. Peel the bag off your foot and repeat on the other leg. This helps you to put on the legs of the wetsuit a lot more easily.

3. Pull it up over your thighs; make sure it's close-fitting in the crotch otherwise the suit will be too tight at the shoulders and chest. Pull the sleeves up over the arms, making sure it's snug in your armpits.

4. Zip up the suit, or ask someone to help, and secure any Velcro fastenings. The strap attached to the zip should be under the fastening and hang over the top.

5. Bend forward and make sure that any ruffles in the neoprene, especially those around your stomach, are worked out by hoisting the material upwards towards the shoulders.

6. Put lubricant around the neck and at the bottom of the legs to help wetsuit removal in transition.

7. On race day, put your timing chip strap under or below the wetsuit leg.

SWIMMING TRAINING

The majority of your swim training will probably be in a swimming pool. Opening times can make access hard, and so scheduling sessions will need to be done with this in mind. Whether in a pool or open water, I would suggest doing some of your swimming in the morning, when you are fresh and also to replicate the start of a race, i.e. training when you are 'cold'. Be aware of any lane designations (e.g. slow/medium/fast), whether you are required to swim in a clockwise or anti-clockwise direction, and rules regarding the use of paddles and fins. Most pools have pace clocks that you can use to monitor your swim speed over a given distance.

We will come on to the different strokes shortly, but one thing that some swimmers do in the pool that they don't in open water is tumble (or flip) turning. A good coach or experienced swimmer should be able to give a helping hand at mastering this skill. The advantages of such turns are that they help maintain fluidity and rhythm, create a more continuous workout (rather than stopping at the end of each length), encourage breathing control and increase swim speed.

While I didn't mind running and cycling alone, I found it more difficult to do all of my swimming without company. Training with others, whether a few friends, a triathlon club or swimming squad, can help with motivation and alleviate the boredom that can come from following the black line. It can also be helpful to have a coach on the poolside to observe and correct your technique and offer encouragement.

STROKES FOR FOLKS: TRIATHLON SWIMMING TECHNIQUE

Front crawl – or freestyle – is the quickest way of getting from A to B, but is *never* compulsory in a race. You can do breaststroke, doggy paddle or, in some races, backstroke, as long as you make the

METHODS TO AVOID THE COLD

> Wear a good-quality wetsuit that fits snugly but not too tightly.

> Pee in your wetsuit.

> Wear two swim caps to help limit heat loss through the head (ensure the coloured race cap is on top). You could put a neoprene cap beneath if the water is very cold.

> Wear silicon earplugs.

> Practise swimming in cold water to breed familiarity and minimise panic.

> Go waist deep into the open water, splash and then slowly submerge your face to alleviate the shock.

> Consider doing a shorter warm-up.

designated swim cut-off time (as stipulated in the race rules). In training, I would do the majority of my swimming front crawl, but incorporate some backstroke to utilise different muscles or the same muscles but in a different way.

While it is easier to maintain a long, smooth, symmetrical and rhythmical stroke in a controlled swimming-pool environment, it is much more difficult during an open-water swim due to the varying conditions, the buoys and the close proximity of other swimmers. For triathlon swimming, we need a technique that's suited to changeable open-water conditions, not easily disrupted by other swimmers and fast yet efficient to enable us to conserve energy for bike and run. The key technique pointers are:

Breathing

Take relaxed, deep inhales and long, full exhales, creating a smooth rhythm. Keep your face and neck relaxed, and don't hold your breath at any point. The question of bilateral (breathing to both sides) versus one-sided breathing is the subject of much controversy. Bilateral breathing is usually done every three strokes (counting both arms) so your breathing alternates from left to right. But equally it could be done every five strokes or even seven if you have the lung capacity of a blue whale. Bilateral breathing does help balance your stroke and create symmetry in your back and shoulder muscles. However, remember that we are endurance athletes and need to ensure sufficient oxygen intake. For some, bilateral breathing can result in oxygen debt.

> " For triathlon swimming, we need a technique that's suited to changeable open-water conditions, not easily disrupted by other swimmers and fast yet efficient to enable us to conserve energy. "

We often have a favoured side and/or rhythm and I would suggest swimming as comes naturally. For example, I breathe every second stroke, always to the right. Even if you do favour one side, you should still practise bilateral breathing in training, as you may need to breathe to your less dominant side in a race; for example, to help with navigation, avoid chop, waves or glaring sun, or face away from another swimmer's flailing limbs. More experienced swimmers might also want to keep an eye on their competitors and respond to attacks and accelerations.

Intermediate and advanced swimmers can practise hypoxic breathing in training. That is, taking fewer breaths to work up oxygen debt in case such a situation arises in open water (e.g. if it is very choppy). An example is a 6 × 100m set in which you breathe every three strokes on the first lap, every five strokes on the second, every seven strokes on the third and every nine strokes on the last lap. Not recommended for beginners, though.

Stroke rate

In open water, the stroke needs to be faster, shorter and continuous to minimise the disruption of forward progress. An overly long stroke (with a long glide) can be less efficient because of the introduction of dead spots and pauses.

Technique

The swim stroke can be broken down into a number of stages, although undertaken as one seamless movement:

1. The hand entry: have a flattish and wide hand entry. If the head is a clock face, your left hand should enter at about ten o'clock and the right hand at about two o'clock.

2. The catch phase: the movement immediately after your hand enters the water. A high elbow is required to provide a strong anchor.

3. Pull phase: a backwards pull that comes straight down the side of your torso (rather than an 'S' shape under the body) propelling your body through the water.

4. Push phase: the final underwater phase, leading with the heel of your hand at the end of the stroke (wrist hyperextension) to increase the length of the propulsive zone and a quick recovery.

5. Exit: your arm, leading with the elbow, and hand exit the water.

6. Recovery: the movement of the arm above the water as you bring it round to enter again at the front. Keep your arm, hand and fingers relaxed. Swimming in choppy conditions may necessitate a higher arm recovery. If it's too low, your hand could enter the water too early or be hit by a wave, causing you to become unbalanced. Use the arm recovery to wriggle your fingers to increase blood flow, especially if the water is cold.

Keep your hand relaxed and your fingers slightly apart. Unless you are turning your head to breathe or 'sight' (see page 110 for information on sighting), your eyes should focus more towards the bottom rather than forwards (which lifts your neck and can cause your legs to sink).

While some triathletes are naturally strong, frequent kickers, this is not absolutely necessary in open water, although an *effective* kick is still important. Kick mainly from the hip, keeping your ankles loose. The downbeat should only be chest deep and on the upbeat your heels should just break the water's surface. The kick should use minimal energy and keep your legs high enough to establish a good body position.

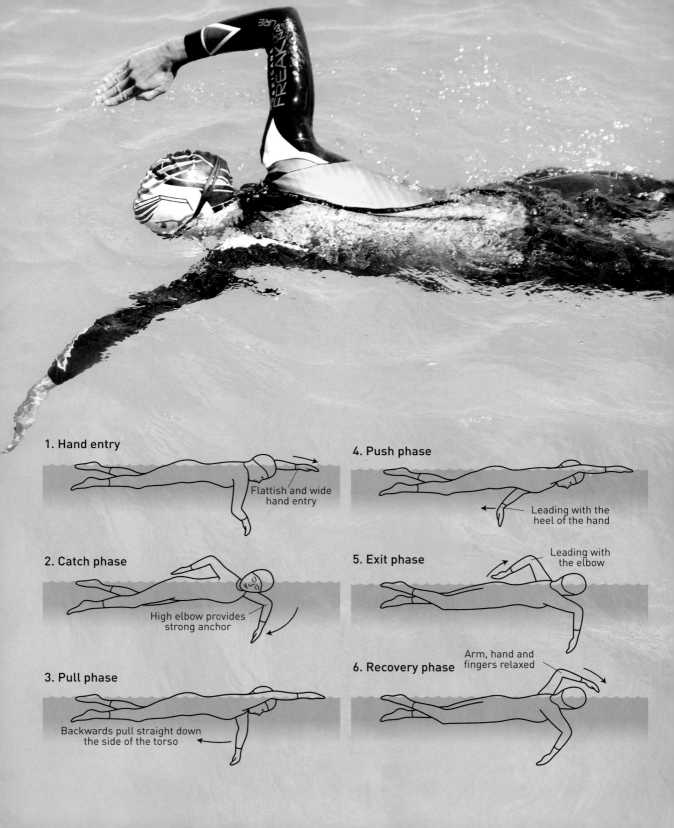

1. Hand entry

Flattish and wide hand entry

2. Catch phase

High elbow provides strong anchor

3. Pull phase

Backwards pull straight down the side of the torso

4. Push phase

Leading with the heel of the hand

5. Exit phase

Leading with the elbow

6. Recovery phase

Arm, hand and fingers relaxed

DAVE SCOTT'S drills

Here are some drills that I give my athletes to improve their stroke. It's always good to do such drills under the watchful eye of a coach to ensure they are done correctly.

1. Swim with a single paddle on one hand. Put the hand with the paddle in front and then take three strokes with the other arm. Avoid dropping the elbow. This enables you to feel more pressure on the front end of the stroke, ensures your hand doesn't slip when underwater, helps develop symmetry and aids focus on wrist hyperextension at the end of the push phase.

2. Switch paddles with someone else. They're usually a different brand and shape and that increases your proprioception ('feel' of the water).

3. Swim with tennis balls in your hands (but don't flex your wrists). Holding tennis balls stimulates nerve endings in the hand and focuses attention on setting the elbow high and engaging the forearm at the front end of the stroke (i.e. the catch). When you remove the balls, you'll recognise the heightened sensation in your palms and be able to better feel the water and hold it to maximise propulsion. Doing this at the start of the session, after a warm-up, can help you retain that feel for the rest of the session.

4. Concentrate on keeping the hand close to the surface and 'lingering longer' at the front of the stroke, with the elbow in a high position. You should feel your lats and serratus (back muscles) engage. This can be done with a single paddle, progressing to a paddle on both hands. A beginner may also need a set of fins/flippers for propulsion.

5. Wearing flippers encourages you to engage your glutes and kick from the hip with a much straighter leg, lifting your heels to the surface. This can also be done on your back to work the core and develop mid-lower back flexibility. Backstroke swimming with fins also works the rotator cuff (shoulder joint) in a different direction to front crawl.

6. Facing upwards, have your legs straight in front of you and your backside down, as if you're seated in a lounge chair. Keeping your feet and ears above the surface of the water, do a quick breaststroke pulling motion with your arms, beginning the pull right next to the side of the knees so that you move down the pool feet first. During this sculling motion, the load is on the arms (specifically the triceps and deltoids) and abs, thereby developing strength in these important swimming muscles.

7. Do butterfly/flutter kicks on your front and back to strengthen your back, core and glutes. This also teaches you to kick from the hips, extend the knee at the completion of each kick and maximise the pressure on the surface of your foot. Proper form requires full arm extension with fingers interlaced or holding a kickboard with your thumbs on the surface. Elevate your knees to the surface, flicking your ankle and toes on each kick.

For a triathlete, one of the biggest swim-related mistakes is to focus solely on technique and swim only 50–100m at a time. Of course, drill work is important, but you need to include longer sets of continuous 200, 400 and even 800m non-drill swimming to ensure you can maintain technique and pace over longer distances. ●

MY FAVOURITE SWIM SET

I love doing the following 2km set, which essentially comprises 50m hard efforts (around 17–18 on the Borg Scale), with steadier swims (around 12 on the Borg Scale) as recovery. *You can alter the send-off times, recovery intervals or numbers of reps to reflect your ability.* Warm up for 500m or so first, and cool down afterwards.

Main set: 40 × 50m as:

> 16 × 50m all off 45 seconds with every fourth 50m HARD (take 3–5 seconds rest after the steady swim, and approx. 8–10 seconds after the hard 50m)

> 12 × 50m all off 50 seconds with every third 50m HARD (take 8–10 seconds rest after the steady swim, and approx. 13–15 seconds after the hard 50m)

> 8 × 50m all off 55 seconds with every second 50m HARD (take 13–15 seconds rest after the steady swim, and approx. 18–20 seconds after the hard 50m)

> 4 × 50m off 60 seconds all HARD (getting 23–5 seconds rest after each)

TAKING TO THE OPEN WATER

Open water. Yes, it can be a scary experience. There's no black stripe to follow and no side/lane rope to hang on to. Aquatic creatures lurk beneath, two-legged creatures flail around you, the water can be choppy and cold and full of floating detritus. But, despite these minor details, open-water swimming can be a wonderfully liberating, fulfilling and enjoyable activity. And even if it isn't, to reach the finish line of a non-pool-based triathlon you will need to get through it!

It's important to feel comfortable in open water before you can enjoy it. And to feel comfortable, you have to understand what the water can do, what you can do, and be confident that you can handle both the expected and the unexpected. Don't go into a race with the attitude that someone will be there to bail you out in times of trouble. Safety personnel are on hand but it is your responsibility to ensure you can complete the swim safely and under your own steam.

Before entering a race, beginners should ask themselves some questions: 'In the pool, do I grab the wall at each turn to rest? Can I stay afloat while coughing after swallowing a mouthful of water, or do I hang on to the lane rope? Can I keep swimming when I get a side stitch, calf or foot cramp? Have I managed to swim the entire race distance in training? Can I swim under water/with my eyes closed for a few seconds without feeling claustrophobic?' Think carefully about your answers, and if you're not confident in your ability to cope with these scenarios then spend a little more time in the pool before you embark on an open-water swim.

If you've never swum in open water, I suggest entering a standalone swim event or a sprint triathlon with more predictable conditions, for example in a sheltered lake, river or canal with no or limited currents. This will help build your experience and confidence. Ocean swims with waves, currents, tides and rips can pose problems for weaker swimmers, and may not be the best option for an open-water novice.

The best way to get used to swimming in open water is to swim in open water, both in training and by gaining experience in races. For safety, it's always a good idea to swim with others. However, don't worry if you can't practise in open water; many of the skills described below can be honed in the comfort of your local pool.

RACE STARTS

Races can have a mass start, when all the athletes start at once, or a wave start whereby groups (or waves) start separately, with a time gap in between. Athletes may be grouped in gender, predicted swim time and/or age-group categories, and each wave often has a different-coloured swim cap. Rolling starts, where athletes decide when to file into the water during a given time window, are also becoming increasingly popular in longer-distance races. The timing chip is activated when athletes cross the timing mat.

There are three types of starts: deep-water (floating), beach (from the beach or ankle-to-knee deep) and dive starts. Given that the latter is unusual in age-group and long-course racing, we will focus only on the first two.

Beach start: Beginners should simply walk into the water until it is deep enough to start swimming. Lean slightly forward to stop any waves knocking you over. If you are more experienced, do a high knee run, lifting your legs out of the water and, when the water is above knee-height, do a shallow dive, gliding for a few yards under water, grabbing the sand to stop you being forced back by a wave and bringing your feet under your hands. Use your feet to push forward at an angle so you break the surface. Then take a breath and dive just under the surface of the water again. These are known as 'dolphin dives'. When dolphining, keep your head tucked between your outstretched arms with your biceps squeezing your ears. When it's deep enough, start swimming.

TRAINING TIP

More advanced swimmers should practise fast starts in training. Do a short warm-up followed by 8–12 × 25m sprints, or 5–6 × 50m sprints, with about 5–10 seconds rest, to replicate the need for speed in the first 200m (as well as accelerating out of turn buoys). This can be followed by some race-paced swimming.

Deep-water floating start: You can either tread water in a vertical position, or lie horizontally and scull with your heels close to the water's surface and your head up and forward (but don't lift your neck too high). You may want to make wide, sweeping movements with your arms and legs to encourage others to keep their distance. Be aware of what is happening around you, and as soon as the whistle, gun or cannon sounds, use a whip- or side scissor-kick to accelerate. This can be practised in the deep end of a swimming pool.

If athletes are grouped in waves, and you're not the first to start, you can watch other swimmers and note the route they take to the first buoy. This will give you an indication of any currents and the best line to take depending on your experience. Beginners should position themselves at the back or the side of the start group to avoid the main melee. You may swim slightly further but you will also reduce the risk of panic or disruption. You could also delay your start slightly to allow the other swimmers to take off, giving you a clear space of water in which to embark on your open-water adventure. Experienced athletes should start in a position that minimises the distance to the first buoy, bearing in mind any currents.

PACING

If you are a beginner, I suggest starting, and staying, at a steady and relaxed pace and intensity. Try to avoid panting or holding your breath, which can increase anxiety and induce panic. If you feel yourself becoming overly anxious, focus on intrinsic factors that you can control, especially calm and controlled breathing, long exhales in the water and smooth hand entry and arm strokes. Starting out too hard can cause your heart rate to spike, leaving you in oxygen debt and fighting for breath. If you find yourself panicking, don't immediately flip on to your back and take large gasps of air. This can result in hyperventilation (taking in too much oxygen), a high heart rate and dizziness. Instead, stay tummy-down, turn your head to get a good breath of air, then put your face in the water and focus on blowing bubbles at a steady rate. If you do want to take some time out, slowly twist your head to the side, breathe and unhurriedly lift your head out of the water. Then either do a few strokes of breaststroke or tread water, take long slow breaths, look around, find your bearings and slowly start front crawl again when you feel ready.

More experienced swimmers should swim at a higher intensity for the first 200m for positioning reasons. This means about 75–80 per cent of maximum 50m effort. You can then settle into your sustainable race intensity and pace, which you would have determined, and internalised, in training.

SIGHTING AND NAVIGATION

It's easy to sight in a pool: you simply follow the black line. Unfortunately, there are no such lines in the open water, so you'll need to be able to stay in a straight line or risk adding a few hundred metres to your race. In open water, you could simply follow the bubbles of the feet in front of you, but you are placing your trust in them to go the right way, so you should be able to periodically 'sight' or 'spot' to make sure you're heading in the right direction. To sight, you need a 'marker'. This can be one of the race buoys or a tall, visible and immovable landmark that you would have identified beforehand (see section on transitions on page 245). In a pack and/or in choppy conditions, it is often easier to sight these land-based markers than the smaller buoys. If you are swimming in a river/canal, look at the bank/towpath as part of your normal stroke to keep you on course.

The world's best triathletes and open-water swimmers can sight without disrupting the rhythm of their stroke or their body position. Press down lightly on the water with your lead arm, lift the head slightly above the goggle line just before you take a breath, look forward and, as you lower it, turn your head to the side to breathe. Don't try to breathe and sight at the same time, otherwise you'll lift your head too high and your hips and legs will drop. It's equally important not to lift your head for too long. The sight–turn–breathe technique should be quick, smooth and fluid, as opposed to three separate movements, to ensure you can maintain your stroke and rhythm.

If you naturally swim straight you can sight every 12–15 strokes. If you have a little more trouble swimming straight you should sight more frequently, say every 7–9 strokes. Sometimes the initial sight gives you only a rough idea of where you're headed, so practise taking two sights on successive strokes.

Another element that affects how often you sight is the weather. If the water is calm with minimal glare, you can sight less as the visibility will be greater and it will be easier to see the markers. However, if there are high winds and the water is choppy, the markers are more difficult to see. If you sight in the trough of a wave you might not glimpse the buoy/marker and may need to take another look after a couple more strokes. If it is choppy, you may need to lift your head slightly higher, resulting in your legs sinking slightly. Counteract this by kicking a bit more.

LOSING YOUR GOGGLES

Although rare, there's always the possibility that you will lose your goggles (or they become dislodged) as a result of rushing water, a flailing arm or a broken strap. Taking to the water with an extra pair of goggles

- In the pool, swim with your eyes closed for 9–10 strokes. This will help you learn to swim straight without looking at the black line on the bottom of the pool. A glance at the lane ropes will tell you which side you veer to, and you can work with your coach to correct stroke asymmetry that might be causing the swerve – often crossing over the centre line at the front of the stroke or under the body. Over time, you should be able to increase the number of strokes and still swim in a straight line.
- Swim normally, but look up to the end of the pool twice every length using the sighting technique outlined previously.
- Water polo drill: swim 15–25m of the pool with your head up. Don't turn your head to the side to breathe. This is a great way to build strength in your neck and make you aware of how your lower body sinks when your head is raised.

wrapped round your wrist or ankle is dangerous and causes unnecessary drag. Instead, practise swimming without goggles and opening your eyes under water, as well as slowly rolling on to your back/treading water to readjust your goggles if they become dislodged. Some swimmers put their goggles underneath their swim cap to reduce the risk of the strap getting pulled or slipping off.

TURNING

Turns during a triathlon swim take place around the buoys. There are generally three types of buoys in a race: the smaller, intermediate buoys, the larger turn buoys and the finish buoys (or archway). Open water is not a controlled environment, and currents, tides and waves can move the buoys. Make sure you know how many turns there are, where they are and how they are marked out (e.g. the colour of the turning buoy is often different from the other course markers). Ninety-degree turns are the norm in an open-water swim (rarely will a triathlon have a 180-degree turn as sending swimmers head-on towards other competitors isn't a great idea).

The area around a turn buoy can be a traffic jam of people with flailing arms and legs. It is important to pick the right strategy depending on your ability. If you swim to the inside (that is, hugging the buoy as close as possible), you risk being caught in the crowd but with the potential to gain on the entire field if you don't get stuck. If you swim to the outside of the pack, you increase the distance swum but avoid the melee. Beginners should remain on the outside to avoid the claustrophobia of too many swimmers. Intermediate swimmers may also want to take the outside path on the first buoy when the pack may be larger and take a tighter line at the latter stages of the swim when the pack may have thinned out. Advanced swimmers will always try to take the shortest route, jostling for position as they approach the buoy.

There are a few ways of getting around a buoy. The first, and best for beginners, is simply to swim around, but twist your body in the direction of the turn. The second method is the sweep turn. Use the arm closest to the inside of the turn as a pivot by keeping it straight and deep through the underwater phase of the stroke. Then, with the outside arm, take wide, sweeping strokes to propel you around the turn. More experienced swimmers may wish to try the much more difficult 'roll' or 'corkscrew' turn, where you roll on to your back mid-turn before turning 90 degrees as you roll back on to your front. For advanced swimmers, the buoys provide a break from the uniform speed/effort and these athletes can utilise pace changes as they negotiate the turn to create/exploit gaps in the field.

DRAFTING

It is legal to draft during the swim portion of a triathlon. Beginners should not concern themselves too much with drafting techniques, but intermediate and advanced swimmers will find this skill extremely beneficial. Studies show that drafting saves around 20 per cent of the energy expenditure of swimming, theoretically leaving you fresher for the bike and run. It can also enable you to swim faster than normal by sitting on the toes of someone speedier.

There are two ways to draft: 1) swimming directly behind another athlete, almost close enough to touch their toes; or 2) swimming in their wake. This involves positioning yourself next to the chest of another swimmer, almost under their armpit. If you decide to use the second method, you may wish swim on the non-breathing (blind) side of the other athlete (if they're not breathing bilaterally) so you can make any tactical moves without being seen. More advanced swimmers should be constantly aware of their competitors and react to changes in pace/direction as necessary. If you find yourself boxed in, or wishing to change to the inside/outside to a position that better suits your breathing pattern, slow down for one/two strokes, quickly dart across the legs of your competitor and kick hard to re-establish your position.

It is important to be aware of the downfalls to drafting. First, you may become complacent and rely on another person to

TRAINING TIP

- Practise turning in deep water, either in the middle of a pool with no lane ropes or at the wall without touching.
- Place a buoy or something similar in the pool. First, practise 90-degree turns solo and then progress into small groups. Experiment with different approaches to the buoy – coming in for a wide turn or cutting the corner as tight as possible. Use the different techniques outlined above.
- Try both left and right turns because, just as we have dominant sides of our bodies, we also have dominant and weak turning sides.

TRAINING TIP

- Most swimming lanes are wide enough to cram three swimmers in side by side. Form an arrow head with those at either side on the hip of the lead swimmer and complete 6 × 25m sets fast. Alternate starting positions, and gain confidence in being able to swim with arms and legs flying around you.
- Practise pace-line sets where groups of swimmers closely follow one another, changing pace and leaders throughout the set.

navigate – so make sure you continue to sight, lest you both head off in the wrong direction. It may also mean swimming at someone else's pace, which may be too slow/too fast.

PRE-RACE SWIM PREPARATION

In addition to technique and skills, there are other swim-specific things to know before race day, which can usually be found on the event website and/or from athletes who have completed the race before (but remember that courses and conditions change):

> the distance you need to swim and whether it is in a pool (and what length pool it is) or open water (e.g. canal, sea, river);

> the swim cut-off time (before entering the race, beginners need to make sure they are able to complete the distance in the allocated time frame);

> the race rules, including wetsuit regulations (e.g. the water temperature cut-off below which wetsuits are allowed);

> the type of start: deep-water, beach or (rarely) dive start and whether it is a mass start or a wave start;

> the start time (of your wave, if applicable);

> whether and where you can do a warm-up and for how long;

> starting mechanism: whistle, a cannon or a shout of 'go';

> the swim course: swim entrance and exit, direction of the swim (clockwise or anticlockwise), number and location of the buoys (and the approximate distances between them);

> conditions such as tides, currents, the ocean floor, any rocks or other hazards;

> the layout of transition, e.g. the swim exit, bike-racking area and change tents.

If it's a major event, there's often time to carry out a practice swim prior to the race. This can be invaluable in helping you establish sight lines and land-based markers around the course, and get a sense of the conditions (although be mindful that these may change come race day).

Fish Out of Water – Swim Training Without a Pool

Q 'I'm currently deployed overseas with the British Army and want to do a half Ironman next year. The swim is my weakest discipline. I'm able to keep up my running and cycling fitness to a degree but I don't have access to a pool or open water while I am overseas. Are you able to recommend any swim-related drills or exercises that I can do in the gym?'

LT CLAIRE JACKSON

A I've come across quite a few people who are unable to regularly access a pool yet want to do triathlon. Not being able to train in one of the three disciplines isn't an optimal situation – but when has optimal ever been possible or necessary? Yes, your swim will probably remain your weakest discipline, at least while you're on overseas deployment, but all's never lost. Focus on what you can do and maximise the opportunities you have.

Remember, too, that even if your swim is relatively slow, your overall tri performance can improve as a result of increased bike and run ability, supported by some targeted gym-based strength and conditioning (S & C) work.

To optimise the benefit of land-based training, select exercises with mechanical relevance to the swimming action. For front crawl, forward propulsion comes from the arm pull and the leg kick, which alternates hip flexion and extension. You should focus land-based training on developing strength in the relevant muscles – including deltoids, triceps, lats, abdominals and obliques, lower back, glutes, quads, hip flexors and hamstrings. Even those who swim regularly will benefit from including these exercises in their S & C sessions. (See Chapter 6 for more details.)

Make sure you warm up first with a spin on the bike, a jog or some star jumps, and then embark on these:

Supermans: Lie on your stomach with arms stretched over your head. Slowly lift your legs, head and arms, ensuring you activate your core, lower back, glutes and hamstring muscles. Keep your neck in a neutral position. Pause about 6 inches off the ground and slowly lower. Do 2–3 sets of 10–15 lifts.

Flutter kicks: These are great for strengthening hip flexors. Lie on your back with your hands underneath your bum. Lift your heels off, maintain straight legs and scissor-kick from the hips with your toes pointed for 20–30 seconds. You can also do this on your stomach with your hands by your hips.

Plank: Balance on your toes, with your upper arms at 90 degrees and your forearms taking your body weight. Keep a strong flat back. Start off at 2 × 30 seconds and gradually increase to 2 × 60 seconds (with a minute or so of rest in between). Side planks with rotation are also beneficial. Turning yourself on to your side, balance on your elbow, keeping a straight line from head to feet. Gradually rotate around your centre line (imagine a line down your spine) towards the floor. It doesn't have to be far – a five-degree rotation is enough. Do 3 × 20 seconds of rotations on each side.

Abs: Do regular and rotational sit-ups slowly and deliberately, concentrating on activating your core.

Shoulders: Hold some small hand weights (4–7lb) at your sides and lift your arms out to the sides (90 degrees) to shoulder height, palms down and lower slowly. Then, keep your arms shoulder width apart, palms facing each other, and lift to shoulder height and lower slowly (two sets of 10–12 repetitions, or reps). Hold slightly heavier weights (10–15lb) next to your head, palms facing a mirror, shoulders and elbows at 90 degrees. Press the weights straight up with extended arms and lower slowly to the start position.

Trapezius muscles: Do seated rows or replicate the motion using dumbbells and a bench. Pinch your shoulder blades together each time (two sets of 10–12 reps).

Lateral pull downs: These mimic the motion of pulling through the water in front crawl. Grab the bar with your arms extended, slightly wider than shoulder width apart, and keep a flat back (not extended or arched). Contract your lower abs to protect your lower back, then flex your elbows and bring the bar down to chest height. It is OK to lean back slightly. Keep your elbows flexed to your sides and hold the weight at your chest for 2–5 seconds before slowly returning the bar overhead. Do 2 × 12 reps initially. Keep the weight challenging, but do not compromise form.

Triceps: A swimmer's press-up is like a traditional press-up, but harder as you should keep your elbows tucked in tight to your sides at all times. Do them on your knees if necessary. Tricep dips on a bench are another option for strengthening this muscle.

You could also purchase some Dryland swim cords – pieces of durable rubber tubing with comfortable handles. Attaching to an anchor point, they allow you to simulate swimming by isolating important muscles while building strength and a better range of motion. They come in different resistances, and I suggest starting with the easiest. There are web-based videos to guide you, or ask a coach to demonstrate the correct technique. (See Chapter 6 for more details.)

Make the most of any time back in the UK to jump in the pool or open water, but don't overdo it and risk injury or overload. And remember that you don't have to swim front crawl in a triathlon. You can always tread water, roll over and rest on your back, or do breaststroke or backstroke (if backstroke is permitted). Just don't risk missing the swim cut-off time.

Ultimately, focus on what is possible and before you know it you'll be powering past people on the bike and the run . . . despite currently being a fish out of water! ●

CHAPTER FOUR

BIKE

I could swim, I could run, but I was 26 years old before my backside first came into contact with a road bike when I bought a third-hand, yellow-and-black Peugeot. It looked like a bumble-bee. It cost £300 and I've still got it. However, upon purchasing said machine I quickly realised that riding the blue shopper with white tassels when I was eight had failed to equip me adequately for a lifetime of serious cycling. I didn't have a clue how to ride my new bee. In fact, many would look at my bike-handling skills and say that I still don't.

OPPOSITE: On the bike at the Ironman World Championship, 2009.

As a poorly paid civil servant with a penchant for charity shops, I had spent, for me, a small fortune on this new steed and hence decided it was all about the bike, and not about clothing or other equipment. I just rode it as was. No clip-in shoes, no bike fitting: I just sat and pedalled. Hard. I remember turning up at the local, Saturday group ride. I was wearing a canary yellow T-shirt and old black running shorts (so continued the bumble-bee theme) and running shoes. The nail in my proverbial group-cycling coffin was that I carried my spares (not that I knew how to use them) in a bumbag. They nevertheless welcomed me into the group, and proceeded to help me turn my bumble-bee cycling from being my amateur Achilles heel to a professional strength. That ability is useful given that the bike section of a triathlon is the longest in both time and distance and hence the one where you can lose or gain the most time.

I can't hope to cover every aspect of cycling here, but hopefully I can shed a lovely LED bike light on some of the more common issues for triathletes to consider when they are tackling the two-wheeled world.

IT'S JUST LIKE RIDING A BIKE: BIKE TRAINING FUNDAMENTALS

EQUIPMENT

Bike

You can grab a bargain or spend several thousand pounds on a bike, but regardless of cost it a) must pass the pre-race safety inspection; b) can't be a fixed wheel (fixie); and c) should suit your race goal. If you're just starting triathlon and only planning to enter one or two shorter events, you can use a mountain bike or hybrid. But if you are thinking of doing more, it's probably best to buy a road bike on which you can train, race and even commute, and which is suitable for a variety of courses. You don't have to buy new. Second- (or third-) hand bikes can be great value – I rode a second-hand bike en route to my World Age Group Championship victory in 2006 – but it's your responsibility to make sure it's roadworthy.

> If you can only have one, I would always choose a road bike. Gear changing and braking are easier, they are safer in traffic and during group training rides and more suitable for technical or hilly courses.

A triathlon bike (also known as a time-trial or TT bike) is the preferred option for many. They are more aerodynamic, but owning a road and a TT bike may make your bank manager see red. You also can't use them in draft legal races (where it's legal to cycle directly behind your competitors, rather than maintaining a designated distance). Ultimately it depends on your chosen type of triathlon, your disposable income and the size of your garage/spare room/lounge. If you can only have one, I would always choose a road bike. Gear changing and braking are easier, they are safer in traffic and during group training rides and more suitable for technical or hilly courses. You can add clip-on aerobars to facilitate a more aerodynamic position. If you want to focus on off-road triathlon, ignore everything said above and get a mountain bike.

Wheels

The type of wheel depends on your budget, and thereafter the course, conditions and you as a rider. Some like to race with wheels with deep rims as they are more

aerodynamic under certain weather conditions, with some even sporting disc wheels. Make sure you practise with your chosen race wheels, and understand that side-winds can make riding wheels with deep rims a bit of a challenge. Disc wheels are banned in breezy Hawaii for that very reason.

Tyres

Tyres are of two main types: clinchers, which allow a removable inner tube to be put inside, and tubulars ('tubs') where the inner tube is sewn inside the tyre, making it a single-piece system. The tyre is then glued or taped directly to the rim and requires a special wheel made for this purpose. The wheels and tyres for clinchers and tubulars are not interchangeable. There is much debate about the pros and cons of each. Some say that tubulars give you a smoother and more responsive ride, and can be lighter and more puncture resistant. However, they are expensive, and can require a skilled person to fit them correctly. Clinchers are lighter on the wallet and sold at every bike shop, and advocates suggest that there is little difference in terms of overall performance. Given the cost and ease of installation, most people use clinchers in training. I also raced with clinchers, given the peace of mind that came from knowing how to change them relatively quickly.

In terms of tyre tread, there are models for all seasons: from tread-heavy winter tyres to smooth racing tyres and everything in between. In general, the smoother the surface of the tyre the faster it is, but the less grip it might have, which can be an issue, especially in wetter weather. However, just to confuse things further, the rubber compound from which the tyre is made is much more important than the tread pattern when it comes to the amount of grip you'll have.

Last, tyre pressure: I would race and train with 110–120psi, but reduce this to 90–100psi if the road surface was wet or the roads were very rough. Pumping up your tyres is much easier using a track (foot) pump than the hand-held variety, but given track pumps don't fit easily in your back pocket you may want to invest in the latter to carry when training and racing. CO_2 cartridges can also be very handy, as (provided they are used correctly) they can inflate the tyre in seconds and are extremely portable. Make sure you know how to use them, especially if you will be relying on such cartridges in a race.

Saddle

Saddles come in a wide variety of shapes and sizes. As the bike-fit section explains, the saddle should suit your biomechanics, physiology and budget, be comfortable and put you in an effective and efficient cycling position. If you wear a race kit with a chamois that is thinner than your regular cycle shorts, make sure you practise training in your kit to ensure that the saddle is still comfy.

Shoes/pedals

Whether you use regular flat pedals or clipless pedals (which you actually clip into) will depend on your cycling experience and confidence. Experienced triathletes use clipless pedals to allow for a full pedal stroke and give them better power transfer from feet to bike. You can, however, simply use the flat pedals on their own or add cages that your forefoot slips into so that you can utilise the upstroke. Cages can be a lot harder to get your feet out of than clipless pedals, though.

Your choice of pedal determines what shoes you wear. With flat pedals, you can use the same shoes for cycling and running. If you use clipless pedals you'll need cycle or tri shoes, with cleats mounted underneath that allow you to clip in. If you're nervous about clipping out, ask a cycle-savvy friend or a bike shop to loosen your pedals (there is a spring-tension system that, when loosened, makes clipping out much easier). Remember to clip out one foot at a time and, if in doubt, practise on a turbo to get used to the motion, rather than at a traffic light.

Helmet

A regular brain bucket will protect your head, as long it has passed the necessary safety tests and fits correctly. While I love a second-hand bargain, it's probably best avoided in this context. An aero helmet isn't absolutely necessary. Yes, if the boffins are to be believed, they may enable you to shave time off your bike split but they always made me feel claustrophobic and I felt that the lack of ventilation could make me overheat, with dehydration striking on the run. In addition, an aero helmet's effectiveness relies on the tail being flat against your back – hard to do if you are looking around, getting drinks at aid stations or climbing a hill.

Clothing

Dress for the conditions. As the saying goes, there's no such thing as bad weather, only bad clothing choices. The following are best avoided: underwear beneath cycling shorts, baggy shorts over tights (aka shites), a jersey that exposes your midriff, shorts that show any sort of crack through well-worn fabric, canary yellow T-shirts, bumbags.

Bike box/case

Extremely useful for transporting your bike to its race or training destination, especially on an aeroplane. They can be bought, borrowed or hired, and can be soft or hard. The former are lighter and usually cheaper, but don't always offer the same level of protection as the hard cases that, although more robust, can be heavier and more cumbersome. I opted for the cheapest version – a free, supersized cardboard box from a bike shop and a roll of masking tape.

Other kit

Carry equipment to change or repair an inner tube, both when training and racing, and know how to use it, otherwise it could be a long walk home. Mudguards are great for winter riding, but most athletes remove them before a race. Have bottle cages to carry . . . bottles, with other hydration systems between your aerobars or behind the saddle (if you're a long-course athlete and need additional means to carry fluid). Remember that the more you carry the heavier the bike. Practise before a race to get used to manoeuvring the bike with added weight. Unless you do all your training on the turbo, good lights are essential. Bike computers range from basic to all singing and pedalling. It depends on what you want to measure. Being more of a back-to-basics girl, mine just informs me of elapsed time, distance and speed. Wearing sunglasses is preferable. Fancy versions come with interchangeable lenses for different conditions.

AERODYNAMICS

'Aero': not the delicious chocolate bar with the lovely bubbles, but the impact of you and your bike on the moving air, aka aerodynamics. Triathletes obsess about it. Yes, it matters. The type of bike, your position on it, the clothing you wear, the equipment you attach to the machine, all determine how fast or slow you go. As I realised, a baggy yellow T-shirt and running shorts created more drag than a queen (bee). Limiting drag is important, but some athletes go to such lengths to be aerodynamic they end up so hunched up over their tri-bars that they get off and promptly seize up. Pure cyclists can get away with more extreme positions because they only have to run a bath after a race, while triathletes still have another discipline to conquer. Striking that balance between being aero, effective, efficient and comfortable over the course of the whole race is the ticket, and this is where a proper 'bike fit' comes in.

BIKE FIT

A bike fit is a way of ensuring that the bike you ride fits you like a cycling glove. There is, however, a range of different methods employed by specialists from a back-to-basics use of the eye to 3D or wind-tunnel fits and everything in between. Some fitters use patented commercialised systems, and others have developed their own unique methods based on individual experience.

I've had my fair share of bike fits in my time, ranging from good to bad and downright ugly in terms of effectiveness. I'm not, however, a guru on the subject so I'm going to defer to someone who eats, sleeps and breathes bike fit, including looking after yours truly in all my wonky glory. What follows is what I've gleaned from Mr Mike 'Bike Fit' Taylor.

Most athletes are wonky, in that the right and left sides of the body are asymmetrical. Bikes, however, are inherently symmetrical. The overall aim of a bike fit is to take the non-symmetrical aspect (aka the rider) of the system and make it meet the symmetrical aspect (aka the bike) in a harmonious way.

Most triathletes would benefit from a bike fit, whatever stage they're at in their sporting journey. If done well, it can help alleviate pain and discomfort, for example numbness in your feet or glutes, hotfoot (a burning sensation through the ball of the foot), sore Achilles, tightness or cramping in the calves or hamstrings, knee or back pain, neck ache, and the much-feared saddle soreness and undercarriage chafing. As importantly, removing pain and discomfort and improving performance can help make cycling – and triathlon as a whole – much more fun.

Mike tries to understand the athlete through an informal interview, finding out their strengths and weaknesses, aims and ambitions, sporting background and medical history, before beginning a physical assessment. Only then does he start to fit you on the bike, using eyes and ears rather than a high-tech computerised system. Whatever method or system is employed, bike fitting must put the athlete at the heart; being tailored to you, rather than 'fitting by numbers' and trying to get the athlete into predetermined position.

Before you hand over hard-earned cash, speak to the fitter to find out their philosophy, what system they use, whether they understand triathlon and the impact of cycling on swim and run and how they ensure an individualised fit. If you have a TT bike, make sure their experience is not limited to fitting athletes to road bikes. Note that an effective position for a sprint race may differ from the set-up for an Ironman.

My bike fit

Throughout my career I had quite a few issues on the bike. Not least my inability to actually handle it, but also aches and pains in my lower back, a tight hamstring and pins and needles in my toes. As a pro, I did my best to manage this, but after I retired myself and a few friends decided to complete the self-developed '4321 Challenge' where we would run up each of the highest mountains in Wales, England and Scotland respectively and cycle the 725km between them – in under 48 hours. This challenge compelled me to get a decent fit on my road bike, and that's where Mike came in.

MIKE TAYLOR on my bike fit

Chrissie was over-reaching on the right-hand side, loading her foot, knee and calf, and not utilising her right glute or upper quadriceps. She tended to slouch and point her toes downwards, both of which further limited the use of those powerful quad muscles. She was constantly moving on the saddle trying to get comfortable, but always favouring the right-hand side. Her shoulders were hunched, her arms were too straight and there was a lack of body weight over the front wheel. Her pedalling on the left side was mechanical and methodical, but on the right was clunky and 'stabbing'. Her right hip was also drawn forward and lower than her left hip. Overall, she gave the impression of being disconnected from the bike, rather than working in harmony.

I inserted internal wedges and arch-supporting insoles to stabilise her pronating feet and moved her cleats back: the left slightly more than the right to even up her pedal stroke, centre her pelvis on the saddle and help her engage her quads. I fitted a women-specific saddle, which was also raised and brought forward, thus opening up Chrissie's hips and enabling a smoother pedal stroke. This also meant her pelvis bones were better supported. The stem was shortened and inverted to raise the handlebars to prevent over-reaching and enable her to relax her arms and have some degree of bend at the elbow. The handlebars themselves were also changed: narrower to suit her shoulder width and with a shallower drop to enable better bike handling.

All adjustments were made individually with an assessment of the impact from the athlete and fitter. Each change then directed the next change required. Part of the art of bike fitting is understanding the sequencing of the adjustments, and these vary from rider to rider.

As a result of the fit Chrissie had much more stability, comfort and connectivity on the bike as well as a more symmetrical pedalling action. By moving her pelvis forward on the bike, we put more weight into the front of the bike so her handling also improved. And yes, she successfully completed the 4321 Challenge, pain-free, in 47 hours! ●

Getting a bike fit from
Mike Taylor for the 4321
Challenge, 2014.

PEDALLING AND CADENCE

With better form, you can achieve greater power output with less input . . . and who doesn't like free speed? If you have traditional, flat pedals on your bike, you'll have little choice but to exclusively push down, but if you have cages or clipless pedals, you can also pull up. Focus on achieving a consistent pull and push, moving the pedal round in an egg-shaped motion. Keep your feet relatively flat and your ankles still. Avoid pointing your toes down at the front of the pedal stroke and pulling up with the heel. Pedalling in circles lessens the 'dead spot', the point where no power is transferred.

Most people have one leg that is slightly stronger than the other. Try to exert the same pressure with each rather than over-relying on your dominant leg, which would exacerbate asymmetry. Relax your upper body (including your elbows) and engage your core (see Chapter 6). No one likes a lazy, floppy torso.

In cycling, cadence is the number of revolutions per minute (rpm) you make – of your feet rather than Elvis-style hip gyrations. You can check yours by counting how many times your right knee comes up in 30 seconds and multiplying by two. It's best to do this on the turbo or a flat road. You could also purchase a cycling computer that does the maths for you. There's no such thing as the correct cadence. It's horses for race courses. I always pushed a relatively big gear (i.e. I had a relatively low cadence of around 70–75rpm) whereas others tend to perform well with a cadence of 90rpm or above. Most people have a cadence of around 80–95rpm. Judge the effect of different cadences on heart rate and, if you have a power meter, on your power. Also, use the brick session to see how different cadences impact your run. Once you've established a cadence that feels good and works best, make sure you've got the bike gearing that allows you to maintain it whatever the course.

GEARING

Know how to use your gears. In the early days, I didn't and tended to try to muscle into headwinds or up climbs in a supersized gear, and ended up straining my hamstrings. I also struggled rather embarrassingly when traffic lights turned green as I hadn't selected an easier gear beforehand. There are lots of gearing options, with different-sized cassettes and chain rings suitable for different riders and terrain. If in doubt, ask at a friendly bike shop or an experienced triathlete what might be appropriate for you.

BIKE-HANDLING SKILLS

Being a confident, competent bike handler isn't just important for safety, it can also enable you to maximise your bike time on hilly, technical courses. Admittedly, I should have invested more time in learning the basics at the start of my career, rather than embedding bad habits, becoming increasingly fearful and generally being a total liability. The advice which follows is what I have gleaned from those who are more proficient than I, including my husband Tom, and will help you corner and descend like Wiggins rather than Wellington.

For cornering, I suggest finding a quiet road, or even a vacant car park, where you can practise. As you approach a corner, lean the bike into the bend by putting your weight distribution on to your inside hand and outside foot; don't try to turn the handlebars; keep the outside leg straight and with most of your bodyweight concentrated downwards through the outside pedal. Preferably, have your hands on the drops (if on a road bike) with your elbows bent, and keep your head vertical rather than leaning with the bike. Go into the corner at a controlled speed. If you do need to use your brakes, do so before the corner and you should feather (apply lightly a few times) the front, and apply the rear with moderation as the rear wheel can skid and slide sideways with too much brake applied. Focus your attention on the end of the corner, rather than looking down. Enter the turn a little wide, and then cut in and hold your line as tightly as possible.

When descending, shift your centre of gravity over the back wheel. If you have a road bike, riding on the drops brings you closer to the ground and helps to maintain traction and keep you and the bike stable. As above, don't grab your brakes, but feather them if necessary. Keep your eyes focused forwards, rather than looking down.

Practise cornering and descending at slower speeds before trying to impersonate Wiggo. If you have a mountain or cyclocross bike then I also suggest getting off-road, even if it's on easy trails, just to get a feel for bike handling on different terrain and without traffic. It's easy to get stressed, stiff and uptight, but try to relax and avoid a vice-like grip on the bars and you'll be careering round corners and descending like a demon in no time.

HILL TRAINING

The nemesis to some, riding hills is essentially a high intensity session because the incline increases the resistance and the descents offer a chance to recover. Hill training can help you become stronger, faster and more powerful, even if you only ever race on flat courses. I reflect on my time in Nepal or when cycle touring in Argentina, weighed down with panniers and grinding up and down mountains. This was hill training at its basic and best, and I believe it's what shaped me into the athlete I became.

In terms of technique, there are a few pointers I can offer. As you climb, use your gears to retain the same cadence and avoid over-straining, keep your body relaxed and pedal stroke smooth. In training, I would do some sections of climbs in the TT position (or on the drops of a road bike) to really work my hamstrings and glutes. I would also get out of the saddle intermittently to vary the position and to increase the power I could exert on steeper sections. When you stand, you should feel like you're running on the pedals, allowing the bike to move, but not rock from side to side. Try to pace your effort, rather than smashing yourself at the start only to be crawling as you near the top. Remember that what goes up must come down, so even if you suffer on the ascent hopefully you'll enjoy the return trip!

INDOOR CYCLING

Indoor cycling can be a friend with benefits for the following reasons:

> It's a highly controlled environment.

> There's no opportunity for drafting or free-wheeling.

> It's time efficient.

> Inclement weather won't stop play given that the likelihood of rain or snow in your garage is low.

> You don't have to navigate potholes, cope with corners or stop, whether that be for traffic lights, flat tyres or cafés with cake.

> It makes simultaneously cycling while watching a video or listening to music possible.

> It helps to train the brain to endure monotony and boredom.

It also comes into its own if (like me) you have a tendency to break bones and can't ride outside.

There are several different devices that enable you to cycle on your normal bike indoors: stationary bikes, such as those you would find in a gym (includes watt bikes); a turbo trainer or rollers. Unless you have a lot of cash to spare, you probably can't afford your own stationary bike. A turbo trainer is, however, well worth the

investment, especially if you live in a country where rain/sleet/snow features heavily on the forecast, you have broken your arm/wrist/hand/finger/rib Wellington style, and/or you don't like cycling in the dark. It consists of a frame, a clamp to hold the bicycle securely, a roller that presses up against the rear wheel, and a mechanism to create resistance when the pedals are turned. There are different types of turbo trainer depending on the latter mechanism. In a wind trainer, the roller drives a fan to create air resistance. You change the resistance using your gears. These are typically the least expensive and noisiest. Magnetic trainers have magnets that resist each other, and are moderately expensive and moderately noisy. Some magnetic trainers have handlebar-mounted devices to change the resistance during a session. Fluid trainers use liquid-filled chambers to create resistance and are the most expensive and quietest trainers. Some trainers are equipped with sensors that monitor power output, cadence, virtual speed and heart rate. You might want to put an old/hard-wearing tyre on your rear wheel – or use a different wheel altogether – to avoid shredding a good tyre.

Bicycle rollers are another option for indoor training. They stay static while you ride, essentially by balancing your bike on top of them. They require the rider to have good stability, focus and a dose of patience in order to master the technique, but they do help improve core strength, your connection with the bike, pedalling efficiency (a more complete, smooth pedal stroke) and bike-handling skills (if you can remain upright!).

DRAFTING

Drafting in the cycling context is when a cyclist rides directly behind another, sitting in the front rider's slipstream. It can help the rear rider save a considerable amount of energy. Triathlons can be drafting (also known as draft-legal) or non-drafting, where drafting is not permitted. In the latter, the race rules will stipulate the size of the draft zone. This is an imaginary rectangular area surrounding each bike, which you must not enter unless overtaking (the manoeuvre must also be completed within a specified time frame). The zones vary in size depending on the race, and there are often 'draft busters' on the course to enforce the rules. It pays to be aware of the rules given that any infringement will likely incur a penalty, which is usually time spent by the side of the road, or even a disqualification.

GROUP RIDING TIPS

Although it's beneficial to do some of your riding alone, especially given the non-drafting nature of most triathlons, there are advantages to group riding, including motivation, camaraderie, skill development and communal cake stops. If you can, find a small group of cyclists to ride with, preferably those who are more practised. More experienced cyclists will also be able to explain hand signals and etiquette so that you don't commit cardinal cycling sins. Some quick tips:

Communication is key. Obvious warnings include 'slowing' or 'braking'. Others to be aware of are: 'car up', meaning there's a car ahead to be aware of; 'car back', meaning there's a car behind that might be trying to overtake; and 'single out', meaning to adopt single file. Use vocal cords or your hand to point out any obstacles, such as potholes or oil.

Try to match your ability with that of the group. If you've any doubts about your fitness or handling skills, always opt for a slower group. Ride consistently and don't yo-yo your pace, brake suddenly or swerve, unless absolutely necessary.

Ride as closely as you can to the person in front, both to get the slipstream effect and to ensure that the group doesn't get strung out. Horse-play is best avoided at all times. If road conditions allow, you can ride two abreast, but make sure you maintain an even pace and stay level with the person next to you rather than what's known as 'half wheeling'. If possible, 'do a turn' at the front of the group even if it's just for a few minutes. Conversely, if you're finding the pace easy don't get to the front and put the hammer down. If this all sounds a bit draconian, believe me, it isn't. Cycling groups are, for the most part, relaxed, fun and friendly places to be and you'll be made welcome, even as a bumbag-wearing novice.

MY FAVOURITE TURBO SESSION

5 minutes at 80rpm with 2 minutes' rest interval

1 × 10 minutes at race pace with 2 minutes' rest interval

5 minutes at 80rpm with 60 seconds' rest interval

2 × 3 minutes at 75rpm with 60 seconds' rest interval

3 × 2 minutes at 70rpm with 60 seconds' rest interval

4 × 1 minute at 60rpm with 60 seconds' rest interval

5–10 minutes' cool-down

66 Cycling groups are, for the most part, relaxed, fun and friendly places to be and you'll be made welcome, even as a bumbag-wearing novice. 99

PRE-RACE BIKE PREPARATION

As with the swim, there are cycle-specific things to be aware of before a race, which can usually be found on the event website and/or from other athletes:

> the distance you need to cycle;

> the bike cut-off time;

> the race rules, including littering, drafting, whether you need to wear your race number on the bike and the use of disc wheels;

> the bike course: bike exit, mount and dismount lines and bike entry;

> the terrain (e.g. hills, corners, type of road/off-road surface);

> whether there are distance markers and, if so, how often they appear;

> location of any aid stations and their provision;

> whether mechanical support is provided and in what form;

> location of any penalty tents;

> when you need to rack your bike and, if the day before the race, what you need to bring to bike check-in (e.g. bike, helmet, race number/s).

Uphill Battle –
Winter Biking Made Easy

Q 'I have signed up for my first Ironman race next summer, which has some steep climbs on the bike course. As most of my bike training during the winter months will be using a turbo, what sessions would you suggest to develop my endurance and hill climbing strength? Being from Norfolk you might understand my concern!'

RENATA GARFOOT

A Congratulations on registering for your first Ironman. What better firework to have up your backside when it's cold, wet or windy outside? That said, cycling is usually the first to suffer with short days and suboptimal weather. However, this needn't be the case, with adaptability, a 'can do' attitude and willingness to endure a little bit of discomfort.

Over the winter, I'd aim for three sessions a week: a longer steady ride, one of 90 minutes with some race-pace work and a shorter 60-minute higher intensity session (see Chapter 2 for more details). You quite rightly highlighted the turbo as being your friend over the colder, rainy months but don't discount outdoor riding altogether. If you can afford it, I would invest in quality front and rear lights, mudguards, winter tyres, layered clothing with a wind/waterproof outer shell, gloves, neoprene overshoes, a thin hat/headband and even a neck warmer. Those little pocket-sized heat packs are also worth their weight in warmth. Wear sunglasses with clear, orange or yellow tints for low-light conditions. Have your bike serviced and give it some TLC after each outdoor session.

You burn more calories in the cold so make sure you fuel sufficiently, and hydration is important even if you don't think you're sweating that much. A CamelBak filled with warm energy drink is an option: a rider's radiator for your back and then your stomach. The winter-warming coffee stop is always something to look forward to. It would be good if you could do longer sessions outdoors and think about joining a group for motivation, camaraderie and safety. An extra bonus would be to find some headwinds or use bigger gear, high resistance efforts of 5–10 minutes during this

ride to simulate climbs. There's a lot to be said for swapping the road bike for a mountain bike, too. They're great for building strength and endurance, and injecting occasional variety can help ward off boredom.

Toughing it out in cold and damp weather isn't always easy or pleasurable but it can be beneficial for the mind, especially if there is the chance that conditions could be similar on race day. You conquer in training. You can conquer in a race. It's all about the having the right kit and carrying a positive attitude in your back pocket.

As the previous section explained, there are also times when you want or need to stay inside on the stationary bike, turbo or rollers. There's a vast range of turbo options, but all you really need is something that gives predictable pedal resistance. Measures of time, rpm, power and heart rate are not essential: it depends on your training philosophy, personality and pocket. For maximum time efficiency, keep your bike set up and ready to go, with a sweat-mopping towel and shoes already clipped in; a mirror is good to check your form; and a fan helps limit Bikram yoga conditions.

Yes, some find indoor training tedious and mind-numbing; however, it's perception and attitude that matter. If you deem indoor cycling dull, it'll be a struggle, but by using motivational tools the sessions will pass more quickly and pleasurably. Stimulation is a matter of choice: I prefer 'We Are the Champions' or 'Eye of the Tiger' to get my pedals turning. Others opt for films and some reach for downloads or technologies that enable you to train on a certain course. Shameless plug: my Tri Harder AudioFuel workouts were designed specifically to give you a music/coaching combo. You could train with others to create a shared steam-room-like experience or opt for spin classes, which tend to be 45–60-minute sessions with high intensity and strength work, often replicating hill climbs of varying lengths.

You've highlighted hills as an area that you want to practise. Indoors, you can simulate hills of varying distances and inclines using your gearing – selecting a harder gear for the duration of your 'hill', perhaps varying it as you ascend, to create slightly flatter or steeper sections. You can alternate between the aero, TT position or (on a road bike) on the drops and top of the handlebars, getting out of the saddle to finish each effort.

In addition to your hills, you could do shorter anaerobic or VO_2-max repeats with a cadence of about 80–90rpm. For example, for the anaerobic work you could do 10–20 × 30–60 seconds, with a one- to two-minute recovery spin in between. Or you can do lactate threshold work to train at your so-called 'sweet spot'; which is

Q&A

an intensity that you can just about maintain consistently for an hour. I used to break this segment up into 20-minute blocks as it enabled me to better maintain the intensity. (See Chapter 2 at page 55 for more details.)

Of course, you can combine some of these sessions, for example doing pyramids with varied gearing and pacing. You can also use the turbo to do a single-leg drill, which can highlight any pedalling dead spots. You'll feel a lack of tension on the chain, feel a small jolt and perhaps hear a clanking sound. Elimination of such a dead spot would be preferable. I wouldn't try this outside unless you like road rash.

You will be able to endure the winter, like thousands of other triathletes do, with some sensible choices, flexibility and a positive mindset. And when you're crossing the finish line at your first Ironman, you'll know it's been worth it! ●

CHAPTER FIVE

RUN

The run: the last discipline to conquer before you cross that finish line and the one where you might feel like you: a) have wooden legs, b) are becoming overly familiar with the inside of a portable toilet, and c) should have taken up lawn bowls. It's also the discipline where races are won and lost, when you can see and interact most with the spectators and which ends with a grand finale – that hallowed finish line. Those aspects – to me – are what makes the triathlon run so special.

You often hear of triathletes bemoaning the fact that they are not 'good runners'. In fact, this perceived weakness sometimes puts people off doing the sport in the first place. However, running after swimming and cycling is very different from running on fresh legs. Remember that just because someone is a great runner doesn't automatically mean they'll be a fantastic triathlete. And vice versa: even though you may not be fast as a standalone runner, it doesn't mean you can't shine in a triathlon. Improving your run is not just down to run training. The decisions we make in the previous two disciplines – in the training we do, the equipment we use, the nutrition and hydration choices we make, the technique we adopt, the bike set-up we have – impact our run performance.

Some athletes do regale stories of heavy legs, stomach problems, blisters and fatigue. However, such problems can be avoided. So how do we perfect the last of the threesome, the run, and ultimately cross that finish line with our arms aloft and a beaming smile on our faces?

OPPOSITE: On the run at the Ironman World Championship, 2011.

BORN TO RUN: RUN TRAINING FUNDAMENTALS

EQUIPMENT

To begin with let's talk kit. One of the great things about running is that you only need a few items of equipment.

Running shoes

Happy feet equal happy triathlete. While the barefoot-running movement is gaining ground, ITU rules clearly state a competitor 'may not run without shoes on any part of the [run] course'. I think this also applies to flip-flops, so ditch the thongs and find yourself a pair of running shoes that work for you.

There is a baffling range of shoes with labels such as neutral, stability, minimalist, racing and off-road/trail, and many different philosophies about how much or little support is required. A good pair of running shoes should provide flexibility, durability and a degree of motion control and shock absorption.

There's no single best pair of shoes – everyone has different needs. Your choice will depend on your foot shape, biomechanics, weight, running form, as well as preferred running surfaces and training and race distances. A male, long-course triathlete weighing 80kg will require a totally different shoe to a 55kg female triathlete who likes to race off-road. Your footwear needs to be a good fit and fit for purpose. You can use the same shoes in training and racing although some triathletes, like me, tend to use a lighter pair for racing (sometimes called racing flats) and do specific training sessions with these shoes to practise and wear them in.

Some runners are prone to overpronation (an inward rolling motion); some to supination (rolling outwards); and others fall in the middle. Some people strike the ground with their heel, others with their mid-foot and the remainder with their forefoot or toes.

Those new to running should visit a friendly, experienced running or triathlon shop for a jargon-busting gait analysis and shoe fit. You can usually test various shoes on the shop's treadmill rather than simply bouncing up and down in front of a mirror. Manufacturers tend to modify their shoes, so if you find a model you like, it may be worth buying extra pairs in the end-of-season sales before they are discontinued.

> " A good pair of running shoes should provide flexibility, durability and a degree of motion control and shock absorption. "

Some other tips:

> Generally speaking, you should replace your shoes after about 800–1,000km (some manufacturers advise even less), but always be alert to wear-and-tear and purchase new ones earlier if necessary.

> If you need new shoes, get them at least four weeks before a race. Buying them two days before, as I did at the Ironman World Championship in 2007, doesn't necessarily equate to happy post-race feet.

> Always wear socks of a similar thickness, and remember that your feet will expand in hot conditions. Shoes that fit really well in the UK winter may not be as comfortable in the 33°C temperatures of Hawaii. Or even Harrogate on a warm day.

> Your heel should be snug and secure but you should still be able to move your toes around.

Laces

Regular laces are fine if speed is not of the essence in a race; however, the quick-tying variety do save time in transition. There are many types. I was a fan of Greepers, which are like real laces with a slightly different – and extremely quick – locking/tying system. Others prefer elastic laces, although I disliked the lack of stability they gave and wouldn't advise using them regularly in training.

Clothing

Dress for the conditions, but remember that your body temperature often increases dramatically when you run and so be able to shed some layers if necessary. Breathable, light, quick-drying fabrics are good, as is bright/reflective material, especially if you are training at dusk or in the dark.

Socks

Socks make for a more comfortable, less-blistered experience although many short-course triathletes prefer to save time and race without them. It depends on whether a) your feet are used to it, and b) shaving seconds off your finish time matters. Practise in training if you intend to go sockless in races, but bear in mind that your shoes may start to smell like a dead rat.

Sports bra

Unless droopy, sore boobs sound appealing to female readers, a good sports bra is a must. It's vital to get one that fits, is comfortable and suitable for the level of impact. I would strongly advise trying before you buy, heading down to your nearest running or triathlon shop for some expert advice and fitting if necessary.

Sunglasses

Well-fitting sunglasses protect your eyes from the sun and keep your eyeballs bee and bug free. Squinting or tensing up the face can impact the whole body, including lower body mechanics, and so sunglasses can also help encourage a relaxed run form.

Headtorch

This is essential if you are running on the roads at dusk or in the dark and don't want to end up like flattened badger roadkill.

Cap or visor

These help to keep the sun off your head or rain/sweat out of your eyes. Note that you rarely see anyone wearing Jane Fonda-style 1970s towelling headbands, unless you're looking at old race photos of Dave Scott. I preferred not having anything on my head, but kept cool in a race by chucking water and ice over my bonce.

Carrier

If you want to carry hydration/nutrition/money/phone/dog food while you run, you can either transport such items in your hands or use one of the many running belts on the market. As with cycling, bumbags are probably best avoided. Remember to practise in training with what you'll use on race day. I carried some of my gels in a small handheld flask, with a couple of extras in my pocket and down my bra (resulting in an abnormally shaped boob).

IMPROVING YOUR TRIATHLON RUN

As Chris McDougall and Bruce Springsteen made clear, we *Homo sapiens* are 'Born to Run', and there are many things you can do to maximise your ability to do said activity effectively and efficiently in a triathlon. Here are a few (non-chicken) nuggets to help you fly rather than flop in the last of the three disciplines:

> Become efficient and strong in the swim and on the bike so that you're less fatigued when you get off it. See Chapters 2, 3 and 4 for more details.

> Include plenty of bike-run brick workouts to get a sense of how it feels to run after cycling (also known as 'running off the bike') so that it isn't an alien sensation on race day.

> Ensure your bike's geometry doesn't cause problems in your back/hips/shoulders or other body parts that can dramatically impact your run. See the bike fit section at page 124 for more details.

> Adopting a run/walk strategy in training can be of use, especially if you're trying to hone your run form, want to eat and drink without spillages, are a beginner and/or you want to increase the distance covered without the impact that running the entirety might have. And the same goes for racing. Indeed, Olympic and Ironman World Champion Jan Frodeno walked through some aid stations en route to winning the Ironman World Championship in 2015.

> As outlined overleaf, try to develop good running form/technique. My right knee had a tendency to collapse inwards Elvis-style and my right arm often swung across my body. Dave and I worked on these little imperfections, particularly through strength and conditioning (see Chapter 6), to reduce the likelihood of injury, prolong my run life-expectancy and give me some lovely free speed.

> I recommend heading off-road occasionally to develop strength, proprioception and inject variety into your training. See page 151 for more details. Make sure your shoes are suited to the terrain.

RUN FORM

We hear coaches and athletes talk about 'run form'; essentially the body's posture and movement of the limbs when running. So, what does good run form look like, and how do we get it?

> Keep your arms relaxed and close to your torso. This reduces over-rotation and opens your chest. Try not to move your arms across your body. Have a small bend in the elbow, with a slight (but not overly exaggerated, 100m Usain Bolt-esque) swing backwards and forwards to assist with balance and rhythm.

> Keep your face, hands and shoulders – in fact your whole body – nice and relaxed. I pretend I'm carrying crisps (not Walkers, ho-ho) between my thumb and forefingers to stop me clenching my fists.

> Imagine you have a string attached to your head, stand tall and lean forward slightly with a strong core. Sloppiness and slouching is best avoided until you've crossed the finish line. A powerful core, combined with glute strength, helps limit knee collapse and means that your feet will ideally land in line with your hip joint and not cross your body's midline.

> Whether you like tango or triathlon, quick and light steps are good. I was fortunate to have a naturally fast leg turnover or running cadence, which helped to limit over-striding and stressful impact with the ground.

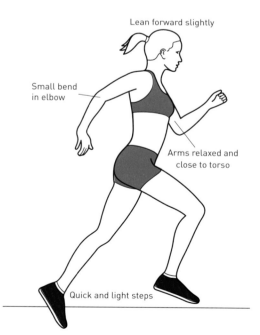

Lean forward slightly

Small bend in elbow

Arms relaxed and close to torso

Quick and light steps

Developing good run form requires practice, constant repetition and focus; think about your form when you train and race, and make subtle corrections if you feel yourself falling into bad habits. It's best not to make any dramatic changes overnight but, instead, concentrate on one or two motions at a time and, initially, practise during shorter, lower intensity runs (or slower sections of a longer run). You'll need to be able to retain that form over the course of the race, so also make sure you try to hold this form during race-paced sessions. Believe me, when combined with some tri-specific strength and conditioning exercises

(see Chapter 6) you'll be bounding along singing 'Baby we were born to run': minus, of course, the towelling Springsteen/Dave Scott sweatband.

HILL RUNNING

Those who live in the shadows of a mountain, hill, fell or even the Himalayas, as I did in Nepal, have no choice but to embrace the art of hill running. Those who grew up surrounded by less lumpy terrain, such as my pancake-flat home county of Norfolk, might not have the same level of experience and love for such lumps. Hills aren't always pleasant: in fact, training on them can be downright uncomfortable. However, if you want to increase strength, improve your form, speed and develop the mental fortitude to cope with discomfort, then hill running is a must.

Hill running is an interval workout that, because you're working against gravity, means you generate far more force than during the same session on flat ground. They may hurt initially but practice and repetition facilitates adaptation and also breeds familiarity, which can give you the peace of mind and confidence that you can tackle anything that a race course might throw at you.

TRAINING TIP

Short bursts of speed of between 10 and 20 seconds, aka strides, are a great drill to incorporate at the end of steady run sessions, or before an interval session towards the end of the warm-up. Start slowly and build to about 80 per cent of maximum effort before gradually reducing your pace. Stay relaxed and try to maintain a fast leg turnover.

There are different types of hill-running session based on the length of the hill, the incline duration and the intensity at which you run. If you haven't got a hill then consider using a treadmill and varying the incline to simulate the required gradient. One of the advantages of a treadmill is that you don't have to run downhill, the impacts of which are discussed on the next page. In addition to treadmill running, you can also climb stairs – Rocky Balboa style – in a multi-storey building or stadium, or find a long, convex-shaped bridge.

There are a few different types of hill sessions, which should always start with a 10–15-minute warm-up:

Long-hill repeats

Climbs of 1–3 minutes, on a 6–10 per cent gradient, using the descent as the recovery, repeated 6–12 times depending on your level of experience. The intensity should be comfortably hard, around 14 or 15 on the Borg Scale. These are great for both strength and endurance.

Short-hill repeats

Select a short 8–10 per cent hill and do 5–8 reps of 20–30 seconds very hard (around 17–18 on the Borg Scale). The climb is anaerobic so use the downhill as recovery, but also add two minutes or so of flat running or walking at the bottom before

starting the next repeat. You can increase the level of difficulty by doing more ascents and/or reducing the rest interval. These are great for developing speed and power.

Mixed hills and flats

I'll always remember my coach Brett Sutton waxing lyrical about the late New Zealand runner-turned-coach, Arthur Lydiard. Born in 1917, Lydiard was famed for his innovative coaching methods and philosophies, which still influence the running and triathlon world today. One such method was to combine hard efforts on the hills and flatter terrain in the same workout, a session that was an integral part of my programme throughout my professional career. For example, when training with Brett in Switzerland there was a 2km loop of hard-packed trail in the forest, which included an 800m hill of about 6 per cent, a

400m rolling section, 800m descent and 400m flat portion. I used to run the hill and the rolling section hard, cruise the descent and then slowly build the intensity on the flat before reaching the bottom of the hill and heading back up. I did this loop 10–12 times.

Hill running technique: top tips

Uphill running:

> Maintain a steady rhythm and intensity of effort for the whole climb.

> Shorten your stride.

> Keep a consistent cadence.

> Maintain a high knee lift.

> Focus on a forceful 'bouncy' push off, engaging your glutes.

> Swing your arms in a relaxed manner.

> Run with an upright torso.

> Relax your shoulders.

> Look straight ahead rather than down at the ground.

> Keep your breathing relaxed.

> Continue to run at the same intensity as you crest the hill.

Downhill running:

Running downhill generates more impact on the body than any other type of triathlon training, so for most hill sessions the downhill should be a gentle recovery. However, some races can involve a substantial portion of downhill running and much time can be gained with effective technique, as well as limiting the likelihood of injury or subsequent discomfort. For example, the Alpe d'Huez triathlon run course is a hilly three laps, with climbs and

MY FAVOURITE TREADMILL SESSION

Even though we were surrounded by hills in Boulder, I also used to do a weekly session on the treadmill that incorporated hills and flatter intervals in preparation for Challenge Roth and the Ironman World Championship in 2011. Here is a favourite session – a fine line between pleasure and pain – that helped propel me to a 2-hour 44-minute marathon in Roth that year:

> Warm up at 2 per cent for 10 minutes – start at 12.5km/h and build to 13.2km/h.

> Set 1: 1 × 30 seconds at 17.7km/h (RI 30 seconds) + 1 × 45 at 18.5km/h (RI 1 minute) + 6 × 1 minute at 19.3km/h (RI 1 minute) all at 2 per cent gradient

> 6 minutes steady at 2 per cent

> Set 2: 12 × 75 seconds as: 3 at 7 per cent at 13.7km/h (RI 30 seconds) + 3 at 6 per cent at 13.8km/h (RI 30 seconds) + 6 at 5 per cent at 13.9km/h (RI 90 seconds)

> 4 minutes steady at 2 per cent

> Set 3: 10 minutes at 14.2km/h at 4 per cent

> 2 minutes steady at 2 per cent

> Set 4: 6 × 45 seconds (RI 30 seconds) at 19.3km/h at 2 per cent

> Cool down for 10 minutes

MY FAVOURITE RUN SESSION

I used to really enjoy, in a masochistic way, this session of Dave Scott's, which I did on a Friday morning in Boulder. It draws on Lydiard's strategy of combining flat and hill running.

> Warm up for 15 minutes, slowly building the pace and finishing at the bottom of a 5–6 per cent hill, then:

> 2 minutes of hard effort on flat terrain at around 16–17 RPE on the Borg Scale (do 1 minute out and 1 minute back to the bottom of the hill);

> 4 minutes hill run at around 16–17 RPE, recovery jog downhill;

> repeat this set 8 times;

> cool down for 10 minutes.

> **Even if you are racing on flat courses, you ignore hill training at your peril.**

descents of around 6–8 per cent. Likewise, the first 10km of the Israman run (in Israel) is straight down the side of a mountain, and so it pays to practise downhill running beforehand. If possible, try to find hills with a gravel or dirt surface in order to help reduce the impact that each stride can have. Take note of the following points:

> Lean forward slightly.

> Step lightly.

> Maintain a short, fast stride.

> Try to stay in control.

> Avoid braking or reaching out with your feet.

I would only ever do a maximum of two hill sessions a week, but suggest that amateurs limit this to one once every 7–10 days. They also require a little more post-workout recovery.

Even if you are racing on flat courses, you ignore hill training at your peril. Yes, they might hurt for those who are uninitiated but trust this Norfolk dumpling, you can grow to love the lumps and the bang-for-buck speed and strength benefits they provide.

DRINKING ON THE RUN

During a triathlon run, drinks are usually handed out in plastic cups. After a race, they usually come in pint glasses, with a smattering of alcohol inside. If you've ever tried to consume fluids on the fly you'll know that it is a notoriously difficult skill to master, and the majority of triathletes end up with liquid anywhere but in their mouths. It's worth, therefore, practising this specialist skill in training and during your lower priority events. A few tips are to:

> tip some water out so the cup is half full;

> squeeze the cup to make a spout;

> try to limit any bouncing (at least through aid stations);

> slow your pace or walk if you have to;

> take smaller sips;

> use a fuel belt with bottles, from which it is much easier to drink.

PRE-RACE RUN PREPARATION

Here are a few run-specific things with which to familiarise yourself before race day:

> the distance you need to run;

> the cut-off time at the finish;

> the race rules, including littering;

> the terrain (e.g. hills, corners, road surfaces, cambers);

> the location of any aid stations and their provision;

> the run course, including the run exit and finish line. (At my first Ironman World Championship in 2007, I wasn't entirely sure of the course, and thinking the finish line was close started to increase the pace and wave at the crowds only to realise I still had another 1km to go!)

Hit the Ground Running – Different Running Surfaces

Q 'I've been a triathlete for five years and I am getting bored of running on the pavements and road. I'd like to try different surfaces but I am also scared of getting injured. Should I go off-road as part of my training?'

TOM FRANKS

A One of the things I love about running is that you can do it on any surface, anywhere in the world! You've got asphalt road or pavement, hard-packed or gravel paths, rocky trails, sand, snow, grass, track, treadmills . . . you name it you can run on it or, in the case of water, in it.

Despite the diversity on offer, triathletes are renowned for being creatures of habit. We have a couple of tried and tested routes that invariably involve large quantities of asphalt. Given that the majority of us race on the road, it makes sense, as you have done, to condition ourselves to this surface. However, there are physical and psychological advantages to be gained from injecting a little variety and adding different surfaces into the triathlon mix.

> " There are advantages to be gained from adding different surfaces into the triathlon mix. "

Physically, running on different surfaces provides different stimuli, including: the way your muscles and tendons are utilised; the nature and level of the impact; the type of environment; and the skills required. In addition, the variety of surface and scenery can help stave off boredom and give a motivational boost. If you have been doing triathlon for a while you might need a little bit of excitement to keep the mojo flowing!

So, what are the best terrains for you, and for other triathletes, who mainly race on-road? I've put together the table overleaf to capture some of the more popular surfaces, together with their pros and cons.

 THE ADVANTAGES AND DISADVANTAGES OF DIFFERENT RUNNING SURFACES

SURFACE	PRO	CON
Asphalt – roads	• One of the fastest surfaces • Distances are measurable • Predictable and hence easier to maintain a steady rhythm • Races are usually held on asphalt roads	• Relatively unforgiving surface and constant repetition can cause injury • Cambers can affect run form and potentially cause injury • Safety issues due to traffic • May be unlit at night (therefore a good headlamp is required)
Concrete – pavements	• Distances are easily measurable • Easily available and accessible, especially in cities and towns	• Unforgiving (10 times as hard as asphalt), which places stress on the body • Obstacles such as kerbs, pedestrians, driveways and dogs can affect rhythm and dodging them may cause injury
Grass	• Softer and with less impact than asphalt and concrete • The forgiving surface can help build strength • Natural surroundings helps alleviate boredom and boosts morale • No traffic to contend with	• Can be uneven and less suitable for those with unstable ankles • Can get muddy and worn in wet weather • May trigger symptoms in those with grass allergies • May be unlit at night
Hard-packed trails/gravel roads/bridleways	• Softer surface lessens impact • Varied, natural surroundings help alleviate boredom and boosts morale • Limited ruts or uneven areas • Less/no traffic	• Can get muddy or accumulate puddles in wet weather • Cyclists, horses or pedestrians can break rhythm • Not always easily available or accessible to those in towns or cities • Unlit at night
Technical, single-track trails and footpaths	• Softer surfaces reduce impact • Can help promote more efficient run form • Helps to develop concentration and awareness • Nice scenery can help with morale • Traffic free	• Uneven and unpredictable ground can increase the risk of injury due to tripping and falling • Require considerable focus and awareness (this can also be advantageous in terms of training the mind) • Not always easily available or accessible to those who live in cities or towns • Other pedestrians can break rhythm • Unlit at night

SURFACE	PRO	CON
Sand – dry and deeper sand further from the sea and harder packed sand close to the water's edge	• Soft, with limited impact • Flat, firm sand close to the water's edge provides good strength training but without the stress on the calves/Achilles from deeper, drier sand • Nice environment – scenery may help improve morale • Traffic free • Limited obstacles	• Soft surfaces (especially further away from the sea) can increase the risk of injury, particularly of the calves and Achilles • Cambers are common and can cause injury • Not always easily available or accessible • Getting sand in your shoes and socks is not always pleasant
Synthetic track	• Surface is relatively forgiving • Easy for a coach to watch and comment from sidelines • Distances can be accurately measured • Flat • Traffic free • No obstacles (unless you try the hurdles or steeplechase) • Safe • Floodlights enable evening/night-time use	• Access may be limited and tracks can be crowded at popular times • Ankles, knees and hips are put under more stress due to the bends and tendency to run in the same direction • Longer runs may be boring unless you have the mentality of a gerbil (this can also be advantageous in terms of training the mind) • Usually have to pay a fee
Treadmill	• Beneficial for those who lack outside running opportunities, e.g. due to excessive traffic, lack of facilities, safety, darkness • Can accurately measure and alter incline, distance and pace, enabling specificity and consistency • Less distractions make it easier to focus on form, cadence and breathing • A coach can observe the session • Can often monitor other data, such as heart rate and calories burned • The belt's cushioned surface can reduce impact and stress (although surfaces vary between models and brands)	• Indoor training can be tedious • Can end up falling off the back of the machine if pace is not maintained • May cause heavy sweating if the area is not properly ventilated • Expensive to purchase or requires payment for gym membership • Access isn't always guaranteed (if in a gym) • Doesn't condition you to running outside and on harder surfaces

Of the three disciplines, running is the highest impact activity, which can place stress on the body, especially the lower limbs. Softer surfaces absorb more of the impact, reducing the risk of injury, helping to develop strength – such as the stabiliser muscles – and facilitating quicker recovery from sessions. Paradoxically, softer surfaces can also increase the risk of injury for some, such as those with weak ankles or those with a tendency to trip over anything bigger than a pebble. Of course, you can have multiple surfaces within one run, perhaps warming up on-road, before heading off to a gravel path to do your intervals.

Without knowing you personally, and your physiology and biomechanics, it's difficult to give specific advice on what surfaces you should train on. Whatever new surface you choose, it's important to start slowly to give yourself time to get used to it, and definitely don't try something new immediately before a race. Hour-long runs on rocky trails when you have only been conditioned to running on-road is a recipe for disaster – believe me, I have had a few falls to prove it!

One thing to remember is that you may need to use different running shoes on different surfaces; for example, your regular shoes may not have the grip necessary to cope with a muddy or rocky trail.

Given that I like to race on-road, I feel it's important to condition my body to withstand the impact and feel 'at one' with this surface come the big day. However, my favourite surface to run on is a gravel path/trail, with just enough give to reduce the impact of the pounding but also away from traffic, in nice surroundings and with limited obstacles. I have been fortunate to live in some wonderful places around the world with such trails on my doorstep, including the paths around my hometown of Bristol.

As a pro athlete, I did quite a bit of my speed work on the treadmill and on the track for specificity. It meant that my coaches could closely watch and monitor my performance and form. Coping with the tedium of the treadmill or track was an important means of strengthening my mind to endure boredom – although, unlike my fellow professionals Bella Bayliss and Hillary Biscay, I never ran marathons on either surface! If you find the track or treadmill boring, then only turn to them for harder sessions or interval training. When your heart rate is being elevated towards its maximum, the bland environment ceases to be a concern.

If I had an injury, I preferred to use the cross-trainer rather than opting for water-running/aqua-jogging, although I know many an athlete who has used the latter to great effect.

So, instead of being a slave to road or pavement I would definitely suggest injecting something different into your tri terrains throughout the season and enjoying the change of sensation and scenery that comes from venturing off your well-beaten asphalt paths. Happy running! ●

CHAPTER SIX

STRENGTH AND CONDITIONING

Most triathletes like the burn. They love to feel their heart rate scaling new heights, relish turning a delightful shade of beetroot and enjoy drowning in salt-saturated bodily fluids. They want to tick the box that says: 'I went faster/harder/longer than I ever have before.' They generally shun anything that encroaches on precious swim, bike and run time or which they believe may make them resemble Geoff Capes. (For those who were born after 1980, Mr Capes was a British shot-putter, strongman and professional Highland Games competitor. He was also very large, muscular and partial to some facial foliage.)

This approach often means that strength and conditioning – or S & C – takes a back seat and is only resurrected when injury strikes. However, as this chapter shows, S & C is neglected at one's peril, for it is the foundation on which hard work is built.

What follows are two main sections, the first containing advice on how and why you should consider incorporating S & C into your overall programme, and the second a contribution from Dave Scott, outlining some of the key S & C exercises that would benefit most, if not all, triathletes.

BUILDING THE FOUNDATION: STRENGTH AND CONDITIONING ESSENTIALS

We are not perfect geometric, superhuman forms – unless your name is Clark Kent – and we all have biomechanical weaknesses. These can be exacerbated by poor posture, sitting behind a desk for hours or carrying the kids/shopping/dog. For many of us this manifests in weak and wobbly body parts, often around the 'core'. Far from being about chiselled abs, the core is essentially a complex group of around 30 muscles working in synergy around the torso – from the superficial to the much deeper muscles. They provide stability and shock absorption for the entire body, facilitating the production of power and speed and enabling correct posture. In short, the core is the central pillar that supports the whole body and its mobility. Yet for the majority of triathletes, it is much weaker than it should be. And it's not just the core that we need to focus on. Triathlon provides an all-over body workout and hence we need to ensure that our entire body, from our heads to our toes, is strengthened and conditioned.

S & C is important for improving range and synchronisation of movement, flexibility, coordination, agility, strength, power, stability and balance. This is especially true as we age when muscle mass decreases, and our mechanical efficiency declines. Strengthen and condition our bodies and we can strengthen our triathlon performance and reduce the risk of injury.

I learned this the hard way. My first coach Brett Sutton didn't place much emphasis on it, although I do remember one instance when he had me doing 50 press-ups on my knuckles. My form was so poor (due to lack of practice), all I got out of it was a gammy shoulder and bleeding, and then scabby, hands! I now realise that neglecting S & C probably contributed to a hamstring injury that plagued me throughout 2009. Under Dave Scott's guidance, I incorporated S & C sessions into my programme, which helped me recover from the injury, address the underlying causes and give me the structural underpinnings to improve. It's worth noting that, up until working with Dave, I also faded in the last 10km of the marathon. Was this glycogen deficiency? Dave thought otherwise, apportioning blame to my weak glute and hamstring muscles that had fatigued and compromised my run form. He prescribed targeted S & C exercises and in time I saw real improvements in my form and performance. I went on to run that 2-hour 44-minute marathon at Challenge Roth in 2011 – and the second half was faster than the first.

More recently I also discovered yoga and Pilates. The latter, especially, I credit for giving me a stronger core that helped me have a trouble-free pregnancy, labour and which facilitated my post-natal recovery (see Chapter 11 for more details).

> Given that most of us are time poor, it is essential to get bang for buck: concentrating on functional movement exercises that will address our personal imbalances, are triathlon specific and can help improve performance and overall health.

Given that most of us are time poor, it is essential to get bang for buck: concentrating on functional movement exercises that address our personal imbalances, are triathlon specific and can help improve performance and overall health. If you have access to one, a good physiotherapist and/or coach should be able to identify your areas of weakness and prescribe a personalised programme. Some of the key exercises that I did, and still do, and which many triathletes would benefit from are provided at page 162.

You don't have to set foot in a gym to be able to do a lot of S & C work. Many of the exercises can be done at home. If your budget allows, stretch cords, a foam roller and a set of dumbbells are a worthwhile investment. If not, you can use household objects for weights. S & C should be done all year round and not just in the off-season. I suggest trying to do 2 × 20–25-minute sessions per week, or more regular, shorter sessions of 10 minutes to suit your lifestyle. Applying the triathlon training principles of variety and evolution, it's important to alter the exercises over time in order to provide different stimuli, address different areas of tension and retain your interest.

Believe me, dumbbells are far from what their name implies. The proof of S & C work is in the proverbial pudding. Incorporate it and your triathlon journey will be all the sweeter for it.

TRI THIS AT HOME: S & C EXERCISES

Where is a vast array of exercises that triathletes could include in a S & C training programme. However, it makes sense to focus our efforts on those that can truly enhance our performance. There's no better coach than Dave to explain the key exercises that benefit triathletes.

Make sure you warm up for at least ten minutes beforehand. There are no prizes for speed but plenty of benefits from doing the exercises slowly, deliberately and correctly, focusing on making the right muscles fire in the right sequence.

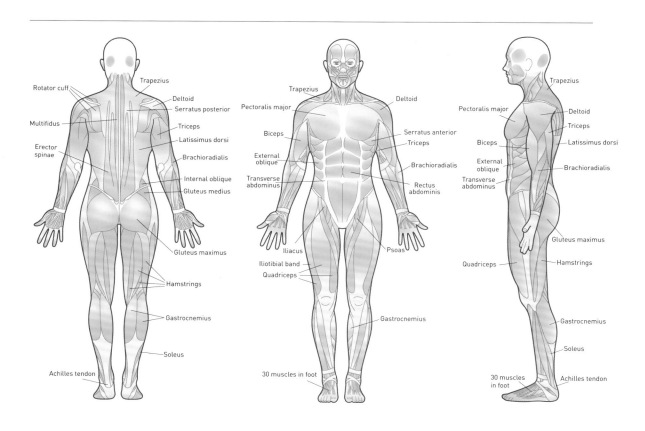

DAVE SCOTT on my S & C programme

We used many of the exercises overleaf to strengthen Chrissie's key areas of weakness. For example, her calves looked magnificent, but they were doing all the work. They are strong muscles, but even stronger muscles – if you can activate them – are the glutes. Chrissie had a right glute that was like butter, with the other only marginally better. To strengthen and utilise her glutes we needed to work those muscles across lots of different angles and directions, not just the unilateral running or cycling planes. This also helped increase her hip mobility and flexibility, stopped her knee rolling inwards and helped release her lower back.

Chrissie was also weak in her serratus and her latissimus dorsi and that was negatively impacting her swim. She had a tendency to press straight down with her hands at the front of her stroke. A tight back meant her hand entry was too narrow and she couldn't retain a high elbow. Both limited the force she could generate. To address this, we incorporated exercises with stretch/tension cords, doing a range of motions, such as rows, butterflies and single-arm freestyle – as described at page 167. She did three sets of 25 of each exercise, but I suggest that beginners start with two or three sets of 10 reps. Stretch cords are also really useful if you are travelling and don't have access to a pool.

Chrissie did three 45–60-minute S & C sessions per week, and stretched every day.

I always advise that athletes stretch after a workout, when the muscles, tendons and ligaments are warm, rather than before when the body is cold and hence more prone to injury. Chrissie did static stretching on areas prone to tightness, such as her calves, quads, hamstrings and lower back, and also used the foam roller, although not over her ITB (iliotibial band) as this band of fibre has limited elasticity and using a foam roller on it can cause injury. She used to put the roller under her backbone and roll down to her lower back, going back and forth across every spinal notch. She would then roll all the way up from her cervical spine, over her shoulders (with her arms above her head), lift up her hips and then roll it all the way down to her glutes. She turned the roller so it was length-wise under her spine, supported by her head and backside, and reached up over her head, first in a backstroke motion and then like a snow-angel to stretch her pecs. Additionally, she used tennis balls to massage her neck, spine, glutes and lower back.

We varied the S & C exercises over the course of the season, but always focused on her tri-specific areas of weakness and asymmetry. Of course, she was doing extraordinarily well without S & C work, but once she realised she could do even better with it, she was conscientious about incorporating it into her routine. That diligence is, in part, why she was a great champion. ●

1. TA ACTIVATION

Sets: 2

Reps: 90 seconds to 3 minutes

The transversus abdominis (or TA) is a slow-acting, deep corset-like muscle that lies underneath your internal obliques. To activate it, stand up tall and draw your belly in, as if wearing tight trousers. Touch your navel and then move your finger 4–5cm either side, where it hollows out. The TA helps stabilise your pelvis and fire your glutes, so you can generate more power from your glutes as opposed to your quads. Keep the gap between your ribs and hip-bones open.

2. SINGLE-LEG SOARING SEQUENCE

MOVE A

Sets: 3

Reps: 12 – pause on even reps for 3 seconds

Pull in your TA and stand on your left leg. Shift all your weight to that leg, tighten your glutes and move your right leg back. Then lift it off the ground and behind you as high as you can, and move your arms straight out to the sides and level with your shoulders. Once you are holding your body weight out in front, you'll feel your TA activate. Repeat on the other leg.

MOVE B

Sets: 2

Reps: 12 – pause on even reps for 3 seconds

Repeat the above exercise but hold 2–5kg dumbbells in each hand. Stand on one leg, contracting your glute and quad. Swing the other leg back and raise it off the ground, keeping your foot flexed upwards (dorsi-flexed). Hips are square. Instead of lifting your arms to the side, point your thumbs forward and initiate a rowing motion by squeezing your shoulder blades tight and lifting them as high as possible. Lower your arms and leg and repeat.

2C

MOVE C

Sets: 2

Reps: 12 – pause on even reps for 3 seconds

Repeat exercise B again, but this time hold the soaring position for three seconds, then swing the soaring leg forward, simulating a bent-knee running position while standing tall. Simulate an exaggerated running motion with your arms. Repeat on the other leg, remembering to keep the TA, standing leg, quad and glute very tight.

3. BENT-OVER ROW

Sets: 3

3

Reps: 12 – pause on even reps for 3 seconds

Stand up tall and hold a dumbbell in each hand. Lightly retract your shoulder blades, keep your elbows close to your torso and bend over about 45 degrees, hinging from the waist, keeping your TA nice and tight, and do a rowing motion with both arms. Focus on activating your mid to upper back, and keep your shoulders soft rather than hunching them by your ears. This is a great exercise for your TA and your back, as it works your mid to low trapezius muscles, which are generally weak in triathletes.

4. GLUTE EXERCISE SEQUENCE

MOVE A: LATERAL DOG LIFT

Sets: 2

Reps: 8–12, holding for 2–3 seconds every third rep

Start on all fours, with your hands under your shoulders and knees under your hips. Externally rotate one knee as high as possible, keeping hips level, like a dog raising its leg while having a pee. Bring it back down and repeat.

MOVE B: LATERAL STRAIGHT-LEG SWING

Sets: 2

Reps: 8–12

Again on all fours, engage the glutes, lift one leg up behind you, keeping it straight, and bring it to the side, taking care not to let the foot drop. Keep your pelvis tucked underneath. Tap the floor with your instep, then bring the leg back to the start position, and repeat.

4C

MOVE C: MULE KICKS

Sets: 2

Reps: 8–12, holding for 2–3 seconds every third rep

On all fours, draw one knee up under your chest, keeping your pelvis level, and then kick the leg straight back, tightening the glute throughout. Flex the knee and lift it behind you, before bringing it back to the neutral position.

MOVE D: GLUTE CIRCLES

Sets: 2

Reps: 8–12

On all fours, extend one leg back behind and rotate it, making circles that focus on the up and outward motion. Squeeze the glute throughout and repeat in the opposite direction, and then switch to the other leg.

4D

5A

5B

5C

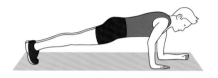

5. PLANK AND PUSH-UP SEQUENCE

MOVE A

Sets: 2

Reps: 10 – pause in plank position for 3 seconds

Start in a plank position, with your legs straight and your weight supported on your toes and forearms, with 90-degree flexion at shoulder and elbow. Support this alignment by contracting your TA, glutes and quads. Allow your chest to drop, releasing the tension between your scapulas. Then contract all the muscles noted above and return to a rigid plank position.

MOVE B

Sets: 2

Reps: 12

In a push-up position (hands and toes), support your body alignment by contracting your TA, glutes and quads. Maintain a straight-arm position, contract your rectus abdominis and come up to a high hip V-position ('downward dog'). Lower yourself to push-up position and repeat.

MOVE C

Sets: 2

Reps: 12

Start in the same push-up position, with your TA, glutes and quads contracted. Drop your left forearm to the ground, then your right forearm (so you're now in the plank position). Push up with your left arm back to push-up position, then with your right.

6. STRETCH-CORD EXERCISES

Stretch cords are relatively cheap pieces of rubber tubing with paddles or handles at either end. You attach the centre of the stretch cord to a bar, fence, tree – anything that isn't going to move. The exercises below should be done fast and forcibly, but without overstraining. Do two or three sets of 10–25 reps for each exercise.

MOVE A: BUTTERFLY

Hold the cords in front of you, facing the attachment point, and stand far enough away to create some tension in the cord. Bend at the waist and keep your head in a neutral position. Pull your outstretched arms to your sides, starting with your palms and forearms as if doing a butterfly stroke. Keep your elbows high (level with your shoulders) and finish with your hands past your hips. You can also do this as a single-arm exercise, focusing on the high-elbowed catch, the pull down and a strong finish beside your hip.

MOVE B: ROW/TRICEP PULL

Start in the same position as the butterfly exercise but keep your elbows tucked close to your sides. With your palms facing each other, press your arms behind you, squeezing your triceps (and your shoulder blades) at the end of each stroke, and release. This can also be done with the attachment point lowered to the ground.

MOVE C: REVERSE/CHEST FLY

Stand upright and face away from the attachment point. Place your hands next to your shoulders, keeping your elbows at shoulder level. Keeping your arms parallel to your shoulders, push your hands forwards until you can press them together in front of your chest, and release.

CHAPTER SEVEN
NUTRITION

We all religiously fill in our training logs for swim, bike and run and may even have another section for any extra comments . . . such as 'I was like Michael Phelps in the pool today', 'Chris Hoy eat your quads out' or 'A plank of wood could have run faster.'

These diaries make clear that our sport comprises three disciplines, but this triad would fall over like a drunken sailor without a few more pillars to hold it up. I am not talking about the greatest race wheels or the newest go-faster Lycra with added anti-chafe; I am referring to one of my favourite subjects – nutrition.

During my decidedly non-athletic university days, my definition of food and of drink was a curry and a Bacardi Breezer. Clearly, these nutritional choices were not particularly performance-enhancing, aside from fuelling my dance-floor antics and 2 a.m. renditions of Starship's classic tune: 'Nothing's Gonna Stop Us Now' (which, unfortunately for our neighbours, was a statement of fact).

When I became an athlete, I embarked on a slightly healthier nutrition plan: courtesy, in part, of the pearls of wisdom imparted by my good friend and nutrition guru, Asker Jeukendrup, whose advice and perspectives pepper this chapter.

What follows are sections on my daily diet and race nutrition, an analysis of Katy Campbell's strategy for the Bristol Harbourside Triathlon, and – to really whet your triathlon appetite – a selection of fantastic, healthy, nutritious and quick recipes for portable foods and drinks, whipped up in collaboration with the author of *Go Faster Food*, Kate Percy.

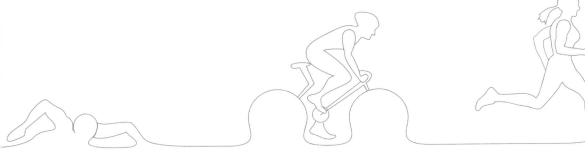

NUTRITIONAL NUGGETS: MY DAILY DIET

I love to eat. Rat, dog and snake were consumed in Indonesia. 'Hoover' would describe my penchant for consuming leftovers. I have even been known to buy, cook and consume sheep's testicles. In Nepal, I started the day with a sweet, milky chiya (tea), bought from a lady with a small stove by the side of the road, which I sometimes washed down with a small bowl of chickpea curry. A few friends and I would then head off on our mountain bikes up and down the hills of the Kathmandu Valley for an exhilarating ride before heading to work. On the weekends, we would venture further afield. We ate and drank whatever we could find in the villages we passed – usually chiya, curry, coconut biscuits, bananas and mountains of rice. Wherever we ended up on Saturday, we would seek shelter in the house of a local person, a small hotel or a monastery. Dinner was always the same, as was lunch during the week: dhal bhat – rice (the bhat), lentil soup (the dhal) and curry. The Nepalese eat it twice a day; Sherpas climb the highest mountains in the world on it. We biked for hours with dhal bhat in our bellies. Likewise, when cycle touring in the Argentinian Andes, we had a camp stove and some porridge, rice, pasta and freeze dried vegetables. And when our supplies ran out we asked a local farmer to slaughter a goat. This was the foody foundation for my athletic career.

Over time, I became more informed about the theories and practices behind sports nutrition, yet my 'keep it simple' philosophy remains. Here are the key lessons I've learned:

> You are what you eat. Food fuels, nourishes and heals.

> Eating for athletic performance is not rocket science and doesn't have to be complex. Keep it simple. I say this with the caveat that I don't have any allergies or intolerances, nor am I vegan, vegetarian or otherwise discriminatory about what I eat. Those who want, or have to, restrict their diet in any way will obviously need to make their own decisions based on what they can and can't consume.

> We are bombarded with messages like 'lose 100kg in 10 days by drinking vile tasting green juice'; or 'eat 20 grapefruits and shed 25 inches in 24 hours'. Fads are there to be ignored.

> Eating is supposed be enjoyable and fun, not stressful or tortuous.

So, taking these philosophies into account, what did my daily diet look like as a professional triathlete and now as a recreational athlete?

Balanced: protein, fats and carbs

I believe my diet is balanced, comprising and combining all major food groups – proteins, fats and carbohydrates. I tend to get my protein from both plant and animal sources, limiting the red meat I consume to once every few weeks (it makes me feel sluggish) and instead opting for poultry and fish. I eat a bucket-load of nuts and seeds, legumes, eggs and also throw in tofu or tempeh (made from soya beans) as alternative protein sources. With regards to fats, I firmly believe that they are not bad for you! I tend to favour sources such as mixed nuts and seeds, avocado, oily fish (for omega 3 and 6), but also have cheese and butter. Coconut, sunflower or rapeseed oil are excellent oils to fry with. Olive, pumpkin seed, flaxseed and hemp oils are good in dressings. I'd say that protein comprises about 35 per cent of my diet and fats 15 per cent, with carbs making up the rest.

66 'Hoover' would describe my penchant for consuming leftovers. I have even been known to buy, cook and consume sheep's testicles. 99

I am fully aware of the controversy surrounding carbs. Are they the devil or the angel? My opinion is that carbs are essential but I keep 'simple', refined ones to a minimum and favour 'complex', wholegrain starchy carbs, such as wild rice, buckwheat, quinoa (also a great source of protein), rolled oats, potatoes, rye and spelt, which also have the added benefit of dietary fibre. I tend to limit my intake of processed, anaemic looking carbs such as white/beige bread, pasta and rice as they induce an energy spike and subsequent crash. I do love a bit of locally bought honey so that's my sweetener of choice.

A rainbow of colours and flavours

I eat fruit and vegetables by the truck-load, especially those that are local and in season. Having a rainbow of colours ensures I get my fair share of antioxidants, including from foods such as blueberries, cranberries, broccoli, red grapes, apricots, peppers, spinach and plums as well as pecans and, of course, dark chocolate. I'm a fan of beetroot, whole and as a juice, which, despite making your wee a perturbing shade of red, allegedly has performance-enhancing properties. I like to add turmeric to dishes and smoothies as it is effective at reducing inflammation. The same goes for pineapple and ginger. Garlic also has a range of benefits; not least warding off vampires . . . and your friends.

Prioritise hydration

I drink about 1.5 litres of water per day, not including training sessions. I sometimes add electrolytes if I have been sweating more heavily. Being someone with excessive tendencies, I was drinking too much coffee and it was affecting my sleep. I decided to limit my intake of said beans to one cup per day, and cut it out altogether when I became pregnant. Now, I either have decaf or pour boiling water into a cup with a piece of fresh ginger and some lemon.

Natural and wholesome

I don't really like ingredient lists that include numbers or names I can't pronounce. Unless it's quinoa, which half the world's population don't enunciate correctly. I try to stay away from processed and packaged foods, sugars and sweeteners, trans fats and hydrogenated oils, and artificial colours and flavourings. Unless it's carrot cake with cream-cheese icing, which is surely one of your five-a-day and helps you see in the dark if you're staggering across an Ironman finish line just in time to beat the cut-off.

Forward planning

Time is limited for all of us, and I prefer the bang-for-buck approach to cooking rather than spending hours slaving over a hot frying pan. Making big batches of delicious meals in advance is great, especially for amateur athletes who are notoriously time deprived. These can be frozen and thawed quicker than you can say microwave.

Moderation

I don't deprive myself of any foods. Nothing is 'naughty' – it is just eaten in moderation. Unless it's the aforementioned sheep's balls, which were a once in a lifetime experience.

The table overleaf adds some meat to the bones, with examples of what my diet actually looks like on a day-to-day basis.

A TYPICAL DIETARY DAY

First Breakfast (about 30 minutes before I step out of the door)	If the first session is short or a run I would have one of the following options: • Two rice, buckwheat or corn cakes with nutbutter and honey; frozen banana (I like the ice-cream-like texture) with nutbutter or tahini and honey • Mashed avocado or banana with cacao powder and agave or honey • Banana and egg pancake (large banana and two eggs) mashed together with some tahini stirred in and lightly fried in coconut oil If my first session was a long ride I would have the second breakfast option below. As a pro, I always had a large cup of coffee, with milk.
Second Breakfast	My second breakfast would be one of the following: • Porridge with another grain (like spelt/buckwheat/quinoa) mixed in and honey on top • Bircher muesli (see recipe on page 196) • Bowl of raw oats, nuts, seeds, dried fruit, coconut and yogurt mixed together • Rice pudding made with black/red rice, coconut milk, chia seeds and coconut sugar My choice depended on whether I was running later in the day (if so, I chose a slightly lower fibre option).
Lunch	• Large baked potato with tuna, cheese and salad • Two wholegrain sandwiches/wraps with hummus or cheese (such as halloumi or feta) and avocado • Brown rice with salad and smoked mackerel • Eggs (usually poached) on toasted and buttered homemade bread, with salad • Bowl of leftovers from the night before!
Dinner	• Baked fish with roasted veggies and quinoa • Stir-fried chicken or tofu with vegetables with buckwheat • Thai prawn curry with brown rice • Vegetarian chilli and quinoa/brown rice mix • 3–4 egg omelette with a jacket potato and salad • Huge bowl of homemade vegetable soup with granary bread
Snacks	• Fruit • Chia or peanut butter balls (see recipes at pages 197 and 201) • Handfuls of unsalted nuts, seeds, fruit and dried fruit • Avocado, cottage cheese and/or nutbutter on rice or corn cakes • Apple with peanut butter • Oatcakes with hummus • Natural yoghurt with some no-added sugar muesli • A small bowl of oats with nuts and dried fruit, yoghurt and frozen berries

DURING TRAINING

But what about during training sessions? The marketeers would have you believe that professional athletes are glugging vile blue-coloured, mouthwash-looking energy drinks and eating plastic-tasting 'sports' bars at every opportunity. The truth is somewhat more nuanced. My opinion is simple:

> > you don't always need such products . . . but
> > there are situations where they are necessary.

Much depends on the nature of the session. If you are doing very high-quality training (such as high intensity interval sessions, time trials/race simulation or much longer rides or runs over 75–90 minutes in length), you will benefit from taking on carbohydrate. On other days, for example ones with cruise/recovery sessions, you may want to train your body to use its stored fuel and no sports drinks/gels/bars are needed as they may dull the adaptation necessary to benefit from such sessions. In short, ensure your use of sports nutrition products is *functional rather than being over-reliant.*

If my training sessions were longer than 90 minutes, I tended to have energy drinks and/or coconut water. While training in the Philippines, we used to stop by the side of the road, buy a coconut, get the shopkeeper to lop off the top and rehydrate with the delicious contents. We also ate the flesh for an added energy boost. I also used to make my own energy drinks, such as the one on page 200. On longer rides, in

> " While training in the Philippines, we used to stop by the side of the road, buy a coconut, get the shopkeeper to lop off the top and rehydrate with the delicious contents. "

addition to an energy drink, I always had a banana and a bar of some sort. I often made my own, such as the ones on pages 198 and 199. On a long run, I would take a gel or two, depending on the mileage. I rarely took on any fuel during my swim sessions, as they were less than 90 minutes in duration.

The important thing to remember is that our bodies are amazingly adaptable and eminently trainable. We can train them to crave or use certain foods and drinks. The more we give them, the more they will want. Feed your body refined sugar in excess, and that's what it will ask for. If you embark on a long ride with five chocolate bars, a whole malt loaf, ten gloopy gels and a few litres of energy drink, and then stop for a doorstep-sized slice of cake and a coffee – guess what? That's what your body will tell you it needs. And it's almost certain that on race day that body will rebel when it doesn't get the usual three-course smorgasbord. It's best, therefore, not to overload yourself during training and, if anything, *teach your body to do more with slightly less.*

RECOVERY

Food isn't just fuel. It's essential for recovery too, and that's where protein comes into its own. When combined with carbs it enables you to build on the hard work you have done and be ready for the next onslaught. Immediately after a hard and/ or long session, I make a smoothie. One example is on page 194; another is a mix of frozen pumpkin or berries, ginger, oats, ground nuts and seeds, blackstrap molasses (high in iron) and water, blended into deliciousness and downed in one. I'd then aim to have a bigger meal within about 45–60 minutes, again with ample protein.

> " It's best not to overload yourself during training and teach your body to do more with slightly less. "

SUPPLEMENTS

Use supplements sparingly, and with due diligence. I always took a high-quality multivitamin, as well as iron when blood tests showed I needed it and calcium as my bone density is relatively poor. If you are feeling rundown, tired, fatigued or are perpetually injured, don't automatically head for a bottle of pills, though. Get your blood and urine tested for any anomalies and then talk to your doctor (preferably a sports doctor) about next steps. It may be that the solution lies in changes to your training or diet, rather than spending vast amounts on costly tablets that simply result in expensive pee.

To conclude, what you consume in your daily diet really can make or break your performance in training and in racing. So, next time you fill in your log book, make sure you've paid enough attention to this hugely important pillar of success. And, if you are in Indonesia, reach for 'rat in a bap'. It never did me any harm!

Insight

ASKER JEUKENDRUP on my daily diet

I first met Chrissie in 2006 and, soon after, she approached me for advice on her daily diet and race-day nutrition. We were (and still are) both members of the Birmingham Running and Triathlon (BRAT) Club; she was preparing for the World Age Group Championship in Lausanne and I was working as a Professor of Exercise Metabolism at the University of Birmingham.

Even as a rookie age grouper, Chrissie realised the importance of nutrition and had read around the subject. We looked at her diet over a typical week, as well as what she had consumed in the few races she had undertaken, in order to develop a strategy that would optimise her performance and her overall health.

On the whole, her daily diet was good. However, I knew that with a few tweaks we could make it even better. She was a creature of habit, and tended to eat the same foods day in and day out. I suggested that she varied her diet a little more, including incorporating more complex, less refined carbohydrates such as spelt, quinoa and buckwheat, and choosing sources of protein other than her default option of chicken and fish . . . such as tofu, eggs, nuts and tempeh.

Chrissie had previously suffered from an eating disorder and still had a tendency to limit her intake of all kinds of fats, and so my advice was for her to increase her consumption of this vital food group, through foods such as coconut, olive, hemp and rapeseed oils, dark chocolate, avocado, cheese, nuts and seeds. Essentially, we had to break old habits and her ingrained food phobias.

Over recent years there has been considerable discussion around low carbohydrate diets, with proponents suggesting that such diets enable the body to become increasingly efficient at fat burning. This is then advertised as a positive effect. The evidence would suggest otherwise: although an improvement in fat burning can be observed by depriving the body of carbohydrate, at the same time it also de-trains the body to use carbohydrate and this is an unwanted side effect. Therefore, I advise athletes to *utilise carbohydrates strategically* and select different amounts and types of carbohydrates depending on the need. For example, in order to train fat burning, you use longer training sessions with limited carbohydrate intake to force the body to use fats and over time the capacity to use fat will improve. One or two days per week of lower carbohydrate intake and little or no carbohydrate during training will do the trick.

However, conversely there are sessions or days when a higher carbohydrate intake is required; for example, to enable an athlete to maintain a higher quality of training, facilitate recovery and, importantly, practise a race nutrition strategy.

I have to stress that foods are not 'good' or 'bad'. It is a case of consuming them at the right times and in the right quantities. If used correctly, there is a time and a place for ingesting more refined sugars, for example during a high intensity or long training session or in a race. However, if used excessively they can lead to a variety of health problems and declining performance.

Chrissie kept improving her daily diet by making small tweaks and monitoring her performance and health indicators; for example, her times/effort levels, her recovery, her sleep, her mood and markers such as iron, calcium and vitamin D which were assessed in routine blood tests.

Race weight

Many athletes also come to me to discuss 'race weight', and specifically how they can determine and then maintain this. It is more common for such athletes to want to lose weight and in such cases I recommend that this be done gradually, rather than through crash diets that can deprive the body of essential nutrients and cause long-term problems, such as reduction in lean muscle, future weight gain and reduced immunity. Although Chrissie tended to gain a few kilograms in the off-season, she tried to maintain the same weight, rather than yo-yoing too much, for the rest of the year. For her, losing weight was never a major issue. The body fat she started with was already very low and as she trained harder towards important competitions, this brought her lean body mass down even more. In Chrissie's case, my concern was more about making sure she had enough to sustain the training she was doing. ●

FUELLING YOUR FIRE: DEVELOPING A RACE NUTRITION STRATEGY

As we have seen, what you eat on a daily basis directly impacts your training and your race-day performance. Yet what to consume on that special day warrants a section all of its own. In my first Ironman in Jeju, South Korea, I was astonished to see the local athletes stopping by the side of the road, miraculously pulling a bowl of rice and cutlery out of their bike-jersey pockets and then sitting down to consume their Uncle Ben-style picnic, before heading off for the remainder of the 180km. Koreans aside, most of us prefer to modify our daily diet and reach for slightly different foods on race day.

Nailing your race nutrition will help you avoid a) head-on encounters with the proverbial wall, b) debilitating dehydration or c) visiting every toilet with gastro-intestinal (GI) issues. There are no one-size-fits-all strategies. Much comes down to your own physiology, the course and conditions, palatability, (in)tolerances and race duration. Although it can seem like a minefield with the mass of products available and what you should take and when and in what quantities, a bit of practice and a 'keep it simple' philosophy can help you navigate this nutritional maze.

Practice and preparation can make perfect

Training is the time for experimenting, learning and refinement, especially during your brick and longer sessions (particularly those with longer race-pace efforts). This includes practising with the nutrition you plan to consume in the 48 hours before the race, as well as during the event itself.

It is important to select foods and drinks that:

> are easy to chew, swallow and digest;

> give you the energy you need: the key being to *consume the least amount possible, but without 'hitting the wall'*;

> contain sufficient electrolytes to replace those lost in sweat;

> are palatable (e.g. you don't want to have a latte-flavoured gel only to realise at 30km in the marathon that the coffee flavour is vomit-inducing).

Monitor your intake, performance and response to selected products during and after your training sessions, bearing in mind these factors. It's worth keeping a log to help you systematically record, reflect and identify any patterns.

Although you can practise in training, it's only in a race situation that you really find out what works, or doesn't. It's a good idea to use the lower priority B and C races as testers, but bear in mind your requirements may vary depending on the course, race distance and conditions. It took me quite a few Ironmans to develop a strategy that didn't leave me dashing for the nearest toilet/bush during the marathon, and that strategy was iteratively developed both in training and through my race-day experiences.

It pays to prepare well in advance. Write a list to help you remember what and when you want to eat and drink. If you are travelling to a race, ensure you pack your required nutrition, rather than purchasing at the pre-race expo or borrowing from a friend. I always took more than I needed just in case of spillages, breakages or mishaps. It is also advisable to find out what will be provided at the race aid stations, even if you don't intend to use them.

Aid stations

All races will have aid – or feed – stations, although they will vary in number and extensiveness depending on the distance and race organiser. Make sure you know where they are located and what products will be available. The provision ranges from water and maybe some energy drink, to buffet-style tables of bananas, energy bars, gels or even pretzels. Given that our demands are very individual, I would caution against relying exclusively on the aid stations, unless you can be sure that the products will be palatable, digestible and meet your energy requirements. Instead, as far as possible, carry what you need for the duration of the race, whether it's attached to the bike, in a pocket or, on the run, in your hands or a fuel belt around your waist. My Ironman strategy (see page 187) was based on the wish to be self-sufficient for everything but water.

Special needs

Find out whether the race will have 'special needs' stations – a specific location on the bike and run course where you can collect a pre-deposited bag containing your own nutrition. They are usually only found at Ironman races. I always put a spare bottle and gel in my special needs bag/s just in case I accidentally dropped a bottle on the bike, lost a gel or the race took much longer than expected. Some races permit a family member or friend to hand you nutrition on the course, but check the rules or this could result in disqualification.

PRE-RACE NUTRITION

I know that some athletes choose Ben & Jerry's finest as their pre-race meal, others head to the Golden Arches for a Big Mac, while one professional athlete I know swears by steak and chips to get him through. In the two days before a race, I stuck to plain, simple food and curtailed my calorific intake slightly given the reduced level of energy expenditure during the final taper. I didn't excessively load up on carbohydrates as it made me bloated and lethargic. Spicy and rich foods are best avoided, unless you like perusing the inside of race-day toilets, nor is it sensible to gorge on every edible handout at the expo. Yes, it can be tempting to try the sugary goo that supposedly gives you wings but, believe me, you're more likely to flop than fly if you overindulge or sample new things so close to the big day.

> Some athletes choose Ben & Jerry's finest as their pre-race meal, others head to the Golden Arches for a Big Mac, while one professional athlete I know swears by steak and chips to get him through.

If you have to eat at a restaurant in the day/s preceding a race, ensure the menu is suitable and be careful with portion control. Buffets, such as those at pre-race carbo parties, can also be a nemesis if your willpower crumbles like the apple-based dessert when faced with excessive quantities of German sausage or cheesy beef lasagne.

The day before a race I'd always have a bowl of porridge with tahini and honey for breakfast. Lunch was a couple of bagels with cheese and olive oil, and maybe some avocado, with a banana on the side. Dinner was a culinary extravaganza: tuna pasta made with a tomato-based sauce, with a sprinkling of cheese and some olive oil. Gordon Ramsay: eat your non-profanitied heart out.

This is also the time to assemble your race nutrition, laying out all the products you might need during the race, and packing them in your bag. If you are not racking your bike until race morning, you may want to attach your nutrition (e.g. stick gels to your top tube or fasten a 'bento box' containing your fuel) beforehand. Prepare your special-needs bags, if applicable.

Some athletes like to make up their energy drinks on race morning, but I preferred to do it the night before and keep them in the fridge to limit my tasks on the day of the race.

RACE MORNING

I had breakfast at least two hours before the race start, which usually meant getting up at the crack of dawn. Don't skip this important meal, even if it is 4 a.m. and your stomach is doing nervous flip-flops.

I favoured rice cereal (finely ground rice that you find in the baby-food department) with honey and tahini stirred in, half a banana and a cup of coffee to get the bowels and whole body moving. A bagel/English muffin/toast with honey and some smooth peanut butter and a banana are other options. Porridge can be good, if the fibre doesn't cause GI issues further down the line. You could also try baby porridge or Ready Brek – very refined oats that might be easier to digest. If you really can't stomach solid food, try a carb-rich (but not dairy-heavy, as this can cause GI problems) smoothie with a source of protein such as peanut butter. You might even add some tofu. Sip water, but don't overhydrate. I would eat the same breakfast regardless of the race distance, but would have a smaller bowl of rice cereal before a short-course triathlon.

I sipped on water before the start, but didn't take on any additional fuel until I was on the bike. Some athletes like to have something light, such as a gel, bar or banana, right before they do their warm-up, but I felt that I had enough fuel on board and didn't need any further top-ups.

DURING THE RACE

It's not uncommon to see triathletes at an Olympic-distance race carrying ten gels, two bottles of energy drink and a banana in their pocket. However, studies show that we have enough stored glycogen to sustain around 75–90 minutes of exercise and hence a portable buffet such as this is slightly excessive. Yes, in an Ironman you will consume more in the way of food and drink than you would in a shorter race, but irrespective of race distance the key is to be able to do your best without needing to consume a substantial meal during the event itself.

My Ironman and half-Ironman race fuel came from carbohydrates and a smattering of fats, derived from a mix of fluids, semi solids (such as gels) and solids. After bouts of GI distress in my first few Ironman races, I had another chat with Asker Jeukendrup and subsequently omitted protein, and generally I advise other athletes to do the same during a race. It's worth noting that I was finishing Ironman races in under nine hours. If you're a triathlete who is closer to the 17-hour mark, it's simple mathematics that your race intensity will be lower (because you are out there for longer). It follows that your energy requirements per hour will also be less, and at the lower intensity your stomach will (hopefully) be more tolerant to solid – and tasty – food.

Given that we can't eat or drink in the swim, the first time you will have the option to take on fuel is in the first transition (T1). Trying to eat or drink when switching from swim to bike may not be easy – especially for those that are clock-watching and want to get through T1 as quickly as possible. It is often worth waiting 10 minutes or so to settle into your cycling rhythm before consuming any calories. If anything, I would grab a cup of water to rinse my mouth – especially if it's been a sea swim.

On the bike, I suggest opting for easily digestible and transportable foods (unless of course you are Korean with a penchant for kimchi or Uncle Ben's), avoiding anything fibrous or excessively chewy. Good options can be: bananas, non-nutty chocolate bars, jellies or gummies, (chocolate-covered) pretzels, Rice Krispie squares or even sandwiches with jam. You could even make your own rice balls (following the recipe at page 201) or combine cooked white rice with honey, melted marshmallow or chocolate. Some athletes prefer savoury snacks and have been known to carry tinfoil-wrapped sweet potatoes.

Relative to the swim and run, it's easiest to ingest calories on the bike. However, it can still be hard to digest solid food if you're in the aero position, and it's difficult to actually chew and swallow if you're working hard. Slower athletes, those who don't use aerobars and those doing races with hilly bike courses may be able to digest solids and can adapt their plan accordingly. If you do take on solid food, do so in the first three-quarters of the ride. Any later and you'll still be trying to digest it on the run, which isn't always easy. Sitting up to eat, rather than staying in the aero position, can help the solids slip down a little better.

During the 180km Ironman cycle, I would have two bottles of quite concentrated carbohydrate-rich energy drink, which I sipped at regular 15-minute intervals; two

gels, which were stuck to my top tube and taken at 90km and 150km; and a small chocolate bar (one bite an hour), which I put in my back pocket in T1. I also used an aerobar-mounted hydration system, which I filled with a couple of inches of water, and drank from this in between the sips of energy drink. Note that carrying extra fluid on the bike will make it heavier, alter the weight distribution and change how the bike handles, so practise with your full-race nutrition set-up in training.

If you are using aid stations, slow down (stop if you have to) as you approach to give yourself the best chance of getting what you need from the volunteers, and use training to practise if you lack confidence in the grab-and-go technique.

Once on the run, I'd have one energy gel every 25 minutes, taken just before an aid station and then washed down with some water. This is often easier said than done, as water tends to be given out in cups and ended up anywhere but my mouth. Like the grab-and-go method, drinking while running is something to practise in training (see page 149). Of course, you can walk through the aid stations to minimise any mishaps.

Don't forget the time-lag between ingestion and impact. There's little physical benefit from taking a gel 20 minutes before the end of the race, with the only potential boost being psychological.

A few words on hydration. Generally, the higher the air temperature, the higher my sweat rate, and hence the more water I needed. However, as Asker Jeukendrup makes clear on page 188, overhydration with water should be avoided at all costs due to the risk of a dangerous condition called hyponatremia (water intoxication or low sodium).

Some athletes like to take caffeine, including in cola and other drinks, gum, tablets, coffee and cacao. Caffeine can have performance-enhancing effects, which is why it was on the World Anti-Doping Agency's (WADA's) list of prohibited substances. It was removed from the list because it is so ubiquitous in everyday food and drink and performance-enhancing doses of caffeine were practically indistinguishable from daily use. Taken in small doses over the course of a long-course triathlon, the quantity consumed can add up. While it can be an ergogenic aid, caffeine can also have negative side effects, such as increased heart rate, palpitations, anxiety and GI issues. As a regular coffee drinker, I always had a cup of joe before races and my gels contained a small amount of caffeine. I did try caffeine tablets in training, but they played havoc with my stomach so were best avoided. The key is to experiment and find out what works for you.

If you do feel stomach discomfort at any point, it's often best to reduce the intensity, sitting up if you are in the aero position on the bike, and giving yourself the chance to let your gut settle. If you also find yourself 'hitting the wall', or 'bonking' as it is also known, prioritise getting some fuel, but don't take on more than you are able to digest per hour; stay calm and positive; reduce your pace (stop or walk if you have to) and the fuel should begin to take effect after about 20 minutes.

Remember that littering will result in a penalty or disqualification and so only discard packages or bottles at the designated points, usually a given distance before and after aid stations. Consult the race guide or ask volunteers if you want clarification.

My energy requirements for shorter races were very different to those in an Ironman. For Olympic-distance races, I only had water and a gel at about 30km on the bike.

For half-Ironman events, I simply halved what I would ingest over the full Ironman distance.

Immediately after an Ironman, I craved chips, a kebab, pizzas or burgers, and tended to indulge in more than one. My world-record-breaking two large burgers, two plates of chips, one plate of onion rings and 15 donuts after Ironman Arizona in November 2010 could have been deemed slightly extreme but post-race excess has always been something at which I have excelled. For more on post-race recovery, see Chapter 10.

However hard you try, it is really difficult to replicate a race nutrition strategy in training. Yes, you can practise and prepare, but sometimes races throw you curve balls, or GI dynamite, that you least expect. Not everything will go perfectly. There will be discomfort, problems and challenges. Back-up strategies help, but ultimately your body can sometimes behave in a way that you do not anticipate. Remember that it's all a learning process, and nutritional perfection is very hard to attain, even when you have a few world titles under your race belt!

MY IRONMAN NUTRITION STRATEGY

Breakfast 2 hours 15 minutes before race start	Bowl of rice cereal made with water, a tablespoon of sunflower butter or tahini and tablespoon of honey. Half a banana. Small cup of percolated coffee with lactose-free milk. Glass of water.
Pre-swim	Approx. 300ml of water in sips before the start
Swim	-
Bike	2 × bottles of energy drink Water as required 2 × caffeinated gels 1 × non-nutty chocolate bar (eaten in 4 stages, one bite every hour)
T2	1 × caffeinated gel
Run	6 × caffeinated gels Water at aid stations Sips of Coke, if required (from 34km onwards)

Insight

ASKER JEUKENDRUP on my race nutrition

Athletes have varying tolerances, preferences and palates as well as having different metabolisms, determined both by genetics and by their daily diet, and so I like to take a very individualised, athlete-centric, yet evidence-based, approach to race nutrition. Chrissie's race-day priorities were ensuring she had enough energy, minimised GI discomfort and stayed hydrated.

In 2006, Chrissie was focused on Olympic-distance triathlon and, taking her background, the race intensity and race duration into consideration, I advised her to take one gel at about 30km on the bike. This seemed to work in her practice races and was therefore the strategy we adopted for the World Age Group Championships that year.

She did her first Ironman race in South Korea in 2007 and didn't have any idea about fuelling for long distance – she simply used the same products as her friend. She still won her first race but suffered from GI problems at that event, as well as subsequent Ironman races. There are several possible nutrition-related causes of GI issues. These causes are extremely individual and what may be problematic for one athlete may not impact another. They can include: a high-fibre, high-fat or high-dairy intake during the preceding days, the use of highly concentrated carbohydrate beverages, consuming too much protein during a race, excessive sodium or caffeine consumption, or taking gels without drinking additional water.

Chrissie and I needed to establish the underlying reasons for her GI issues and, by removing the potential causes one by one, we started to find the solutions. For example, she was using a sports drink that contained a significant amount of protein. There is little evidence that protein during exercise improves performance, but there is plenty of evidence that it will slow down gastric emptying and the delivery of other nutrients. We therefore opted for a drink that contained a mix of fructose, glucose and electrolytes, but no protein. We also reduced her fibre intake in the day before the race.

Evidence has shown a so-called 'dose response' relationship between carbohydrate and performance – that is, increased carbohydrates can lead to improved performance. However, there is also a limit after which performance can diminish due principally to the increased risk of GI issues such as sickness and/or diarrhoea. I tend to advise that athletes consume between 60 and 90g of carbohydrates per hour during longer distance races. Research that I have undertaken (and was later corroborated by others) has also shown that if you combine glucose and fructose you can absorb more carbohydrate per hour than if you only use a single sugar, such as glucose alone. Hence, I suggested to Chrissie that she used drinks and gels that comprised both sugars.

Chrissie's specific energy needs for the Ironman were calculated based on numerous factors, most importantly: her physiology, her goal/s and the duration and the intensity at which she was racing. For the bike and run, her intake was approximately 60g of carbohydrates per hour. This is at the lower end of the scale, largely because Chrissie had trained her body to be extremely efficient at using body fat as fuel.

Besides energy, it is important to stay hydrated to replace water lost, principally, in sweat and urine. Sweat rates vary between athletes, with excessive sweating sometimes leading to dehydration. Severe dehydration can have a significant impact on performance. Sweat rates can be calculated by measuring nude bodyweight before and after training. Note that it will vary between swim, bike and run as well as under different environmental conditions. The difference, corrected for fluid intake and urine losses, is mostly sweat loss. For instance, if your body weight before a two-hour bike session is 75kg and after is 74kg and you have drunk two 0.5-litre bottles, your sweat loss would have been approximately: $(75-74) + (2 \times 0.5) = 2kg$ or 2 litres. This equates to 1 litre per hour. From frequent measurements in different conditions you will be able to predict your sweat losses with reasonable accuracy. It has been shown that 2–3 per cent reduction in body weight will negatively impact performance. To prevent dehydration, you will have to drink amounts that are similar to your sweat rate.

Just as we should avoid dehydration, it is also important to avoid overhydration and weight gain. Not only would an athlete unnecessarily carry extra weight, which can impede performance, it can also be dangerous to drink too much. Hyponatremia (low blood sodium) is an incredibly serious condition and is the result of drinking too much water. There are many ways to achieve proper hydration: sports drinks and water are of course the most common ones. Chrissie used water and energy drinks on the bike and water on the run.

It's also vital to consider your sodium intake. Sodium losses can be very high in athletes who sweat heavily and whose sweat has high sodium content. As an indicator, these athletes will often have white crusts on their clothes after training. In my opinion, many athletes take too much sodium during races, especially in the form of concentrated salt tablets. This increases the osmolality (density) of the stomach contents and may have negative effects on gastric emptying and can be the cause of GI problems. Most drinks and gels have moderate amounts of salt (sodium), which is generally sufficient for most athletes, although the heavy sweaters may wish to consume slightly more by adding regular table salt to their drinks.

It is possible to undertake a sweat test that measures how much sodium you are losing. Based on this test, an estimate of sodium losses can be made and a supplementation plan formulated. I have developed tools that can enable me to do this, but for Chrissie it was never an issue as she had an extremely low sweat rate and we never considered sodium, either excess or deficiency, to be a problem. ●

One-on-One

Chewing the Fat: Race Nutrition with Katy Campbell

Katy raced the Olympic-distance Bristol Harbourside Triathlon in June 2015 as her B-race preparation for the Alpe d'Huez Long Course seven weeks later. Based on her training and the course profile, we thought her splits would be roughly as follows: 30-minute swim, 1-hour 25-minute bike and 49–50-minute run. Matt Edwards and I wanted Katy, who is a vegetarian, to practise her race-day nutrition. We asked her to plan what she would eat and drink in the day before the race, as well on race day. We then discussed her choices and finalised a strategy that would hopefully suit her needs. Here is Katy's own plan, with our comments on the choices she had made.

KATY CAMPBELL'S RACE NUTRITION PLAN

	KATY'S INTAKE	OUR COMMENTS
DAY BEFORE:		
Breakfast	Muesli (with oats, nuts, seeds and dried fruit), berries and yogurt, plus a latte.	A carbohydrate-rich breakfast is great if you are doing a harder or longer session and have time to digest it; however, given you will be doing a run soon after, you could have something lighter and simpler, with less fibre and dairy to minimise GI distress – and a more substantial breakfast after.
		Good options are rice cakes or toast with peanut butter and honey/agave syrup, a banana with tahini, homemade rice balls with coconut and honey. Have a less milky coffee, like an Americano with a dash of milk.

	KATY'S INTAKE	OUR COMMENTS
25-MINUTE RUN		
Post-run second breakfast	Oat and apricot slice and a latte.	Opt for another lower-fibre breakfast, such as eggs on toast with avocado and a banana. Sip on water, but not excessively, and ditch the second coffee of the day!
Lunch	Homemade hummus, tabbouleh and large mixed salad.	Could be simplified. Have a bagel with egg, adding avocado and spinach if you crave the 'green' fix.
45-MINUTE BIKE		
Snack	Homemade bars with dates, almonds, banana and peanut butter.	A great, healthy, carb-protein rich snack, following the short bike ride. You could also have rice cakes, as per the first breakfast, or a banana.
Dinner	Cheesy pizza.	Pizza can be good, but: limit the amount of cheese as dairy can cause GI problems, don't overdo the toppings or have an oily, processed base. Homemade would be best. You could also try pasta, a herby tomato-based sauce and some tofu; or a risotto (but not too creamy) with peas.
RACE DAY:		
Breakfast (2 hours 30 minutes before the start)	Muesli, berries and yogurt, and a latte.	Eat between 2 hours and 2 hours 30 minutes before the start. Try something less complex and easy to digest, yet carbohydrate rich: toast or a bagel with peanut butter and jam or honey or porridge made with a splash of milk but mostly water, a homemade chocolate muffin, or even baby rice cereal. Have a banana if still hungry. Sip water, but don't overhydrate. As you normally drink coffee it's OK to have one, but an Americano rather than a latte.
Snack before race start	Malt fruit loaf.	Breakfast should sustain you until you get on the bike, and this is probably unnecessary.
During race	Bike: Two fruit and oat bars, 500ml half apple juice half water and 10 Haribo. Run: nothing	You could add a few pinches of salt to diluted apple juice to replace that lost in sweat (especially if it's a hot day), or we can use some training sessions to find a commercial energy/sports drink that you like. Another option is diluted coconut water. Haribo could be hard to chew. You could have a gel instead, at about 30–35km, to tide you over for the run. One bottle of energy drink and a gel would probably provide sufficient carbs for this race, but you could have one fruit and oat bar in your back pocket in case of an energy lull.

	KATY'S INTAKE	OUR COMMENTS
Post-race	Gatorade, chocolate milk, fruit scone with clotted cream.	Ingest carbs and protein within 20–30 minutes of finishing. Homemade chocolate milk is a good option: just combine your milk of choice (cow's, soya, rice, almond, coconut), some cacao powder, honey or agave syrup, with banana/berries and coconut if you fancy it, and have this delicious beverage in your post-race bag. Watermelon or coconut water is great for rehydration.
Three hours after finishing	Jacket potato, beans and cheese; chocolate and Guinness cake and I'll probably have a glass of Prosecco!	A great post-race meal with ample carbs and protein, although you may wish to eat this a little earlier, perhaps 60–90 minutes after finishing. Other options are: large hummus sandwich with spinach, tofu and pasta/quinoa/bulgur wheat with some feta cheese, a lentil burger, eggs on toast with avocado.
Snack	Tabbouleh, crisps	Tabbouleh is great, although crisps are salty (which you might crave post-race), they are nutritionally poor. That said, post-race is the time to let your hair down, and so a crisp or ten won't derail your recovery.
Dinner	Vegetarian sausage roll, peas and oven chips.	Good choice, but best if the veggie roll was homemade rather than an overly processed shop-bought variety.

Post-race reflections

Katy followed our advice and performed really well: having a great 29-minute swim where she overcame her nerves and gained huge amounts of self-belief. She was comfortable and confident on the bike, with a split of 1 hour 24 minutes, and maximised her strength with a 48-minute run, finishing in a time of 2 hours 45 minutes, sixth in her age group and 11th woman overall. It was a fantastic result, and helped inform both her nutrition and overall race strategy for Alpe d'Huez five weeks later.

> " A fantastic result that helped inform both her nutrition and overall race strategy for Alpe d'Huez five weeks later. "

TO THE FINISH LINE RECIPES

Although I'm no Jamie Oliver, I much prefer to whip up my own food, rather than be overly reliant on relatively expensive, sometimes over-processed sports nutrition. As I explained earlier there is a place for using such products when training and racing, but you can also work real-food miracles with natural, wholesome ingredients in the comfort of your own kitchen. I've been fortunate to work with nutritionist and author of *Go Faster Food*, Kate Percy, to develop some recipes for tasty, healthy, nutritious and performance-enhancing snacks that are easy and quick to make. They are also portable, meaning you can shove them in a swim bag, in the back pocket of your bike jersey or even carry them in your hand on the run. I hope you enjoy making and consuming them as much as I do!

BEETROOT AND ALMOND MILK RECOVERY BLAST

This juice really packs a punch when it comes to recovery. Beetroot contains nitrates, which, once converted to nitrite and nitric oxide in the body, enables muscles to work more efficiently and demand less oxygen. In fact, an Exeter University study found that beetroot juice enabled cyclists to exercise for up to 20 per cent longer than when they had a regular fruit juice. To gain the most advantage, it's best to consume beetroot as a juice. However, I realise it is an acquired taste! Combining the beetroot with almond milk, fresh cucumber and red pepper not only renders it more palatable, but really light and delicious too. Loaded with healthy carbohydrate to replenish depleted glycogen levels, protein to help muscle recovery and regeneration, and minerals such as sodium and potassium to replace those lost through sweat, it's great to consume after a heavy workout to optimise recovery. The turmeric and ginger are optional but using them will increase the juice's anti-inflammatory properties. If you would like to increase the protein content, add a tablespoon of chia seeds or natural yoghurt.

Preparation time: 5 minutes

NUTRITION PER SERVING

Energy 245kcal

Protein 4g

Carbohydrate 52g of which sugars 37g

Fat 4g

Salt 0.4g

Fibre 6g

INGREDIENTS FOR ONE LARGE SERVING

4 ice cubes

200ml unsweetened almond milk (fine to substitute with cow's, rice or soya milk)

250ml unsweetened apple juice

1 medium cooked beetroot, peeled (about 60–80g)

60g cucumber

60g red pepper

1 tsp turmeric

5g fresh ginger, peeled and sliced finely

METHOD

1. Add all the ingredients to the blender and blend for a few minutes until really smooth.

2. Pour into a long glass and enjoy!

AVOCADO AND CUCUMBER LASSI WITH TURMERIC AND MINT

Rich in potassium, calcium, B vitamins, vitamin E and monounsaturated fats, this is a light and delicious recovery drink. A powerful antioxidant and anti-inflammatory, turmeric is an excellent spice to include in your training diet.

Preparation time: 5 minutes

NUTRITION PER SQUARE

Energy 185kcal

Carbohydrate 14g of which sugars 7g

Protein 6g

Fat 12g

Salt 0.5g

Fibre 4g

INGREDIENTS FOR 2 GLASSES

1 small avocado, chilled, peeled, stone removed and cut into cubes

½ cucumber, sliced

Good pinch of salt and freshly ground black pepper

1 tsp ground turmeric

6 fresh mint leaves

200ml fresh milk or unsweetened almond, soya or rice milk

1 heaped tbsp natural yoghurt

8 ice cubes

Ground cumin or ginger, stick of cucumber or ginger to serve

PREPARATION

1. Blend the avocado, cucumber, mint, salt, turmeric, milk and yoghurt in a blender.
2. Add the ice cubes and blend again until all the ice is crushed.
3. Pour into two tall glasses and decorate with a little ground cumin or ginger and a stick of ginger or cucumber.

BIRCHER MUESLI

What I love about this muesli is that you can prepare it the night before and all you have to do in the morning is take it out of the fridge, stir in yoghurt and apple, and eat! Originally created by Dr Bircher-Benner in the 1890s as a healthy meal for patients in his Zurich hospital, this muesli provides an excellent balance of heart-healthy, sustaining nutrients, including slow-releasing carbohydrate, good-quality protein and omega-3 fatty acids. It's also a great source of vitamin E, potassium and fibre; a super breakfast (or a small bowl would be a great snack!) to support your training.

Preparation time: less than 5 minutes plus overnight soaking

NUTRITION PER SERVING

Energy 240kcal

Protein 8g

Carbohydrate 36g of which sugars 23g

Fat 6g

Salt 0.2g

Fibre 4g

INGREDIENTS FOR 2 SERVINGS

120g unsweetened muesli with fruit and nuts (or, if you'd like to use individual components: 80g whole rolled jumbo oats, 20g chopped mixed dried fruit, 20g chopped mixed nuts and seeds)

Enough milk, or non-dairy alternative, to cover the oats

Splash of apple or orange juice

¼ tsp grated nutmeg, ground cinnamon or cardamom

1 crisp, fresh apple, grated

1 tbsp natural yoghurt if required

1 tsp runny honey

METHOD

1. Mix the oats, nuts, seeds and dried fruit (or pour out the desired quantity of muesli).

2. Pour over enough milk to cover the mixture generously and add a splash of apple or orange juice.

3. Add grated nutmeg, ground cinnamon or cardamom.

4. Leave for a couple of hours, or overnight, in the fridge. When you are ready to eat your Bircher muesli, remove from the fridge and stir in the grated apple.

5. If required, add a dollop of natural yoghurt and a good drizzle of honey.

CHIA-SEED ENERGY BALLS

These bite-sized balls of nutritious deliciousness work incredibly well as an on-the-bike energy booster or a speedy pick-me-up before an early morning session when you've no time for a sit-down breakfast. A staple of the Mexican Tarahumara tribe of 'barefoot' running fame, chia seeds are a rich source of protein, carbohydrate and omega-3 fatty acids as well as minerals such as potassium, calcium, magnesium and iron. They are quite pricey, though, so swap them for flaxseed if you like. Use toasted sesame seeds, desiccated coconut or ground golden flaxseed as an alternative to raspberry powder if you prefer.

Preparation time: 5–10 minutes

NUTRITION PER BALL

Energy 40kcal

Protein 1.6g

Carbohydrate 6g of which sugars 3g

Fat 2g

Salt trace

Fibre 1.3g

INGREDIENTS FOR ABOUT 25–30 BALLS

90g soft pitted dates

80g soft dried apricots

100g sultanas

10g chia seeds

20g porridge oats

20g pumpkin seeds

40g sunflower seeds

2 tbsp freeze-dried raspberry powder to coat

METHOD

1. Place the seeds and porridge oats in the food processor and blitz until roughly chopped.

2. Add the dried fruit and blitz again until the mixture starts to stick together to form a dough.

3. Roll into small balls in the palm of your hands, about 1.5cm in diameter, 12–15g in weight.

4. Pour the freeze-dried raspberry powder into a small bowl and then roll each ball in the powder to cover completely.

5. These will keep for a couple of weeks, stored in a sealed plastic bag or airtight container.

CHOCOLATE, FIG, GINGER AND ALMOND BOOST BARS

Figs are rich in potassium, vitamin K and fibre, and are a great source of carbohydrate, calcium, magnesium and iron. Blended with melted dark chocolate, crunchy toasted almonds and fiery fresh ginger, they make a tasty base for these little squares of energy, loaded with anti-inflammatories, anti-oxidants and healthy monounsaturated fats. I like to eat one late afternoon as a pick-me-up before an evening session.

Preparation time: 10 minutes and 30 minutes to chill

NUTRITION PER SQUARE

Energy 158kcal

Carbohydrate 25g of which sugars 17g

Protein 3g

Fat 6g

Salt trace

Fibre 3g

INGREDIENTS TO MAKE 8 SQUARES

70g dark chocolate (preferably around 70–80 per cent cacao content), broken into squares

200g dried figs

100g dried apricots

20g fresh ginger, peeled and finely grated

½ tsp ground ginger

50g whole almonds, skins on

METHOD

1. Preheat the oven to 180°C. Lay the almonds on a baking tray and roast for approximately 5 minutes (remove from the oven the moment you smell the delicious aroma of roasted nuts, otherwise they will burn). Leave to cool for a few minutes.

2. Melt the chocolate in a heatproof bowl over a pan of simmering water. Remove and leave to cool for a couple of minutes.

3. Line a small tray, about 15 × 15cm, with a piece of greaseproof paper.

4. Take a chopping board and roughly chop the almonds using a sharp knife (you want them to add crunch to the bars). Remove and set aside.

5. Place chopped figs and apricots in a blender, and blend until they bind together.

6. Add the cooled chocolate, add the grated and ground ginger and the almonds and blend to combine.

7. Spoon the mixture onto the greaseproof paper and flatten the surface with the back of a spoon (or your fingers). Decorate with a few extra pieces of almond.

8. Refrigerate for 30 minutes to allow the mixture to firm up, and then cut into 8 squares. These will keep for several days in an airtight container, but I like to keep them in the fridge as they taste so good cold!

MALTY FRUIT BARS

If, like me, you love malt loaf, then you'll love these fruity bars. Soft, chewy and nicely balanced with carbohydrate, protein and fats, and rich in vitamins A and C, calcium and iron, they make very tasty fuel, especially during longer bike sessions. Use really ripe bananas; in fact, it's a great idea to keep a stash of overripe bananas in the freezer to defrost for use in cakes and banana bread. Malt extract can be found in most health-food stores and larger supermarkets, but use molasses or honey as an alternative if you like. Also, experiment with the dried fruit content to suit your taste and energy requirements, too; use more dates for post-exercise bars as they provide faster releasing carbohydrate to help muscles recover quickly, or dried apricots, which are slower releasing, to provide a more sustained level of energy.

Preparation time: 10 minutes / Cooking time: 35–40 minutes

NUTRITION PER BAR

Energy 254kcal

Protein 5g

Carbohydrate 31g of which sugars 17g

Fat 13.5g

Salt trace

Fibre 4g

INGREDIENTS FOR 16 BARS

200g wholemeal spelt flour

2 tsp baking powder

2 tsp mixed spice

170ml cold-pressed rapeseed oil or coconut oil

2 large ripe bananas, peeled and mashed with a fork

2 heaped tbsp malt extract

4 eggs

600g dried fruit (try a mix of currants, cranberries, sultanas and dates)

Zest of 1 orange

50g walnut pieces

METHOD

1. Preheat the oven to 180°C.
2. Put the flour into a bowl with the baking powder and spices.
3. In another bowl, beat together the oil, banana and malt extract with an electric whisk for a couple of minutes, until the mixture thickens a little.
4. Add the eggs and whisk until well combined.
5. Using a large metal spoon, fold in the flour mixture and then the dried fruit and orange zest.
6. Pour the mixture into the tin and smooth the surface. Arrange the nuts on top.
7. Turn the oven down to 160°C and bake for approximately 35–40 minutes, until a skewer pierced through the centre comes out clean.
8. Cool in the tin on a wire rack and then cut into bars when cool. These keep for several days in an airtight container or can be wrapped individually and frozen.

HOMEMADE ISOTONIC DRINK

Isotonic drinks are formulated to provide minerals (electrolytes) to replace quickly those we lose through sweat, and a boost of carbohydrate to replenish depleted glycogen stores. This incredibly straightforward and tasty homemade sports drink is just as effective as the commercial variety, containing minerals such as sodium, calcium, potassium, iron, manganese and magnesium, as well as vitamins C and B6. And it's a whole lot cheaper!

Preparation time: 1 minute

NUTRITION PER 500ML

Energy 123kcal

Protein 0g

Carbohydrate 31g of which sugars 28g

Fat 0g

Salt 1g

Fibre 0g

INGREDIENTS

250ml unsweetened apple juice

250ml water

Pinch salt (c. fifth of a tsp)

METHOD

1. Measure out 250ml apple juice. Add 250ml water to make a total volume of 500ml.

2. Add a pinch of salt and shake well. Chill in the fridge until required.

PEANUT BUTTER RICE BALLS

If you find sweet gels and energy bars on long rides hard to stomach, then these delicious savoury peanut balls make a really effective alternative. White short-grain rice is loaded with fast-releasing carbohydrate, which will top up depleted glycogen levels efficiently, as well as providing healthy unsaturated fats, potassium, sodium and vitamin B6.

Preparation time: 5–10 minutes

NUTRITION PER BALL

Energy 127kcal

Protein 3.2g

Carbohydrate 23g of which sugars 2g

Fat 3g

Salt 0.5g

Fibre 1g

INGREDIENTS FOR ABOUT 10 BALLS

2 tbsp (50g) whole nut crunchy peanut butter (no added sugar variety)

4 dried apricots (use the soft variety), chopped very finely

Zest of ½ lime, finely grated

250g cooked sushi or pudding rice

METHOD

1. Combine the peanut butter, apricots and lime zest in a small bowl.
2. Place one teaspoon of cooked rice on a sheet of cling film.
3. Spoon a small amount (less than ½ tsp) of the peanut butter mixture into the middle of the rice and then cover with a little more rice.
4. Pick up the cling film to form a parcel, so that the peanut butter mixture is enveloped inside, and shape the rice into a ball, or whatever shape you prefer.
5. Twist the top of the cling film to form a tight seal.
6. Refrigerate to help the balls firm up.
7. Peel off the cling film, and enjoy!

CHAPTER EIGHT

PSYCHOLOGY

Preparing your mind is as important as preparing your body. This is part of training – the part that people don't put in their logbooks; the part that all the monitors and gadgets in the world can't influence or record.

We will all face adversity at one time or another, and conversely there will be highs that can also derail us if we let them. Our sport is as much about mental strength as it is physical strength; and sporting success rests on having the mental fortitude to overcome fears, hurt, discomfort, self-doubt and more. It sounds simple but is so easy to forget. If we let our head drop, our heart drops with it.

Some people are born with ample determination, positivity, motivation and drive, others embody composure and placidity; some may be ruthlessly competitive while others are more passive. We may be able to endure boredom and isolation while our neighbours fear it. It is unlikely that we were born with all the required psychological traits and, hence, if we are to reach our potential, all of us need to invest time in training the brain.

The importance of the mind in sports is being recognised like never before, with increasing numbers of employed by professional teams and individuals to try to provide a vital performance edge. My own coaches were masters of sports psychology, and I learned so much from working with them. This chapter will shed light on some of my own tools, strategies and philosophies; as well as advice on learning to love your body, musings about the concept of sport as an addiction and a special homage to those who have inspired me along my life and triathlon journey.

It will help you develop a mind that is as strong as your body, because in triathlon this can be the most powerful weapon of all.

MAXIMISING YOUR MOJO: MOTIVATION METHODS

The most common question I am asked is: 'How do you stay motivated?' People tend to assume that professional athletes are blessed with unwavering and limitless drive, determination and vitality; that we never feel lethargic or lazy, that we don't become despondent in the face of injury, and that the thought of donning a onesie and performing a sofa-slump never crosses our minds. This couldn't be further from the truth. I, like the rest of the human race, suffer from motivational ebbs and flows. The key is that we learn to prevent or else recognise, manage and mitigate mojo-malaise – stopping it from totally derailing us from the pursuit of our goals.

> ❝ I, like the rest of the human race, suffer from motivational ebbs and flows. The key is that we learn to prevent or else recognise, manage and mitigate mojo-malaise. ❞

So how do we solve the case of the missing mojo, put a *Chariots of Fire*-work up our onesie-wearing backsides and quash the voice that says, 'Put your feet up. Have a donut!'? This is where mental strength comes in. Without mental discipline these minor speed bumps turn into mental monsters.

The following are some of my tips for inserting fireworks where the sun doesn't shine and getting you out of the door faster than you can say 'Mr Motivator's brightly coloured spandex'.

A clear, realistic, yet ambitious goal

What's your dream? Lounging in a hot-tub with Richard Gere is an admirable aspiration, but you may want to think slightly less *Pretty Woman* and more *Iron Man*. Set and then recall your A-race goal. As Chapter 1 made clear, have constant, visible reminders: stick a note on your front door, make it your screensaver, go public on social media, get a pre-emptive triathlon-related tattoo. Never lose sight of your dream.

Know your motives

Remember why you set the goal in the first place. For instance, the goal might be to complete your first half Ironman, and the reasons – or motivational carrots – might be to improve your health, meet new people, to prove to yourself that you can meet the challenge, to honour a loved one's memory or raise money for

OPPOSITE:
Motivational words got us through the 4321 Challenge.

charity. If ever I am struggling, I recall Florence and the Machine's perceptive advice in 'Dog Days are Over':

> You better run.
> Run fast for your mother, run fast for your father.
> Run for your children, for your sisters and brothers.

Wise words indeed, although she forgot to add '. . . for the post-race pizza and a large beer'. In addition to the carrots, also recall the stick of being fed up with the status quo (not the rock band with a penchant for using only three chords and having dodgy barnets) or memories of when things may not have gone so well, so-called 'failure' that you'd prefer never to repeat. When you're overcome with inertia, use these carrots and sticks to propel you into action.

Just start

Starting is often the hardest part. So, do just that. Start. Remember that around the two-minute mark your cells more easily utilise oxygen as a fuel, muscle temperature rises and exercise becomes easier.

Rungs on a ladder

In training, if you have a set of intervals, focus on completing only one. Then as endorphins flow, begin number two, then three . . . And, bingo! You've done ten. Or play mind games. Tell yourself you can stop after two intervals. You'll do those two, and then the mind games can start again, 'just get to five'. I bet you make it to ten! I would do something similar within races. For example, during the Ironman World Championship in 2011 I endured the pain by breaking the race down into separate stages – whether it be the next swim buoy, getting to an aid station or even just taking one more step forward. I promised myself that at that point I could either a) stop or b) keep going. Giving my brain the reward of having completed these smaller goals creates positive momentum. And yes, the answer is always b) keep going.

On a broader scale, set small tasks or stepping-stone goals to make the longer-term ultimate goal seem less overwhelming, and ensure that you can enjoy the journey

with successes along the way. These stepping-stones can be difficult training sessions or B races en route to your big A race.

Create a practical plan

A daily, weekly and monthly strategy and plan provides direction and structure, and gives you milestones en route to your goal. The plan should be realistic and tailored to you and your life. So, if your goal is to complete a 5km run, develop a daily programme enabling you to realise that dream. Help can be found in Chapter 2.

Time efficiency

Make training as convenient as possible. For example, find a gym, running track or pool that is accessible and financially affordable; keep your running clothes at the office so you can do a quick session in your lunch break; bike to work to get bang for commuting buck; keep your swimming paraphernalia in the office so you can delve into the pool without going home first. Going to bed in your training gear is probably one step too far.

Mix it up

Motivational malaise can strike when the regimen becomes too . . . regimented. An occasional injection of session spice will keep you physically and mentally fresh and stop you getting stuck in a rut. Maybe you can run on forest trails, instead of pounding the same old roads. Swim in open water instead of the pool. Head out on new bike routes, or with a different group of people – or even use a mountain bike instead. Perhaps you could also consider doing some different races, for example duathlons, off-road triathlons, aquathlons or even some cross-country running. Maybe it's even worth – heaven forbid! – taking some time out from triathlon altogether. Yes, it's a fantastic – and addictive – sport but a break may help rekindle that fire, or else make you realise how much you prefer doing something totally different.

Use music, movies, poems, inspiring stories

It was 2006 and I was en route to Geneva to race at the ITU Age Group World Championship. I was bubbling over with excitement and decided to follow the advice of A Very Experienced Person (aka my housemate) and listen to motivational tunes. My friend had kindly made me a compilation of songs, including some by Eminem. I didn't really see myself as a fan of gangsta rap until I listened to the lyrics of two of his songs: the first being 'Lose Yourself' and the second entitled 'Till I Collapse'. The latter ditty goes a little something like this:

> Cause sometimes you just feel tired, feel weak,
> And when you feel weak, you feel like you wanna just give up.
> But you gotta search within you, you gotta find that inner strength
> And just pull that sh*t out of you and get that motivation to not give up
> And not be a quitter, no matter how bad you want to just fall flat on your face and collapse.

Who'd have known that gangsta rap could have summed up a triathlete's experience so eloquently? This, and others, have found their way on to my training and racing playlist at page 211. While I wouldn't expect you to have the same bad taste in music as me, I would nevertheless suggest creating a playlist of songs that will get you jumping, moving and grooving.

In addition to music, I write the words of Rudyard Kipling's 'If' (see page 227) on my race water bottles. Watching uplifting movies or YouTube clips of others overcoming hurdles to achieve their dreams can also ignite your fire. Ditto goes for standing at the sidelines of the London Marathon. A quick peek at Ironman World Championship videos the night before a race never fails to get my blood pumping. Podcasts can be good (although I haven't found BBC Radio 4's *From Our Own Correspondent* to be particularly useful). Be inspired by words. Be inspired by others. If they can, you can.

Keep a log

Chart your progress in a log, ensuring you bank feelings of euphoria on which to draw in future. Make sure you highlight any accomplishments and successes and note how they make you feel. When you find your mojo flagging, look at that book, and recall difficult times when you have struggled but overcome lethargy, tiredness or discomfort – and know that if you have jumped those hurdles in the past, you can do so again.

Reward yourself

A little bit of bribery never hurts, so occasionally reward yourself with flowers, a trip to the theatre, a manicure or a new aerodynamic bike toy. Take time to celebrate what you are achieving along the way.

Friends with benefits

Sometimes we need others to help motivate, guide and encourage us. De-friend naysayers, pessimists, braggers and whiners, and instead surround yourself with those who offer good guidance, support and encouragement – a coach, a training partner, family members, a local sports club, online forums and upbeat friends who have their drink bottles half-full.

Make intentions public

Extrinsic motivation can also come from broadcasting your intentions. The next time you're wavering about a workout, post on social media/your blog/an online forum or call your best

THE CIRCLE OF LIFE

'The Circle of Life' on *The Lion King* soundtrack is a favourite song of mine. Prior to Challenge Roth 2011 I was chatting to Felix Walchshöfer, the race organiser and owner, and he asked me whether there was a special song that they could play at the race start, just before the cannon fired – a song that meant a lot to me, and which I would immediately know was being played in my honour. There was only one choice – 'The Circle of Life'. And as I sat there peacefully before the start, 'my song' came on. The other 4,000 competitors must have been baffled to hear it replace Euro-pop on the loudspeaker, but I smiled and knew from that moment it was a very special day.

TOP: Katy Campbell's mantra inscribed on the headset of her bike.

friend and tell them, 'I'm just about to do this session' or 'I am going to sign up for this race'. This social expression will give you the urge, and accountability, to deliver on each step, and update people on progress towards your goal.

Positive mindset and mantras

Replace energy-sapping thoughts of 'I'm knackered, I want to sit down and eat a donut, it's raining and my new shoes will get muddy' with positive affirmations, images of sunshine and smiles or your personal mantra. I write 'Never Ever Give Up and Smile' on my race wristband and my water bottles. And don't forget to spend time on visualisation. Picture yourself training and racing. See yourself as being strong, confident and successful. Imagine how it will feel to cross the line, hear the roar of the crowd, fall into the arms of your loved one and taste the huge post-race burger. You are only as powerful as your mind.

We all suffer from motivational ebbs and flows. It's normal, it's natural, but it is also under your control. You can crack the case of the missing mojo, and doing so will ultimately be a key pillar of your success.

CAN'T STOP THE MUSIC: MY PRE-RACE PLAYLIST

Uplifting, inspiring, funky, groovy or downright cringeworthy, here's the list of songs that I always listened to before every race.

'With or Without You'	U2
'We Are the Champions'	Queen
'Wait and See'	Shihad
'Under the Moon'	Jim Major
'Mr Jones'	Counting Crows
'Tonight, Tonight'	Smashing Pumpkins
'Romeo and Juliet'	Dire Straits
'Mr Brightside'	Killers
'Learn to Fly'	Foo Fighters
'I Just Can't Wait to Be King'	*The Lion King* Cast
'Lose Yourself'	Eminem
'One Moment in Time'	Whitney Houston
'Basket Case'	Green Day
'Local Boy in the Photograph'	Stereophonics
'I Alone'	Live
'Girl from Mars'	Ash
'Every You, Every Me'	Placebo
'Everlong'	Foo Fighters
'Come Back to What You Know'	Embrace
'Eye of the Tiger'	Survivor
'The Circle of Life'	*The Lion King* Cast
'Chasing Cars'	Snow Patrol
'Can You Feel the Love Tonight'	*The Lion King* Cast
'Bend and Break'	Keane
'Till I Collapse'	Eminem
'Where the Streets Have No Name'	U2
'Be Somebody'	Kings of Leon
'Angels Fall'	Jim Major
'Angels'	Robbie Williams
'Ana's Song (Open Fire)'	Silverchair
'Sunrise'	Arno Carstens

UNSELFISH SPORT: MY SOURCES OF INSPIRATION

I have always been passionate about sport and about development. In 2001, I was fortunate to make the latter topic my career when I got a job working as an advisor to the UK government on international sustainable development policy and, later, when I managed water, sanitation and health projects in Nepal. At that stage in my life, I combined my development-related work with a recreational passion for endurance sports. It was the best of both worlds. In 2007, I left my civil service career to become a full-time triathlete, putting my ability to undertake development work on hold – or had I?

I thought the single-minded pursuit of an athletic goal was an incredibly self-centred endeavour. This notion hit me like a thunderbolt during a training session and I was overcome with a sense of guilt and impotence. I remember saying to my then coach, Brett Sutton: 'I don't know how long I can do this. I am so selfish; everything I'm doing is for me and me alone.' And he replied quite simply, 'Chrissie, just you wait. With your sporting achievements you will be able to change people's lives in ways that you may never have thought possible.'

Little did I know it then, but Brett's prophetic words were to become reality.

Triathlon has given me a unique and valuable opportunity to combine my two great passions – sport and development; a chance to raise awareness, to speak about things that I care about, to be a role model and an ambassador for causes like gender equality or children's participation, and to inspire others. It is a platform for positive change. The part I play is small, but I derive a huge amount of satisfaction and pleasure from encouraging others to find their passion, test their limits and get to their finish line. My achievements have given me a chance to make a potentially selfish, self-absorbed existence . . . unselfish.

And this doesn't just apply to me. I believe that we *all* have this opportunity. Through triathlon every single one of us has the chance to impact others in a really positive way: by being role models, by encouraging people to face their fears, by racing for a charity, by volunteering at an event . . . the list is endless.

I hope we all see the sport not only for what it gives us, but what we can also give to others through our participation.

OPPOSITE: With my wonderful parents at the finish line of the Ironman World Championship, 2009.

For every person you inspire, there are those who will do the same for you. Reflecting on my life, I thought I would mention just a few of my own 'guiding lights'; those who, in one way or another, have selflessly devoted their lives to others and in doing so have lifted me to greater heights.

First, my parents, who gave me opportunities to grow, to learn, to make mistakes and to explore. They have helped to nurture and shape me into the person and athlete I am today. The same goes for my husband Tom and our daughter Esme, who have taught me what it means to be selfless, to be calm, to appreciate the small things and try to stay in the moment.

And then there are the thousands of age groupers who train and race, conquering challenges along the way. I see them cross finish lines with elation and pride etched on their faces; the boost and pleasure this gives is unparalleled. The same goes for the para-triathletes, including those who competed at Rio 2016 in the inaugural Olympic para-triathlon. Awe-inspiring.

I often think of Dick and Rick Hoyt, a father-and-son endurance team. Despite Rick being born with cerebral palsy in the 1960s, the Hoyts have completed more than a thousand races – including marathons, duathlons and triathlons (including six Ironmans). In 1992, they biked and ran 6,010km across the USA in 45 days.

Those who watch me race will have also seen me roll across the finish line in memory of the late Jon Blais. Jon was an American amateur triathlete who contracted motor neurone disease (or ALS – amyotrophic lateral sclerosis), defying all odds by finishing the Ironman World Championship in 2005, where he symbolically rolled across the line. Jon's last days were devoted to establishing a charity to raise money and awareness about the disease. Then there's Sister Madonna Buder who, in her 80s, sets the triathlon world on fire. Or a woman I met once in a restaurant in Texas. She came up to me and said, 'Chrissie, I just want you to know – I took up triathlon aged 73 and I have never felt better!' Just wow.

TOP: The inspirational 'ALS Warrior' Jon Blais.

ABOVE: Marilena (middle) and I with Roseann Dougherty, the founder of cancer charity Team Inspiration.

Another of my shining lights is a woman you have probably never heard of: my friend, Marilena D'Amone. Marilena had completed countless marathons and dabbled in triathlon before being diagnosed with an aggressive form of breast cancer in July 2013, aged 37 – six weeks before she was due to do her first Ironman. Treatment comprised two operations, intensive rounds of chemotherapy and a course of radiation. In August 2013 – the day before chemotherapy began – she completed a 100-mile cycle sportive and, soon after, finished two half marathons. In 2014, she set a goal of completing 14 races – including half Ironmans, short-course triathlons, the Ironman Wales training weekend and a marathon. Despite the challenges she faced, Marilena never once complained: her unrelenting, effervescent positivity and compassion for others is an absolute inspiration. Fortunately, Marilena's cancer is now in remission. She celebrated that news with several endurance events and continues to enrich the lives of everyone she meets.

We can also look to organisations – which are comprised of passionate, dedicated individuals – such as parkrun. Set up in 2004 by the incredible visionary Paul Sinton-Hewitt CBE, parkrun is changing lives through physical activity and volunteering in the UK and around the world.

Or what about those outside of the sporting fraternity? One of the first people to teach me to follow my dreams and encourage me in the pursuit of excellence was a man called Don Feltwell, the headmaster at my primary school. Mr Feltwell sadly passed away in January 2011, but I carry his wisdom, support and encouragement in my mind and heart.

So, while professional athletes – or those who have retired – can hopefully motivate others through their sporting feats, there are those who do the same for us. Recalling those on my list never fails to lift me when I feel low or elevate me to even greater heights. Maybe you could also write and carry such a motivational list – including those you have helped and those who have helped you.

Ultimately this section is an opportunity for me to extend my deepest gratitude to those who selflessly inspire and support me. As they say in Hawaii, 'Mahalo.'

TRIATHLON HIGHS: SPORT AND ADDICTION

I'm an addict. My addiction has brought me World Championship crowns, some records of the non-vinyl variety, chafing and huge oversized calves. The drug? Sport. And like any addict, when I don't get my fix I become Cruella de Vil (cruel, devilish and with a decidedly dodgy haircut). I get grumpy; I throw my toys out of the pram; I suffer cold turkey; I chew on my nails – basically metamorphosing from a relatively stable person to some kind of Godzilla that is impossible to be around.

I am sure many of you can relate to this. We all do sport for different reasons. To get fit, to challenge ourselves, to justify vacuum-cleaner style eating habits and, yes, for the undisputed 'high': the satisfaction of treading that fine line between pleasure and pain, the masochistic seed that only a good hard training session or race can cultivate.

I've always had an addictive personality but this obsession with sport didn't develop overnight. Retrospectively, I gradually morphed from a once-a-week kind of gal to a full-blown 'must-get-the-daily-fix-sport-junkie'.

I often pondered the link between sport and addiction, but was compelled to put fingers to keyboard after reading a CNN piece entitled 'Former drug addicts find new fixation on triathlons' (5 June 2009). The article told of two former drug addicts who used triathlon to rebuild their lives. In their case, the 20-year high from heroin had been replaced by the rush of endorphins.

The same was true of a man, Matt, whom I met at Ironman Australia in 2008. Having reached a heroin-fuelled rock bottom he decided to change his life – coming off illegal drugs and taking up triathlon. I was fortunate to watch him cross the finish line and realise his dream of becoming an Ironman. He was still an addict – he had just changed his drug of choice. Fulfilment through sport, and the many benefits it brings, became the goal, rather than securing the next artificial, illicit hit.

Many triathletes would probably admit to having addictive personalities and, while the word addiction often comes with negative connotations, in the sporting context it can be a healthy obsession. However, like any good thing – chocolate, caffeine, *The West Wing* boxset – we can have too much of it. Triathlon can change from a positive to a negative addiction when fulfilling the craving overrides everything else.

The obsession with filling that logbook compels us to run when really our Achilles/calf/hip/back is saying – sofa! We end up nursing a zero-fun Achilles/calf/hip/back injury for the ensuing month. We might choose to do a scheduled five-hour ride instead of going to an important family reunion. Or, exhausted from an overseas work trip, we nevertheless drag ourselves out for that swim – only to succumb to a cold the next day. We might come out in hives at the thought that the pool might be closed on Christmas Day and spend the festivities worrying that we haven't done the 3km we said we would. Then there is the link to food. A day or two without exercise may mean personal punishment in the form of cutting calories or other disordered eating patterns. Addiction. Believe me. I've been there.

This trait came to the fore in 2010 when I had my arm in a cast. I had to go through a painful process of cold turkey, cue feet-stamping and self-pity. Worrying about where and when I would be able to get my next endorphin fix became the focus on which my emotional state depended. The compulsion to train overrode the more rational side of my brain that said 'rest'. I decided to swim one-handed, with a plastic bag around my cast. The bag, unsurprisingly, leaked. The wounds in my wrist became infected and, to add insult to this injury, I hurt my other shoulder. Reflecting on my seemingly irrational, addictive behaviour, I realised I had become wedded to the triathlete label. It was how I defined myself and this guided every action I took. I knew I had to step back, re-establish perspective and regain control of what was controlling me.

Unlike glugging a bottle of whisky, injecting oneself with opium or eating ten large bars of chocolate a day, exercise addiction can be harder to acknowledge given that sport is generally seen as a splendidly healthy activity in which to engage. For those who recognise themselves in the above anecdote, it is nevertheless very real. However, there are a few ways I found of preventing a sporting addiction becoming a negative force.

Listen to your body

By listening carefully and honestly to my body I am learning when I can push it that little bit further but also when to back off and rest. There were times during training when I felt fatigue building up: not just physically but mentally. Although, as a professional athlete, I rested about 18–20 hours a day, I remember a time in 2011 when I hadn't had a full rest day for over five weeks. After consulting with Dave, I took two. I lay on the sofa all morning. Then went for lunch at a café, and back to the sofa. And did the same the next day. I needed it. And I didn't feel in the least bit guilty. I had put in a solid month of training and I knew that my body deserved that break. I often have to remind myself, even now, that more isn't necessarily better, and that recovery is part of training and not an add-on or 'nice to have if you get time'. Of course, I came back after a two-day break all the better for it. The key was to listen to what my body and mind were saying and try to override that compulsion to exercise.

Be flexible

Be prepared to change and adapt. I hark back to when I had my broken arm and couldn't train as I wanted. This disrupted my routine and, for an obsessive-compulsive person, it was hard to bear. After the swim-with-the-cast debacle, I finally accepted the need for change rather than neurotically ploughing on regardless. The best course of action was to focus on what I could rather than what I couldn't do: using the cross trainer and the turbo and prioritising S & C.

Listen to those you trust

It's often difficult for triathletes to be objective – about our fitness, bodyweight, personality and attitude – and many of us need a second pair of eyes to spot potential warning signs. If you do have an addictive personality, surround yourself with family, friends, coaches and others who can be those eyes when you are blind to yourself. Just as importantly, be prepared to listen to and act on advice and trust that these mentors have your best interests at heart.

Triathlon can be an addiction. You try it once: you're hooked. And, for most of us, triathlon is ultimately one of our healthier infatuations. However, it can still take over your life, and occasionally we need to step back and reflect on our thoughts and actions. Instead of satisfying that sporting urge, sometimes we need to break open that bar of chocolate, take a rest day or go to the family reunion, even if every fibre of our being is screaming 'put your running shoes on'. You are, after all, so much more than simply a triathlete and our lives are all the richer for carrying that healthy dose of perspective along for the ride.

BODILY LOVE: BATTLES WITH BODY IMAGE

You don't often hear people exclaiming, 'I love my body!' – at least not in public. Why is this? Do most people not love their bodies, or does it sound arrogant to verbalise that you actually do? Of course, people's views of 'body beautiful' vary over time, across the sexes and between cultures. However, in the West at least, it is more common to hear 'I hate my body, my legs, my backside, my . . .' and find men and women taking a variety of actions to alter their appearance in the hope that they might be happier – a happiness that may prove ellusive.

But what does 'love' mean in this context? As both a verb and a noun it means many different things to different people. I love my daughter, my husband, my friends and I also love racing and eating avocado – but the love I have for avocados isn't the same as the feeling I have for my husband (although if I was to eat an avocado with Tom, now that would send me into a state of euphoric delirium!). To me, love is adoration, respect, faith, happiness and acceptance.

We are not islands, and true strength also means knowing when to reach out and lean on others for support.

And, moreover, what do we mean by 'our body'? When we talk about 'my body' we're invariably referring to the colour, shape and the contours of our skin. The outer shell – the external image – becomes the benchmark by which we judge ourselves. But many of us tend to ignore, myself included, what's on the inside; the body that we don't see – the bones, the nerves, the ligaments, the tendons, the blood, water, the veins, the arteries, the muscles and the organs. Working in unison, these comprise our body, enabling us to live, eat, sleep, and, assembled in slightly different ways, make us all absolutely unique.

The relationship I have had with my body has changed over time, and hasn't always been an easy one. For some of my young adult years I disliked many aspects of my external body. I compared myself, self-deprecatingly, to others. I would stand in front of the mirror, my mind full of criticism at the image that stared back at me. I ignored the fact that I had a body that enabled me to achieve high academic grades, to play sport, to climb mountains, to be a sister, daughter and friend and to always live my life to the full.

It was that desire for a 'perfect' body, coupled with a tendency towards obsessiveness, control and perfectionism, that drove me down the path of an eating disorder in my late teens and early twenties. I used to spend every waking hour worrying about what I was or wasn't going to eat; the illness had a causation and impact that went far beyond the physical. Eating disorders stretch their tentacles into every area of your life.

Those who have read my autobiography will know of this struggle, and the fact that triathlon helped me become healthier, mentally and physically. I knew I needed to fuel myself correctly in order to be able to perform and this, coupled with the realisation that I was hurting those who loved me the most, gave me the impetus to change my behaviour and channel the desire for control into another, more beneficial pursuit.

I would never claim to be totally free of the thoughts that compelled me to adopt disordered eating practices, but with the support of my friends and family I now know what to look out for, how to manage them and ensure that they don't take over my life.

Accepting help from those around me was hard. I wanted to appear strong, resourceful and self-reliant. To suffer was, to me, to appear weak. Something I couldn't abide in myself. I know differently now. We are not islands, and true strength also means knowing when to reach out and lean on others for support.

It wasn't – and isn't – easy, but today I have a very different relationship with that same body. I try not to pass judgement on its external appearance, but instead focus on what it does for me, day in, day out. As well as enabling me to produce a new life – in the form of our daughter – I also see my body as a unique combination of my mother and father. To criticise my body is to criticise them – and that is something I would never do.

I never again want to carry the burden of this problem on my shoulders, or impart that problem to others through my behaviours. I want to be free of concerns over what I eat and how much I eat and love the image that stares back at me when I look in the mirror.

> **For everything that my body has enabled me to achieve, I am so grateful.**

I push my body and mind to its limit, and even though I haven't always treated it with the respect it deserves it has never let me down (aside from a few niggles and broken bones). It heals itself, withstands the pressures it's faced with and as such I have come to trust it.

Of course, I am never satisfied, and I continue to strive to get more out of myself and my body – testing it, challenging it and reaching for the stars. I don't look in the mirror and think I am gorgeous – but I am slowly developing a love for the image that stares back. For everything my body has enabled me to achieve, I am so grateful.

Fighting the Fear –
Building Self-esteem

Q 'I'm new to triathlon and feel very self-conscious about how I look in my tri-suit. If you're not confident in how you feel when standing on the start line, how can you have the confidence to perform?'

DAVE RAMUS

A Thanks so much for this (brave) question. You're definitely not alone, as many athletes and people generally deal with similar concerns and fears. Even professional triathletes, with their toned and honed physiques, sometimes feel imperfect, inadequate, insecure and anxious.

I speak from personal experience. For some of my young adult years I was self-critical of my body and, even as a pro athlete, I looked at my peers and worried that they looked so much stronger, more chiselled and fitter than me!

But, really, our bodies are not the external form, but the internal – the muscles, bones, blood, tendons and, of course, the mind. Our focus should be less about what our bodies look like, and more on what we can do with them each and every day. That holistic perspective is what enabled me slowly to develop an appreciation for the mirrored image. Whether I fit into a small/medium/large item of Lycra or weigh 60kg or 65kg is irrelevant: it's whether those pounds are serving my goals that truly matters. I've seen enough six packs DNF'ing in an Ironman to know that chiselled ab muscles don't always lead to better race performances.

It's not a beauty contest that you're entering. It's a test of mind. The focus must be on training that brain so that it is capable of withstanding self-doubt, wobbles in self-esteem and discomfort. Developing the self-assurance to wear your tri suit with pride is part of the triathlon challenge, and one at which you can succeed.

Take heart from doing something that so many would not dare to do . . . That is, enter triathlons. This, in itself, means you have courage and confidence. The next step is to view your body less as an external, visible image and more as a unique, special vehicle that will help you to achieve your sporting goals. And, like cars, these triathlon vehicles come in all shapes and sizes: from the trucks that go all day to the speedier racing variety, and everything in between. We are all individuals. Even at pro level we're all built differently, so try not to compare yourself to your peers. There is no one ideal triathlete shape or size and, if you wait until you are a target shape or weight to do anything, you could be waiting for ever. The time is now!

Of course, through triathlon your body shape may alter but it is the internal changes that are key: the development of strength in mind and body, power, and the happiness and enjoyment that comes from training and racing. You will continually develop self-confidence and self-belief through challenging yourself, testing your limits and achieving your goals. It may also come from joining a club and leaning on those around you for support and encouragement.

> 66 It's not a beauty contest that you're entering. It's a test of mind. 99

When I have self-confidence wobbles I remind myself that I am not alone in having these feelings and no one is looking at me in the same way as I look at myself. I also recall the inspirational people I've met. For example, children, supported by the US-based Challenged Athletes Foundation, who were born without legs, yet whose bravery, confidence and determination are limitless.

Come race day, you'll be more focused on your last-minute preparation and your race plan than you'll be on the reflection in the mirror. And, what's more, at 5km into the run everyone is in the same boat. Cameras will capture hilarious facial expressions, bloated bellies that look like you have swallowed ten pints of beer, stains from sweat, blood and other bodily fluids, mad hair . . . this is part of the sport that we all love to do!

I have seen people who are 50kg and those who are 110kg complete triathlons. We must celebrate our individuality and be grateful for the amazing opportunity we have to do this sport; to be healthy and active, to train and to race, to be with friends, visit new places and challenge ourselves and our limits, mentally and physically. Whether or not we have a spare few pounds around our waist should not define us or our emotions. So please – *be kind to yourself.* With your body – the body you have clothed in Lycra right now – you can achieve great things, inside and out of sport. So wear that tri suit with confidence and go out there and strut your training and racing stuff with pride! ●

Race Report

Smelling the Flowers: Musings following a world record

Most triathletes are focused on getting faster. We are obsessed with splits (times, rather than actually doing the splits, which could cause all manner of groin injuries), PBs and finish times. We also have a tendency to rush from one activity to the next, determined to hit our goals and fill every waking moment with something we can write on Facebook. We have our heads down in our aerobars or focused on the black line of the pool. We might even do a run without truly seeing things along the way. I am no different. In fact, I am the proverbial Duracell bunny that can never sit still: I find it hard truly to just 'be'.

Most sports psychologists can tell you how to motivate yourself and cope with nerves, but what if you also need to learn how to rest your mind, to be still, to slow down, to just be in the moment?

Here is my blog following Challenge Roth in 2011, when I reflected on my world record, the passing of time and the need to celebrate and smell the flowers each and every day.

I lie face down on the ground, tears of relief, pride and joy dripping on to the carpet, the clock above my head reading 8.18.13. I stand up, wobble, embrace those I care about most and prepare for the deluge of photographs and interviews. Cameras, microphones, Dictaphones, mobile phones and old-fashioned notebooks are thrust under my nose, and within seconds I'm asked the question: 'Chrissie, can you go faster?' Part of me wants to respond with 'There are always areas of improvement, so yes, of course!' but the other half thinks 'Please, just slow down, let's all sit back and celebrate this achievement.'

Time conscious, adrenalin loving, speed seeking; like many of us, I live my life at warp speed. I always have done since I was a small child. Why walk when you can run? Why chew your food when you can do the 'snake swallowing a whole rat' trick? Why fold your clothes when you can simply throw them into a drawer? I was constantly thinking of the future, wondering what it may bring, impatiently planning what I would do next. And, worried that I wasn't making the most of everything that was on offer, I spent years living in London frantically catapulting myself between work, the theatre, sports events, dinners, concerts and training sessions. And in my rush, I would fall over, break bones, slice my tongue (that's another story) and cover myself in unsightly bumps and bruises. I resembled an Energizer Bunny – always running – figuratively and literally.

And, despite the passing of the years, not much has changed. I am still like a Formula 1 driver on amphetamines. My clothes are never folded and always creased, I still eat my dinner like the presenter of *Man v. Food*, shoving as much as I can into my mouth without it even touching my teeth (I make for a delightful dinner guest), I try to finish an Ironman distance race in 8.18, and afterwards I can't even slow down enough to pour the huge vessel of beer into my mouth – instead sending it cascading over my head. (I smelt like a brewery at the press conference, but was as sober as a judge.)

Yes, I'm still racing through life like a frenzied bargain hunter at a jumble sale.

However, even I am starting to recognise the need to slow down, take a breath and to savour the moment.

When I sliced my hand with a knife four days before Alpe d'Huez Long Course Triathlon in 2007 (in a rushed attempt to hack my bike-computer zip ties off), Brett had no sympathy. His words: 'You think things just happen to you by accident. They don't. You deserve the misfortune because you are not methodical or calm in your body and mind.' Too true. He then imparted a few words of wisdom: 'Learn to hurry – slowly.' More recently, in my boyfriend [now husband] Tom, I have seen calmness incarnate. He is still seven minutes faster than me in an Ironman, but he teaches me every day what it means to be unruffled, patient, orderly and, yes, how to fold clothes.

And so, post-Roth, I took a leaf out of his book and used that leaf to really smell the flowers. Instead of my long run I did a hike in the mountains around Boulder. I went on my own, with my water bottle and camera for company. The first few hours I spent climbing, rushing up the side of the hills as fast as my legs would carry me (not that fast, given post-race fatigue), but then I got to the top and paused, taking more than a moment to savour the spectacular view. I journeyed on and began to *really* look at my surroundings. Not just seeing, but soaking

Celebrations at the finish line of Challenge Roth, 2011.

up the landscape and the amazing minutiae of the natural world – in particular, the plethora of flowers that were growing around me. I didn't know their names, but the varied shapes and rainbow of colours amazed me. And instead of rushing past, I stopped, and photographed as many as I could. I saw butterflies flirting with each other, and being more measured, quiet and patient, I didn't scare them off; instead they perched unperturbed on the purple petals, sampling the nectar. And as I descended into the forest I resisted the customary Chrissie urge to run – instead appreciating how the dappled sunlight made beautiful, intricate patterns on the ground beneath me. Gandhi was right, 'There is more to life than increasing its speed.'

So, going forward, I am trying to incorporate a little of this experience into my everyday life. To chew my food; to avoid simultaneously watching television, surfing the web and talking on the phone; to rest and recover my mind as well as my body; to understand that I cannot do everything and must learn to say no; and to appreciate the moment for what it is, rather than what it is leading to.

Yes, I live my life for racing. But this doesn't have to mean living my life like it is a race. ●

One of my race water bottles, inscribed with the words of 'If'.

'IF' By Rudyard Kipling

If you can keep your head when all about you
Are losing theirs and blaming it on you,
If you can trust yourself when all men doubt you,
But make allowance for their doubting too;
If you can wait and not be tired by waiting,
Or being lied about, don't deal in lies,
Or being hated, don't give way to hating,
And yet don't look too good, nor talk too wise:

If you can dream – and not make dreams your master;
If you can think – and not make thoughts your aim;
If you can meet with Triumph and Disaster
And treat those two impostors just the same;
If you can bear to hear the truth you've spoken
Twisted by knaves to make a trap for fools,
Or watch the things you gave your life to, broken,
And stoop and build 'em up with worn-out tools:

If you can make one heap of all your winnings
And risk it on one turn of pitch-and-toss,
And lose, and start again at your beginnings
And never breathe a word about your loss;
If you can force your heart and nerve and sinew
To serve your turn long after they are gone,
And so hold on when there is nothing in you
Except the Will which says to them: 'Hold on!'

If you can talk with crowds and keep your virtue,
Or walk with Kings – nor lose the common touch,
If neither foes nor loving friends can hurt you,
If all men count with you, but none too much;
If you can fill the unforgiving minute
With sixty seconds' worth of distance run,
Yours is the Earth and everything that's in it,
And – which is more – you'll be a Man, my son!

227

CHAPTER NINE
AT THE RACES

W hile there may be a few reading this who prefer never to enter a race – instead simply enjoying the challenge of training for swim, bike, run – for the majority of triathletes training is a means of getting to our ultimate destination: the race finish line. It is the racing, and especially our A race, that is our ultimate focus and challenge, the culmination of everything we have worked so hard for, the moment where we want to perform to the very best of our ability and celebrate the journey we have taken and what we have achieved.

For me, racing was my time to perform on some of the world's biggest stages, the opportunity to battle, and test myself, against my competitors, to answer my own questions and, hopefully, realise my dreams. My race performances were also a publicly visible means of inspiring others, both those whom I raced alongside and spectators, near and far. Through competing I wanted to convey the message that more truly is possible. Yes, the journey to get there was incredibly valuable and enjoyable, but it is the races that are some of my proudest achievements.

This chapter comprises sections on a variety of subjects related to racing, including practical tips for your pre-race preparations, mastering the art of transitions, coping when races may not go well or reflecting back on your performances as a stepping-stone to future success. I include reports from some of the more important moments of my career: the Ironman World Championships in 2007, 2010 and 2011, and reflections on Katy's A race, the Alpe d'Huez Triathlon in 2015.

OPPOSITE: The famous Solar Berg climb at Challenge Roth.

PRACTICAL PREP: PRE-RACE PLANNING

You've entered the race, you have a training programme and, best of all, you're managing to follow it. That's the exciting and fun part! The less stimulating task is arranging the logistics so you can actually get to that start line, on time and with everything you need.

If you've entered a local race, the logistics are relatively simple. You can stay in your own bed the night before; you don't need to travel too far or transport your bike long distances. However, many of us relish the opportunity to travel to different parts of our home country or even abroad: in which case, there's a little more to think about.

> " Forward planning breeds peace of mind and helps minimise any last-minute panic so you can focus on getting yourself in race shape. "

An opening word of advice: don't leave your preparation to the last minute. Forward planning breeds peace of mind, helps minimise any last-minute panic and enables you to focus on what matters most – getting yourself in tip-top physical and psychological race shape.

So, with that in mind, here are the main things to factor in as the months, weeks and days tick by to the Big Day.

Accommodation

Book well in advance. Consider whether you would prefer a hotel/motel/B & B or self-catering accommodation, what facilities you need (e.g. restaurants, wi-fi, cleaning services, a gym), cost and what type of environment you prefer (e.g. peace and quiet, lively and loud). The location is important, especially the ease of getting to the race start (which is often very early in the morning). Big events usually have a list of hotel partners and these can be the first to fill up. Speak to those who have done the race before to get an idea of accommodation options.

KATY CAMPBELL'S
preparation for the Alpe d'Huez Triathlon

As part of her preparation for the Alpe d'Huez Long Course Triathlon Katy booked a holiday to the Alps with her husband Ed in order to train on the course in a relaxed, non-race environment. Aside from on race day, swimming is not permitted in Lac du Verney and so Katy could only admire the beautiful Alpine water from the shore. She was confident in her ability to tackle the run, but it was the hilly bike course that made her most nervous. To help quell self-doubt and develop her hill climbing strength and technique, she did several bike sessions on sections of the course so that, by the end of the week, tackling the route became second nature. Consequently, Katy was confident that she could finish and even enjoy the hilly course – an invaluable psychological boost as she prepared for the race. Through this training holiday she also acquainted herself with the race site, practised exercising at altitude and learned where the facilities (e.g. shops, registration venue, her race accommodation) were; all of which gave peace of mind.

Travelling to the race

Decide how you will get to the race and, if necessary, book public transport, a hire car or flights as early as you can. Flights, especially, can get busy if hundreds of athletes are travelling from the same airport to a popular destination. Bear in mind that delays can put a spanner in the works of any best-laid plan so it's sensible to leave some pre-emptive wiggle room.

Course recce (part 1)

Although most events will be marshalled, ultimately it's every athlete's responsibility to know the route, and recceing the course gives you first-hand experience of the conditions and terrain. Unless you live near to the venue, the recce can be done by taking a special trip (or even a holiday) and training on the course. Note that some open-water locations are only accessible to swimmers at selected times, so check with the landowner before jumping in. Rather than biking and running, you could choose to drive around the course instead. Some organisers arrange recces in advance of race day; for example, a training weekend is held in Tenby a few months before Ironman Wales where athletes can complete the 3.8km sea swim on Friday evening, the 180km bike on Saturday and the marathon on Sunday, or choose to do shorter distances over part of the course.

Bike servicing

I always get my bike serviced a week or so before a race, giving the mechanic time to deal with any problems.

Transporting your bike

If you are flying or taking the train you will often have to book – and pay for – bike space, as it can be limited. This should be done as early as possible, ideally when buying your ticket. A box is the safest way of transporting your precious cargo, but practise dismantling and reassembling your bike beforehand, as it's not always an easy task. If you are planning to drive make sure your bike – in its box if necessary – fits in your vehicle (including if it's a hire car) or on a bike rack. If you can afford it, you could use a specialist company to transport your bike to its destination.

Peruse the race guide

Read and re-read the race guide to familiarise yourself with the essential information. This includes: the rules, the race course, aid-station locations, road closures and car parking, start times, as well as any pre- and post-race events that may be organised. It is often mandatory to attend a pre-race briefing; if so, find out where and when it is.

Food for thought

As explained in Chapter 7, plan your race-related nutrition well in advance. This could be for consumption while travelling (unless you love aeroplane food you may want to pack some of your favourite fodder) as well as at the race destination itself. If you have booked self-catering accommodation, find out where the nearest supermarkets are and, if you are going to eat in restaurants, check the opening times and menus to ensure there is something to whet your pre-race appetite. If you are staying in a hotel, find out what they serve for breakfast, and whether they will accommodate any dietary requests (remember that not every hotel will be able to provide breakfast at the required time on race morning). Much of this information can be gleaned over the telephone or internet before you even get to the race site.

Get your kit in order

Using the pre-race checklist at page 338, assemble and then – if you are travelling away from home for the race – pack your kit, clothing and nutrition. You can't control whether the sun shines, but you can bring clothing and equipment that is appropriate for the conditions. For example, if it is due to be hot, you may wish to pack sunscreen or a visor, and if the forecast has a big black cloud, you might want arm warmers, a waterproof jacket or a gilet. To err on the side of caution, I included items to cover all meteorological eventualities. I laid everything out in separate pre-race, swim, bike and run piles, double-checking that I had everything I needed and that it was in working order. I also labelled some items with my name and race number in case they ended up in lost property.

Having arrived safely at your race destination, there are a few more logistical boxes to tick.

Bike building

One of the first tasks should be to unpack and build your bike. This way, if something has happened to your prized possession in transit, you have a bit more time to deal with it. I strongly recommend asking a mechanic to do a final check of your bike, once fully assembled, to make sure everything is in working order. There are usually mechanics at the race expo, or there might also be a friendly bike shop in the vicinity that can do the job. Be warned, though, they are usually busier than a hive of bees and queues for servicing may be long.

Registration and race-pack collection

If you haven't been sent your race pack in the post, it will be necessary for you to collect it during registration at the race venue. The race website will tell you when registration will open and for how long, so make sure that you don't miss it. The volunteers will also ask you to sign a disclaimer, if you haven't already done so. You will need to take a form of photographic identification, such as a passport or driver's licence, as well as your national governing body (NGB) membership card if you have one and, sometimes, your race entry confirmation email. For insurance purposes, you may be required to pay for a day-race licence if you are not a member of an NGB. You usually (but not always, so please check!) register on race morning for short course triathlons, a day or two before a half Ironman and one to four days before an Ironman race.

The race pack will contain all/some of the following:

> race number/s;
> timing chip often with a timing-chip strap;
> race number stickers and/or tags for helmet and bike;
> coloured race swim cap;
> transition bags to put clothing and equipment in for each discipline (only for Ironman races);
> race information (such as course maps);
> a variety of leaflets advertising all manner of triathlon related products;
> some goodies – avoid eating/drinking/using these before or during the race unless you are familiar with them.

Check that all the numbers you have been given correspond with your designated race number.

Course recce (part 2)

If you can – and want to – swim-, bike- or run-recce the route on arrival, but ensure that any training session fits into your taper. For example, it's definitely not advisable to cycle the entire 180km Ironman bike course days before the race. You may not want to sit in a car for a few hours to do the recce either, so perhaps you can peruse a specific section of the course, or even look on the internet for race videos. As a pro, I had the luxury of travelling to Ironman distance events at least a week in advance and trained on all – or some – of the race course as part of my taper. In Kona, I used to do some of my runs on Ali'i Drive – the first and final part of the run course – and listened to my pre-race playlist. I then identified landmarks with certain songs and, come race day, mentally replayed those songs as I ran past those markers. Swimming in the ocean in Hawaii is also great for learning about the current and the conditions, as well as being one of the best natural aquariums in the world. At Challenge Roth, however, the canal is out-of-bounds to swimmers until race day, and so all my pre-race prep was done in the open-air 50m pool. If permitted, it's also good to peruse transition to familiarise yourself with the layout.

Equipment inspection

Do one last check of your clothing and equipment to ensure that you have everything and it's in working order.

Check the forecast

This will enable you mentally to prepare for what is coming, and finalise what clothing and equipment you will use. Accept that you cannot control the weather and can only control your approach and perception.

Getting to the race start

Arrange how you will get to the start on race morning, organising transport and car parking if necessary. If you are driving, remember that there may be road closures and traffic jams, so factor in a large time buffer.

Bike check-in

For long-course races, you usually rack your bike in transition the day before the race (known as bike 'check-in'). Make sure you know what time you need to do this, and take your helmet along for a safety inspection. Attach the numbered helmet/bike stickers and the bike tag (if applicable) to your bike before heading to check-in.

That just about covers the essential pre-race practical prep. If you can't bear the thought of having to book flights or piece together a dismantled bike before a race, then you could consider paying someone to do it for you. Specialist tour companies offer a package of services that can include race entry, accommodation, transport, food, massage, bike servicing and race-course familiarisation – but this is usually only an option for athletes doing major events, such as popular Ironmans or World Championships. The companies often arrange pre- and post-race get-togethers for the whole tour group and can be a great way to make new tri friends, find training partners or meet a future spouse.

Those who haven't bought a race support package and don't have a personal secretary will, however, need to add personal planning to the triathlon mix. Booking flights, packing your bike or checking out car-parking options are not the most exciting tri-tasks in the world, but any preparation pain is worth it for the huge race gain that comes at the end!

Mind Over Matter – Coping with Pre-race Nerves

Q 'I am new to triathlon and always have concerns about my preparation. I'm only competing in triathlons for fun and can't imagine what it is like for serious athletes. Once the gun goes off I know the nerves will go, but how do you cope with pre-race mental battles and banish self-doubt?'

KURT SWALLOW

A You're not alone. Everyone gets nervous, even the more 'serious athletes' to whom you refer. This is part of race preparation; it is a sign of your passion, commitment and effort. I bite my nails to the bare bone before races! If you were not apprehensive, I'd be more concerned. Nerves stimulate adrenalin production, which is vital for propelling your body into action. The key is to control those nerves and, importantly, banish self-doubt so that they don't become debilitating. Here are just a few ways of doing this:

> Remember that your butterflies always fly away after the start. Anticipate and embrace the nerves, but trust that they are ephemeral.

> Recall times when you have been uncomfortable or thought you couldn't finish, but pushed on and managed to succeed. If you have a training log, look back and remind yourself of past achievements – and know that if you have conquered hurdles in the past you can do so again. Bank those memories and hold them close.

> There are some things you can't control, like the weather, but you can control your thoughts and the way in which you perceive things. This includes replacing negative self-talk with positive affirmations. For example, substitute 'I'm not strong enough to do this' with 'I'm strong and powerful and I will finish this race'. And have a mantra to repeat meditatively.

> In addition to Rudyard Kipling's 'If' (see page 227), I carried a collection of motivational greeting cards that people have given me over the years and put them up around my race accommodation. Watching uplifting movies or videos of others overcoming hurdles en route to their own finish lines gave me confidence that I, too, could succeed.

66 Spend time on visualisation. This is the simple act of closing your eyes, relaxing your mind and then going through each stage of the race one step at a time. 99

> Spend some time on visualisation. In training, when travelling, while in bed, during work meetings. This is the simple act of closing your eyes (although this is not recommended while on your bike or in front of your employer), relaxing your mind and then going through each stage of the race one step at a time. You can draw on the visual images (the finish line), the feelings you experience (energy surges) or the sounds you hear (roars of the crowd), as well as imagining the possible problems you might encounter and a strategy for dealing with them. That way, when you race, you have the confidence that you have already conquered the challenges.

> Do calming breathing exercises: lie down, close your eyes and focus on the slow rise and fall of your torso as you inhale and exhale deeply and rhythmically.

> Don't be afraid to speak to those you trust – a coach, a training partner, friends or family – about your fears. Their reassurance and encouragement can do wonders to calm nerves and ease self-doubt. Avoid naysayers or wet blankets.

> Nerves strike when we worry about something going wrong and derailing us. However, whether you're an age grouper or professional, preparation and races rarely go exactly as planned. Instead of searching for that perfect preparation and/ or race, trust in your ability to overcome any problems – perfectly.

> We invest a lot of energy, emotion and resources into the sport and want to reap the rewards, but triathlon should never totally define us. It is one cog in the wheel of life. The outcome of a race – while important – isn't the be all and end all. When nervous, I remind myself to retain this perspective and it helps relieve some of the anxiety.

> You mention worrying about your preparation. However, there are things – in addition to your thoughts – that you can control and which, if done effectively, can eliminate panic and give peace of mind. For example, planning your taper and organising pre-race logistics, such as transport and accommodation. These are considered at pages 230 and 240. Have practical 'to do' and equipment lists to provide direction and structure, and don't try or buy anything new close to race day, as unfamiliarity can also breed anxiety and doubt.

As you stand on the start line, be confident that you have done all you can to prepare – physically, psychologically and practically – and all you can do is your best on that day, in that very moment. And believe me, those butterflies will undoubtedly propel you to heights you never could have imagined! ●

TAPER TIME: THE ART OF TAPERING FOR A RACE

Race week was always something I looked forward to. Of course, I had nerves like anyone else, but I relished the excitement and the anticipation as D-Day neared. I also enjoyed race week for another reason: it was the chance to reduce the amount of training and get more rest: in triathlon parlance – taper time!

The taper enables you to prepare physically, psychologically and practically for a race, helping you recover from any training fatigue (both mental and physical), and replenishes the musculo-skeletal, cardiovascular, metabolic, respiratory and nervous systems.

There are more philosophies about how best to taper than I've had pasta dinners. However, most coaches and athletes agree on one thing – tapering can make or break an athlete's performance. Lab-coated experts have conducted insightful studies suggesting performance improvements of up to 6 per cent from the perfect taper – meaning triathletes can shave off substantially more than the hairs on their legs.

The practical side of preparing for a race has been covered on page 230, and so this section focuses on the physical and psychological aspects of tapering.

PHYSICAL PREPARATION

Tapering is about changing the frequency, intensity and duration of training – otherwise known as the training load. Factors to consider are:

> normal training load;

> ability to recover from specific training sessions;

> the type and duration of the event;

> other commitments or stresses in your life;

> the amount of travel to get to the race;

> level of priority attached to the race (e.g. A, B or C race).

Some athletes choose to have a shorter – or even no – taper before their lower priority races because they want to retain consistency in their training, practise racing when tired or use the event as a training session. For example, in July 2006 I entered the Salford Olympic-distance triathlon as a B race. I trained as normal in the week preceding the event and actually did an aquathlon (as a C race) the day before. This was because my priority was the World Age Group Championship six weeks later and Salford Triathlon was a means of experiencing race conditions and practising my race-day plan without disrupting my training programme. However, if it is an A race or you want to use a lower priority race specifically to practise your taper, then it pays to develop and follow a strategy to maximise your performance.

While not an exact science, there are some universal tapering principles that you can apply to help develop an approach that works for you.

Duration

Reducing the duration (time and distance) of training sessions has a much bigger impact on performance than lowering intensity or frequency. How much should you reduce duration by and when? It should be done in stages rather than trying dramatically to cut down from one day to the next, and proportional to what you are already doing. An effective taper should involve a reduction in training volume of around 60–70 per cent over the course of the taper period. I suggest that most athletes start to reduce the duration of their sessions two weeks before an Ironman, ten days before a half Ironman and seven days before an Olympic-distance event; the volume should be reduced by approximately 40 per cent in the first third of the taper and another 20–30 per cent in the second third, leaving you with 30–40 per cent of the pre-taper volume in the lead-up to race day.

Frequency

I tended to retain the same session frequency in the lead-up to a race. For example, if my normal programme included a swim and brick session on a Wednesday, I would still do those sessions but the *duration* of the workouts would be much shorter. I always had a full day off. Given that I, and many athletes, tend to feel sluggish after a rest day, I took this on the penultimate day, rather than the day before a race. On that final day, I included a few higher intensity efforts within short sessions of swim, bike and run.

Intensity

This is key. Maintain some higher intensity segments in your sessions right up until race day, but decrease the duration of each hard effort and the overall session, and increase the rest interval. The revving of your engine keeps you neuro-muscularly sharp and ensures your body remains alert.

Type

I maintained my swim, bike and run sessions but cut out S & C work in the week preceding the race. Another consideration is that running, which is weight bearing, results in greater muscle impact than swimming and cycling, so you might want to be more conservative with run volume in race week.

Triathletes are renowned for their masochistic tendencies – their puritanical desire to go longer, harder and faster. They are typically less adept at easing off; scared that their fitness will miraculously disappear if they don't do one last five-hour smash-fest bike ride, followed by a 20km run and a 'little' swim as a confidence-giving backslap. You will probably feel more lethargic, sleepy sloth- and slug-like than superstar during your taper. This is normal. However, the risk of overcooking yourself is far greater than any mental and physical boost a final validation session may give.

MENTAL PREPARATION

The taper gives you the chance to have a psychological rest from training. Yes, having more time to think can be detrimental if your nervy brain goes into overdrive but, if applied correctly, you can relax and refresh the mind and get in the best psychological state to perform. Now's not the time to compare yourself to other athletes or fret over what you have or haven't done, nor is it the time to spend sunbathing or souvenir hunting. Use the taper to relax, read a good book, watch a film, chat with friends and generally stay off those compressed feet.

> " Many athletes struggle to sleep in the days before a race. I was no different. I was lucky if I had four unbroken hours the night before some of the biggest races of my career. "

A few words on sleep: many athletes struggle to sleep in the days before a race. I was no different, with dreams/nightmares of missing the start/forgetting my wetsuit/losing my bike being all too common! I was lucky if I had four unbroken hours the night before some of the biggest races of my career. I accepted this was normal, tried to bank as much as possible in the preceding days/weeks and trusted in my body to still perform on race day.

So, to summarise: reduce the volume, maintain the frequency, keep some higher intensity work and try to switch off mentally. Your aim is to get to that start line with a refreshed and honed mind and body; the hard work is in the bank and now all you need to do is have fun drawing on those funds!

EXAMPLES OF TAPER WEEKS

Overleaf is my typical taper for an Ironman, although bear in mind that this taper directly relates to the volume and intensity of the training I ordinarily did on a weekly basis. Rather than modelling your taper on that of a pro athlete, ensure that your taper reflects your training, your race and your life. Also, note that I had to factor in travel – which, for all Ironmans other than the World Championship, I did on the Sunday preceding the race – as well as any pre-race obligations such as the press conference and pre-race briefing. Also overleaf is my mentee Katy Campbell's programme for the week preceding her A race, the Alpe d'Huez Long Course Triathlon.

MY IRONMAN TAPER WEEK

	MORNING	MIDDAY	AFTERNOON
Monday	**Swim:** 3km including 1km total of lactate threshold-zone work and 300m total of VO$_2$-max repeats	**Bike:** 2 hours including 4 × 3 minutes at lactate threshold (RI 2 minutes) and 3 × 6 minutes of effort just below lactate threshold (RI 1 minute)	
Tuesday	**Run:** 45 minutes including 5 × 3 VO$_2$-max efforts (R1 3 minutes) and 5 × 30-second strides to finish	**Swim:** 3km including 1km total of aerobic and threshold work	
Wednesday	**Swim:** 1km cruise	**Bike/Run Brick** Bike 90 minutes including 20 minutes broken down into 1 × 10 minutes and 2 × 5 minutes at race intensity, followed by a 35-minute run including 4 × 500m swing pace at 4 mins/km and 3:50 mins/km pace (RI 3 minutes)	
Thursday	**Bike:** 2 hrs including 5 × 2 minutes at lactate threshold (R1 3 minutes)	**Swim:** 2km including 500m total of threshold and aerobic work Massage	
Friday	Day off		
Saturday	**Swim:** 2km cruise with 10 × 25m quick efforts (but not all out) (RI 50m easy)	**Bike:** 75-minute cruise with 3 x 3 minutes at race intensity	**Run:** 25-minute cruise with 5 x 30 seconds strides in the middle at 4 mins/km pace
Sunday	Race day		

KATY CAMPBELL'S TAPER WEEK

	MORNING	AFTERNOON
Saturday	**Brick: bike/run** **Bike:** 90 minutes with 30 minutes cruise, 30 minutes as 5 x 5 minutes race pace (RI 1 minute). Cruise 30 minutes **Run:** 30 minutes, building to race pace for last 15 minutes	
Sunday	Active recovery: hike or bike, very easy	
Monday	**Swim:** 30 minutes including 5 x 200m (alternate easy/hard every 25m) with RI 1 minute	Massage
Tuesday	Travel to France	
Wednesday	**Bike:** max 60 minutes with a few switchbacks of Alpe d'Huez	
Thursday	**Swim:** 15–20 minutes including 7 x 50m at race pace	**Run:** 15 minutes (3–4 short 30 second strides)
Friday	Race day	

TRANSITIONING TO TRI:
PERFECTING TRANSITIONS

Three sports become one through the oft-feared, seemingly frantic and sometimes
confusing fourth discipline: 'transition'. In a tri context, it is both a verb and a noun.
Transition from swim to bike and then bike to run is what you do, but it's also the
place in which you do the said manoeuvre.

Transition is sometimes identified by the array of flailing body parts, funky-chicken
dances, airborne clothing and a feeding frenzy akin to the most disorganised of

zoos. If you've never been to a triathlon, imagine an H &M changing room during the Boxing Day sales. Yet, fear not, for what appears to be bedlam can be made simple, methodical and orderly with a few words of wisdom and some practice. So, let's strip bare (although not literally as birthday suit antics are likely to result in a penalty rather than rounds of applause) and get back to basics.

First, a definition. Transition is where you demonstrate the art of moving as swiftly as possible from:

a) swim to bike, otherwise known as Transition 1 – or T1;

b) bike to run, otherwise known as Transition 2 – or T2.

Transition is also the place where you will get ready before the start. It tends to resemble a bike-storage facility, a changing room and a canteen, and so understanding the art of transitioning is something in which every athlete should invest time.

What are the key things that every transitioning triathlete needs to know?

It's part of the race

The clock does not stop in transition; therefore, any time spent in transition is taken into account in your final time. The faster you are in T1 and T2, the faster your race. Some people like to be relatively pedestrian, taking a while to lube up, change their wardrobe and leisurely consume fuel – however, if you're focused on speed, then it pays to try to get through swim/bike and bike/run as quickly and safely as possible.

Practise practise practise

Transitioning from swim to bike and bike to run is a skill. Train to hone the necessary transitioning skills so you can undertake the process as smoothly and rapidly as possible. For example, practise removing your wetsuit without tears (either of the crying or the ripping-of-neoprene variety) or mounting your bike without looking like a drunkard.

Transition can be 'split'

That is, when T1 and T2 are in different locations. This means you change into your bike kit in TI and your run kit in T2. Race organisers often transport your running stuff so that it is ready for you in T2 when you arrive, but check the race website or speak to the organiser for more details.

Different areas of transition

There will be a clearly marked swim exit, a bike exit and a bike 'in' and run exit. There will also be a mount line you must cross before you can jump on your bike, and a bike dismount line for the return trip. Mount too early or alight too late and you risk a penalty. There is no need to cut it too fine as you won't save time, and giving yourself a few metres' grace can mean more space for a flawless manoeuvre. Spend time before the race familiarising yourself with the entries, exits and lines, and going through each stage in your mind so you can picture exactly where you need to go and when.

> 66 Transition is identified by the array of flailing body parts, funky-chicken dances, airborne clothing and a feeding frenzy akin to the most disorganised of zoos. 99

Nudity is not allowed

If in doubt, err on the side of caution and avoid showing a butt cheek or nipple. This means thinking about what clothes you want to swim, bike and run in and, if you don't want to wear the same outfit for the whole race, how you are going to change attire. In Ironman events, there are usually separate male and female changing tents, and so you can strip off more clothing than you can in a shorter distance race where any wardrobe change has to be done al fresco.

Clean and tidy

Each athlete gets about a metre of space in which to rack their bike, store their clothes and kit, and get changed. Keep this area clean and tidy otherwise you may incur a penalty.

Transition bags

Some long-course races provide transition bags (at registration) for you to put your kit in. The race website will let you know if this is the case.

The above provides some basic info but what, I hear you cry, do I actually have to do in this zoo-like zone called transition?

BEFORE THE RACE

Visual map

> Check out the race-course map beforehand to see where transition is located.

> Once at the event, if possible, recce transition to locate the entrances, exits and mount/dismount lines.

Know and remember your spot

> You may have an allocated space on a bike rack, corresponding to your athlete race number. Some races aren't as organised and prefer the free-for-all approach.

> Transition can become an unsolvable maze in the heat of the action. You're not allowed to put any markers down to help you, so make a mental note of your spot by memorising the row/letter number and using fixed landmarks. Having a dayglo bike or vibrant running shoes can help in identifying where your possessions are.

Go through the safety check

> There's often a safety check on your bike and helmet as you enter transition, either the day before or the morning of the race. This is to make sure the bike is roadworthy and your helmet has passed the necessary safety standard, as indicated by the sticker inside.

Body marking

> It's usually mandatory to have your race number inked on your body, commonly on the upper arm and the back of the thigh. You may either be given a temporary tattoo to put on beforehand or there are designated 'Body Markers'; volunteers who do it for you.

Rack your bike

> Place your bike on the designated area of the bike rack by the handlebars or the saddle. Some race organisers will stipulate which of the two options they prefer; others leave it to you to decide. I tended to hook mine by the saddle as it was easier for me to remove the bike quickly. I faced the handlebars in the direction of the bike exit so I could steer straight out of transition.

Get your bike and bike gear ready

> Pump the tyres up first so that you have more time to sort out any unforeseen problems (having your own track/foot pump is a good idea). Note that if you rack the bike the day before, and it's hot weather, take a bit of air out of the tyres to reduce the risk of an unfortunate blowout due to internal pressure changes.

> Put the bike in an easy-ish gear.

> Secure your spares to the bike.

> Reset your bike computer if you are using one.

> Put your (unbuckled) helmet upside down on your handlebars or aerobars.

> Make sure the lenses of your sunglasses are clean and then put them in the helmet with the arms open; place your number belt (if you are wearing one) upside down on top with the clasp open. If it's windy, you may wish to place them on the floor to reduce the risk of them going airborne.

> If you wear bike shoes, sprinkle talc inside and loosen the straps; then either a) clip them into your pedals (some athletes attach their shoes to the bike with elastic bands to keep them upright when running to the mount line), or b) place them next to your bike. If you are doing an Ironman you may have put your shoes in your bike-transition bag.

Get your running kit ready

> Place a small towel next to your bike and your running shoes on top (if you are doing an Ironman your shoes will be in your run-transition bag).

> Make sure that the tongue and laces are open and put one sock in each shoe (if you plan to wear socks).

> I also sprinkle talc inside my running shoes (and socks) to help soak up excess water and prevent blisters. This can be done the day before.

Get your nutrition ready

> Secure your bottles/gels/bars, etc, to the bike and place any run nutrition next to your running shoes.

Get ready for the start

> Focus on yourself and don't watch what others are doing. Yes, the bike next to you might be slightly more bling than your antique penny farthing, but it's the engine that counts. Now is not the time for tri perving. Save it for after the race. Close your eyes, relax, breathe and accept that a few nerves are normal!

> Leave time to get into your wetsuit (if you are wearing one). Top tips for successfully donning the neoprene can be found on pages 98 and 99.

> Don't forget to put your timing chip strap under or below the leg of your wetsuit.

> Swing your arms slowly (forward and back) to loosen them before entering the water.

> I always did a 10-minute swim warm-up (with some 10–15-second, higher intensity efforts). Some athletes also like to do a short run beforehand.

TRANSITION 1 (SWIM TO BIKE)

> Swim toward the finish, making sure you sight correctly, using obvious landmarks. Kick a little harder at the end to fire your leg muscles, but remain calm and prepare yourself mentally for the next stage.

> If in the ocean, use the waves to propel you forward, body surfing as you near the beach. You may need to increase your stroke rate and kick faster to catch the wave.

> Don't stop or stand up until your fingers scrape the bottom/you reach the exit steps/ramp, then take a deep breath and pull yourself up slowly. There are sometimes volunteers to hoist you up but don't rely on this.

> Start to walk (more experienced athletes jog or run) and lift your goggles on to your head. I removed my hat and goggles at this stage.

> Unzip your wetsuit with one hand, remove your arms one at a time and pull the suit down to your waist. You can strip down in the change tent or by your bike.

> Run or walk to where your bike is racked. If doing an Ironman, you will go through the change tent before getting to your bike and it's in this tent that you will remove your wetsuit and change into any cycle clothes.

> Pull your wetsuit down in one smooth motion so that it is below the knees. Step out of one leg, and tread on the wetsuit to help pull the other leg out. Don't panic if you can't get your wettie off immediately; relax, breathe and try again – sit down if necessary.

> Remove hat and goggles if you haven't already done so.

> Put your sunglasses on first, then the helmet. This way they will be under the helmet straps and won't get knocked off when you take your helmet off in T2.

> Put your race belt on, with the number on your back (if you haven't attached your number on to the back of your outfit using safety pins).

> Apply sunscreen, if required.

> Quick-dry your feet if you want to, and put on your shoes (unless they are attached to the pedals).

> Unrack your bike and – if you can – wheel your bike by the saddle not the handlebars, to help prevent the pedals bashing your legs en route to the mount line.

> Don't jump on your steed until you cross the mount line.

TRANSITION 2 (BIKE TO RUN)

> Increase your cadence in the last 500m.

> Loosen the strap on your bike shoes about 100m from T2, slip your feet out and place them on top. Slow down and dismount barefoot, so you can run or walk swiftly through transition. If you are not confident doing this, simply dismount the bike with your shoes on. If you are wearing your running shoes for cycling, ignore what I've just said.

> Push your bike to your racking area. Make sure you retain total control and don't impede other competitors.

> Don't unclip your helmet until you have racked your bike.

> Put on, as necessary, socks, shoes, hat or visor and nutrition belt.

> Apply sunscreen, if required.

> Rotate your race belt so the number faces forward (or put on a number belt if you didn't wear one on the bike) or wear clothing with the number already pinned to the front.

> Take a few deep breaths and run or walk towards the run exit.

> Smile, the last discipline is underway and, next stop: the finish line!

It may seem like a lot to take in, but once you've done it once or twice it will become second nature and funky-chicken wetsuit-removal, wearing your helmet backwards and navigational numptyness will be a thing of the past. Never be afraid to ask for advice from more experienced athletes and also from the volunteers at the race itself. Remember, practice really does make perfect and before too long your transition will be as smooth as a triathlete's legs, and you'll be knocking minutes off your PB without even needing to invest in swim, bike or run effort!

ROBING FOR RACE DAY: COMPETITION CLOTHING

In the 1980s swimsuits reigned supreme when it came to race day clothing. The skimpier, it seemed, the better with body parts squeezed into postage stamp sized outfits that left little to the imagination. Nowadays, however, the shelves are flooded with different styles, colours and fabric features. The two basic tri-suit styles you'll see are a one-piece suit – where the top and shorts are combined and there's a zip on the front or back – and a two-piece suit, with separate shorts and top. The tops can come with sleeves (short or long) or without (for example, a vest) or, in a two-piece, also a crop top. Tri-specific shorts have a chamois, but it's much more minimal than in regular cycling shorts – enabling you to run without feeling like you're wearing a supersized, soggy nappy. It is never necessary to wear underwear under your shorts. Some tri-suits have an in-built bra that may offer sufficient support for some women but, if not, buy one without and wear a separate bra.

Of course, there is always the swimsuit option – but there can be some trade offs, specifically around comfort, coverage and practicalities, mentioned below.

Tri-suits come with a range of features and properties such as compression, chlorine resistance, sun protection, cooling, wicking, quick-drying and more. If you can, head to a shop to try on any new clothing, rather than purchasing on the internet. Some of the key things to think about when making your choice are:

Comfort and fit

Select an outfit that is not restrictive, has the properties you require and minimises the risk of chaffing and general discomfort. The last thing you want is for your race to become unpleasant because your shorts feel like sandpaper on your thighs, your shoulders are sunburnt and your nipples are red raw. It's a good idea to minimise speed-reducing drag by choosing a suit that fits snugly and doesn't flap in the wind.

Practicalities

Ideally you'll wear one outfit for the whole race, rather than getting changed in T1 or T2. You'll also want to think about how you might perform body functions (i.e. toilet trips) on-the-fly – with a two-piece suit making toilet trips a lot easier; as well as whether you need pockets to carry any nutrition, and where on the suit you prefer them to be located.

Coverage

Think about the weather conditions, sun protection and your own preferences for exposing different areas of your body. Rules exist regarding the display of body parts, with nipple or butt cheek sightings sometimes incurring the wrath of race referees. You can always layer-up if it's cold, wearing arm warmers and a gilet on the bike for example. On the subject of coverage, remember that opaque white fabrics could quickly become transparent when wet.

Type of swim

If you are not wearing a wetsuit it makes sense to avoid suits with pockets that might collect water or looser clothing that can create drag. If it's a non-wetsuit swim you could swim in your tri shorts (and, for women, also a sports bra) and then put a top on in T1.

Budget

In the lead at the Ironman World Championship, 2007, wearing my friend's shorts.

If you're watching your pennies then it can make sense to simply use a tight t-shirt, vest or cycle jersey that you can also wear in training, and only invest in a pair of tri-specific race shorts. Keep an eye open for end-of-season bargains or even, as I did, borrow from a friend. Indeed, I won my first Ironman and the 2007 World Championship in a pair of shorts that I borrowed from a teammate. It was a long-term rental as I still have them!

Ensure you give your race wardrobe a few practice swim/bike/runs, and wash it to soften the fabric and seams. One last thing about tri-attire, don't worry about what you look like. Athletes come in all shapes and sizes, and there's clothing to suit all body types. As I said, it's a race course not a catwalk so dress for your own success, hold that head high and go out there and strut that swim/bike/run stuff.

THE NEED FOR SPEED: HOW TO PACE YOUR RACE

It was 2004 and I was living in Nepal. Myself and two friends, Tina and Billi, travelled to Langtang in the north of the country, bordering Tibet. Our aim was to summit an unconquered 6,000m peak. It was my first time at high altitude. We walked up the valley over five days and gradually gained height, reaching 4,500m. It was at that point we decided to climb what looked like a relatively easy hill, albeit one whose summit was 5,300m above sea level. Me being me, I decided to see how fast I could get up it. Sure enough, I beat Billi and Tina to the top and celebrated

among the coloured prayer flags. Bravo. However, it was downhill, literally and figuratively, from there. My head felt like it was in a vice; the blood inside it started to pound. By the time I arrived at the trekking lodge, I couldn't lift my head at all and sat for hours slumped over my haunches, my brain feeling like it was exploding, thinking I was going to die. Fortunately, I lived to tell this tale. The problem was not that I couldn't adapt to altitude; I had gone up too quickly. I may have reached the top first, but Billi and Tina had won. It taught me so much: not least a lesson about pacing that subsequently served me well.

Becoming proficient at pacing means distributing effort in such a way as to maximise performance while avoiding premature fatigue. One of the most common questions posed by triathletes is how to pace their race to cross the finish line in one piece rather than crashing, burning or horrendously bonking – or else finishing feeling that they have a lot left in the tank. The information below should shed some light on this important issue.

VARIATIONS IN PACE

As we saw on page 48, pace is impacted by the course and conditions. For example, the bike and run at the Alpe d'Huez Long Course Triathlon are both extraordinarily hilly and consequently pace varies wildly with each climb and descent. Or inclement weather may result in wet roads and increased caution – slowing your pace. These variations also mean that finish times are relatively inconsequential in triathlons. For example, my PB at Challenge Roth was over 30 minutes faster than at the World Championship; this was affected more by the course and conditions than any change in fitness or ability. Given this variability, I predominantly used RPE to guide my effort when racing.

PREDICTING PACE

Pace can, however, be a useful measure on courses that are flattish, not technical and without too much wind. Selecting your specific swim, bike and run race pace is highly individual and is based on a variety of factors (in addition to the course and conditions) – including the race distance, your training and level of experience. For example, my coach Dave Scott thought that at Challenge Roth, for the wetsuit-legal swim in the calm waters of the canal, my pace could be 1:18–20 mins/100m; the run is almost flat, with 60 per cent on hard-packed trail and the weather usually temperate, so he anticipated that I could run 3:55 mins/km pace for the marathon. As it turned out, his predictions were almost spot on as I swam 49 minutes 49 seconds for the 3.8km (1:18 mins/100m) and ran 2 hours 44 minutes (3:53 mins/km) for the marathon!

Look at your training log and, specifically, your race-pace work, brick workouts and longer sessions for a good indication of what you can comfortably sustain for each discipline. Think back to sessions or races where poor pacing choices may have resulted in you hitting the wall or finishing feeling like you were overly conservative, and those where you hit the pacing nail on the head. Then ask: what pace was I doing? How did it feel in terms of RPE? What factors influenced my pace? Were these controllable? The answers should help guide your future pacing strategy.

Race distance

Generally, the longer the race, the lower your RPE and the slower your pace. Put another way, I wouldn't be able to speak during a sprint race and it would feel 'hard' but during an Ironman I could hold a short conversation and the effort would feel 'comfortably hard'. In terms of RPE (using the Borg Scale on page 48):

> Sprint: 16

> Olympic: 15

> Half Ironman and Ironman: 13–14

Do your research

Research the course beforehand so you know what to expect, especially in terms of factors that can affect pace, such as the open-water conditions and, for the bike and run, climbs, descents, tight corners and surfaces.

Use training and racing to hone your skills

Race intensity should be determined and practised in training and during B and C races.

Stick to your plan

Although your pace may deviate slightly from what you predicted, it is unlikely to miraculously alter so, as long as you have factored the course and conditions into the plan, stick with your prearranged pace. For, example, don't try to ride an average of 40km/h if you've trained to sustain 30km/h. This means focusing on yourself and not what everyone else is doing, staying calm and not letting the ego and adrenalin take control. You are your only competition. Your game plan is what matters if you want to get to the finish line.

PACING THE THREE DISCIPLINES

There can be a mismatch between RPE and pace, especially at the start of each discipline – that is, a fast pace might feel relatively easy. Hence, be a little more conservative at the outset of each discipline as there are far more negative repercussions from going out too fast (which can feel easy) than a little too slow. I always ask people to imagine themselves in the later part of the race. Will they still be going at the same pace? If the answer is 'No way!', they are going too fast, even though it may feel OK at that point in time. For the swim and the bike, mete out a consistent effort to reach the run in the best shape possible. On the run, and provided you want to finish the race a spent force, you should expect to see the RPE rise as you tire: i.e. running at 5 mins/km for the first kilometre should feel more comfortable than the same pace in the last kilometre. Remember, the closing stages are not supposed to feel easy, but it makes reaching the finish line even more satisfying.

Specific swim, bike and run strategies include:

Swim

In an open-water swim, it's impossible to measure pace without a pace clock or distance markers and hence you have to go on RPE to gauge your intensity. Pack dynamics, adrenalin and freshness may mean that you go out far too fast, causing a heart-rate spike, which can impact your entire race. Try to start the swim at a steady, controlled pace, quelling any anxiety or adrenalin-fuelled urges to sprint. Your breathing should be relaxed and you shouldn't feel that your heart is pounding. If your normal pattern changes and you feel yourself gasping for air, ease back, concentrate on your breathing and regain your composure. The only exception to this rule is if you're an accomplished swimmer who wants to start faster for tactical, positioning reasons, before settling into your race pace.

Be careful not to get stuck in a swim pack – or on the feet of a swimmer – moving at a faster pace than you can sustain. As you near the swim exit, it's OK to kick that little bit harder to get yourself ready for a run to your bike and the next discipline, but don't increase your pace significantly as this will waste valuable energy for little gain.

Bike

Putting the bike in an easier gear before the race will prevent overstraining or frantic, uncontrollable spinning in the first few hundred metres. Give yourself time to adjust to being on the bike, and start conservatively and slowly build the pace. Aim to minimise huge variations in effort, and hence energy-sapping heart-rate spikes. If the bike (and/or run course) is hilly, it's best not to work overly hard on the climbs, only to take your foot off the gas completely on the downhills. On the bike especially, it's tempting to let ego or competitiveness get the better of you. Race your race and not your competitors – they might come zooming past at 45km/h, only to be staggering or DNF-ing 3km into the run. Also, try to rely on your internal computer, the brain, rather than being wedded to a gadget to gauge your effort. Your pedal strokes should be smooth and rhythmical and use your gearing to ensure you can retain the required RPE on any ascents and descents. If you start to feel overly fatigued, back off slightly. As you approach T2, use your gearing to increase your cadence and prepare for the run.

Run

My perception would always seem to be a little skewed at the start of the run, largely because I would have been cycling at much faster speeds. Although my legs would feel a bit wooden, I would often run faster than I intended to – and thought I was – in the first few kilometres. I suggest taking the first 500m in a sprint distance, 1km in an Olympic distance and 2–3km in a half Ironman or Ironman a little more slowly, and build into the final discipline. Focus on your rhythm and cadence, opting for shorter, faster strides if you can, and lean slightly forward. You may wish to adopt a run/walk strategy. If you feel you have the energy, pick up the pace in the final few hundred metres of the race, being careful not to go too fast too soon and risk not crossing that finish line.

Pacing for success isn't always easy. It's often only by trial and error that we know what we are truly capable of. However, the thousands that cross triathlon finish lines show that it's a skill that you can definitely master!

PERFECTION, PRACTICE AND PERSEVERANCE: COPING WITH RACE-DAY PROBLEMS

Every athlete dreams of that one special day, when the jigsaw pieces fall into place, creating the perfect finish-line picture. Challenge Roth in 2011 was as close to a perfect day as I think I will get. Like gold dust: celebrated, remembered and treasured. However, there were still things that I look back and think I could have improved upon.

I am a firm believer that we can never have a so-called 'perfect race'. Triathlon is not a 100m sprint, with no room for error. No matter the distance, it's an endurance sport, with the added complexity of being made up of three disciplines. Mr Dickens hit the nail on the head in stating: 'It was the best of times, it was the worst of times . . . it was the spring of hope, it was the winter of despair'. Whether a world champion or novice, we will experience racing highs that must be savoured and endure lows when things don't go according to plan.

So, what problems might we encounter during a race? They might be *psychological*, such as crippling self-doubt and a desire to quit; *practical*, for example, flat tyres and mechanical failures on the bike, dislodged goggles in the swim or a dropped water bottle; we can also encounter *physical* issues, such as GI trouble, the pain of injury or energy lulls. These are often interlinked; for example, a physical problem can lead to a psychological slump. Success, or otherwise, is largely determined by our approach to such obstacles. If we are able to overcome such imperfections perfectly therein lies the holy grail: our 'perfect race'.

Fortunately, there are tools and techniques that will enable you to cope with whatever a race throws at you. Note, however, that *race day is too late to be developing these*: it must be done in training. You don't want to be stranded on the side of a road in a race, thinking that you really should have learned how to change a flat tyre; or wanting to DNF after 3km on the run and not knowing how to quash that negativity. Training is about teaching yourself to endure, whether this is strengthening the mind to cope with discomfort or self-doubt or changing that pesky puncture. If you invest the time beforehand, you'll get to the start line armed with the weapons needed to battle any problems. Here are just some of the ways that you can endure the troughs of the racing rollercoaster:

ENDURING THE TROUGHS

Stay calm

Panic expends unnecessary and valuable energy, so always stay calm and composed. For example, if your goggles get knocked off as mine did at Ironman South Africa in 2011, relax, breathe, find a quieter area of water to replace your eyewear and rejoin the other swimmers a stroke at a time. Or if you get a flat tyre, don't panic that your race is over, as I showed at Ironman Korea in 2007, the Alpe d'Huez Long Course Triathlon in 2008 and the Ironman World Championship later that year. Provided you have packed a repair kit or, as a last resort, receive mechanical support, you can solve the problem. Think and act methodically and rationally – go through the necessary steps and use the opportunity to refuel and/or hydrate and get respite from the cycling position. And once back on the bike, remain calm and don't ride like a bat out of hell to make up for lost time.

Substitute negativity with positivity

There are varying ways of banishing self-doubt or coping with discomfort. I always find that a smile is the best remedy of all. Having a mantra to repeat during the race can also help. Those, like me, with memories similar to a goldfish can write the refrain on their water bottle, bike, hand or another body part. If you use permanent marker, be prepared for the wording to stay there long after the race has ended (and that you might receive strange looks from colleagues when you return to work with 'You can do it!' tattooed on your arm). Draw on your bank of positive mental images, for example of family and friends, of previous races, of beautiful scenery, of big plates of greasy chips. Anything that will make you smile, lift your spirits and your energy levels, especially if the 'I am knackered. I want to stop. Why did I enter this race? I must be mad' thoughts start creeping in. Importantly, draw confidence from instances in training and life where you have successfully endured discomfort and perhaps achieved more than you ever thought possible; serving as a reminder that you can do so again. During the tougher times, recalling some of my motivations also gave me a huge boost, for example racing to inspire others and raise awareness of causes I care about.

Constant change

Over the course of a triathlon, emotions, situations, conditions and feelings will ebb and flow. You may be experiencing shoulder pain in the swim, which will disappear when you start cycling. All too often we start the run with peg legs, only for this sensation to fade a few kilometres later. Or it might be pouring with rain when you get on the bike, but the sun emerges as you go through the 20km point. If you latch on to, and worry about, what might be happening now and what might happen in the future, you'll dig yourself an emotional hole. Simply focus on the immediate controllables: your form, breathing, effort and thoughts at that one moment in time. This leads us on to the next point . . .

Stay in the moment

Focusing on the process of racing, rather than the outcome, can help. I have a photo from the Ironman Australia run course as my computer screensaver. It is a painted rock and says 'Be happy for this moment. For this moment is your life.' I always remember that when I am racing: doing the best I can at that very moment is all I can ask of myself.

A painted rock on the sidelines at Ironman Australia, and my computer screensaver.

Compartmentalise

As mentioned in Chapter 8, if you need a target to aim for, dividing the race mentally into smaller, bitesize chunks can make it less overwhelming than simply focusing on the finish line. For example, when the going gets tough on the bike, I concentrate on getting to the next aid station and on the Ironman run I think in terms of 10km increments, rather than the whole 42.2km, as well as targeting lampposts, other athletes, aid stations or even places where my family and friends might be standing. For example, seeing 'Team Welly' on the sidelines cheering, waving banners and acting like loonies was the wind under my wings, especially during tougher times. I simply focused on getting to them, before setting another marker.

Just as we encounter problems, there will be plenty of times when you feel strong, powerful and confident. These 'highs' are to be treasured but try not to get too carried away and lose focus. Remain in the now and concentrate on what you can control and never lose that smile.

I hope this advice provides some gold dust so that you too are blessed with that elusive 'perfect day'. Not the one when everything is flawless, but when you overcome imperfections absolutely perfectly.

One-on-One

'A' was for Alpe: Race Reflections with Katy Campbell

August 2015 marked the end of the fantastic 12 months I spent mentoring novice triathlete Katy Campbell and guiding her to the finish line of her A race, the Alpe d'Huez Long Course Triathlon. As such, it was an opportune time for reflection and celebration. Katy wrote a blog summarising her thoughts about the race and the year she spent working with myself and coach Matt Edwards.

What follows are excerpts from her post-race report (in the left-hand column), with combined comments from Matt and myself (in the right-hand column). We did, of course, go out for a celebratory pizza and glass of wine to toast the year and all Katy had achieved!

KATY CAMPBELL'S POST-RACE REPORT

KATY'S REPORT	OUR COMMENTS
I'd been focused on the Alpe d'Huez race since before Christmas, but before I knew it I was packing. And yes, I packed everything but the kitchen sink!	Before the Bristol Harbourside Triathlon we encouraged Katy to write a list of all the necessary equipment, and then analysed this. As a result, she realised how many items she would have forgotten, including her race belt and bike pump! For Alpe d'Huez she wrote a comprehensive checklist to cover all eventualities and minimise last-minute panic.
My taper started the fortnight before – bliss! I flew to Geneva the Tuesday before the race (which was on the Friday) with my husband and my parents. The rest of the 'K-team' support crew arrived after that. I felt ready and raring to go.	Katy booked her travel months in advance, and borrowed a bike box a few weeks before to practise packing and rebuilding her bike. For the taper, we reduced the volume of her training, but retained some intensity until race day. Travel meant she didn't do any training on the Tuesday. We were happy that Katy's friends and family had chosen to come out, as we knew she thrived on their emotional and practical support (doing her grocery shopping for her, for example).

KATY'S REPORT	OUR COMMENTS
On Wednesday I did two sessions: a short ride including some Alpe d'Huez hairpins. I registered and collected my race pack on Thursday. While there, I met with a couple of Exeter Tri Club members – new friends with whom to share feelings of trepidation! I had a simple, quiet dinner back in Huez – pasta and tomato sauce with no onion – followed by an early night. Everything was packed and I knew what I needed to do.	Katy followed our advice and stayed off her feet as much as possible. On the Wednesday, she did a short ride to get herself moving after the travel, and the day before the race she did a short swim and run. Her brother Greg is a mechanic and he gave her bike one last check too. Packing her bags the day before gave her vital peace of mind. Katy had learned from a previous pre-race experience, when she went out to eat at a restaurant and couldn't guarantee the menu or the quality of the food, and this time she brought food from home. She was, quite understandably, a little nervous but also confident and relaxed in her preparation. A far cry from the high levels of anxiety and self-doubt she had at the start of the year. Being part of Exeter Tri Club had done wonders in this regard, and some of her club friends being there was an added bonus.
I got up at 6.30 a.m. (three hours before the start), ate my pre-race breakfast and cycled to the start. I racked my bike, set up my equipment, queued for the loo, put on my wetsuit and listened to the race briefing.	It's very hard to replicate race-day conditions – physical, mental or indeed meteorological – but having practised in training and previous races, Katy had a solid, simple plan. She left plenty of time to get to the start and calmly prepare in transition, following her step-by-step checklist. The Alpine temperatures can be cold and so Katy wore plenty of clothes to keep warm.
I got in the water and did a short warm-up. All 1,200 athletes went off together but I positioned myself further to the back, to avoid the crowd and make sure I had a clearer space of water; 2.2km and 51:17 minutes later I exited the swim and, with slightly wobbly legs, I walked through transition.	Katy had learned how to control her nerves in her B race and during practice open-water swims – and put this to good use on race day. Swimming more than 2.2km in training gave her the confidence she could complete the distance and she developed strategies to cope with glacial water (see page 106). Staying to the edge of the melee is best if you are more nervous about mass starts. Going from horizontal to upright can be strange, so don't feel the need to run immediately after exiting the water.
I managed to remove my wetsuit standing up, put on a few warm clothes, grab my bike and head for the bike exit. I was glad I didn't have my shoes clipped to my pedals, as the bike route starts with a fairly steep ramp.	Remain standing during transitions if you can, to save time, keep momentum and minimise the chance of seizing up (especially in cold weather). Katy sensibly wore arm warmers at the start of the bike due to the colder temperatures. She made the right choice, based on the course profile, to put her bike shoes on in T1, and run in her shoes to the mount line. If you do pre-clip your shoes, make sure you practise mounting beforehand, and remember that you have to get your feet into them when surrounded by other cyclists and potentially on a gradient.

KATY'S REPORT	OUR COMMENTS
The first section is flat or downhill – a good warm-up, and then it's time to attack the Col de l'Alpe du Grand Serre. A climb of 15.3km, 1,003m ascent and an average gradient of 6.5 per cent. I maintained a steady pace, focused on just getting around each bend and even overtook a few people. I arrived at the top in good shape. The views on the descent were beautiful, and I even whooped with delight at one point! The second climb up the Col d'Ornon was a little shallower, but I have to admit to feeling sluggish at that point, and after a downhill and a period of flat riding I reached the bottom of Alpe d'Huez itself. It was amazing to be riding up the iconic 21 switchbacks, and see my family with about six bends to go. With a bike split of 7:02 hours, I was placed 843rd, although my climb up the Alpe was a more respectable 768th.	Having smaller goals, like an aid station, a tree, or an Alpe d'Huez bend can be a useful way of motivating yourself and dividing the race up mentally. Yes, you can use other athletes as targets, but it's also important to race your own race and not over exert yourself to catch someone else. Katy's bike strength and handling has improved dramatically. For example, she knows how to use her gears to maintain a consistent intensity; especially important on hilly courses. This had also given her confidence. Ten months ago, we rode with Katy and she bailed on what she thought was a steep hill. In comparison to the monster that is Alpe d'Huez, it was only a little lump. Katy is now a hill climber!
Now on to one of the hardest runs I've ever done. It's three laps, with a lot of climbing and descending, with parts being off-road. The support from fellow competitors, including my new friend Ian from Exeter Tri Club, was so important, as were the cheers from my family and friends. I saw them at least six times, cheering and waving pompoms. Chrissie and Matt also offered a few words of advice as I passed. I had to dig deep and remind myself of why I wanted to do the race as well as just focusing on getting through each lap, rather than the finish line.	It is an incredibly tough run course due to altitude and the hilly terrain (and having the 2.2km swim and equally mountainous 115km bike ride beforehand). Katy had done hill sessions in training, and had also practised running off-road to give her a feel for the conditions. She didn't give up, and remained calm even during times of discomfort. Recalling pre-race motivations was important, especially when her body was tired. The crowd support can be really valuable, whether it's from strangers or from your own support team, and Katy let our cheers lift her spirits. The three-lap run meant that we could see and speak to Katy relatively frequently and this enabled her to compartmentalise the run into 7.3km increments. We encouraged Katy to periodically check her form and gave a few reminders to relax her arms.
Aside from the last hill on the final lap, I managed to run all the way. I completed the 22km in 2:35 hours, shuffling down the blue carpet to high-fives galore with 10:09:31 on the clock. Exhausted but smiling from ear to ear . . . I did it!	Katy went from being a novice triathlete to completing one of the hardest races on the global triathlon calendar, all in the space of a year. She conquered self-doubt and pushed beyond what she thought possible. The finish line was the culmination of all that effort as it was incredibly special to watch Katy achieve her dream.

We wish that were the end of the story, but post-race things didn't go exactly to plan. At the finish, Katy seemed fine. Tired, yes, but happy and totally coherent. She gobbled down a small plate of pasta, had a pre-prepared smoothie and, after chatting with friends, went home to have a shower having firmed up plans to go out for a celebratory meal. We had no inkling of what was to come. Katy started feeling unwell soon after arriving back at her accommodation. Although she did manage to eat and drink a small amount, nausea prevented her from refuelling properly. After going to bed, Katy also experienced diarrhoea and vomiting and, in the early hours of the morning, suffered a seizure, breaking and dislocating her shoulder in the process. An ambulance was called and took her to Grenoble hospital, where she received fantastic medical care. It was obviously heart-wrenching, worrying and concerning for Katy and all involved and, to this day, we don't know exactly why it happened. Hospital tests showed that she had hyponatraemia – usually caused by over-drinking and hence diluting your sodium levels. We've assessed Katy's race-day nutrition, and it seems highly unlikely that this was the case; her electrolyte intake was adequate, and, if anything, she said she was a little dehydrated. However, it could be that the failure to refuel combined with a very upset stomach may have contributed. Fortunately, Katy has now made a full recovery and is back training and planning new adventures.

It was an honour and joy to work so closely with Katy, Matt and the rest of the 'K-Team' to help Katy achieve her goals. That's not to say I wasn't nervous beforehand. Having never formally mentored anyone, this was a whole new experience, and one that I approached with a mix of excitement and trepidation. Did I have what it took to help Katy? Could we develop a strong relationship? What if she didn't like me? What if I didn't know the answers to her (many!) questions?

Katy, too, was fearful. She was worried about failing, scared of what people would think, concerned that she was 'not worthy', nervous about giving up her life for triathlon and riddled with self-doubt. But for both of us, these fears were unfounded.

I personally gained as much from working with Katy as I hope she did from me. I was impressed and inspired by her insatiable appetite to learn, her inquisitiveness, her ambition, her tenacity and her bravery. To be able to watch her race the Alpe d'Huez Triathlon and see her cross the finish line and achieve her goal was the absolute icing on this wonderful cake. My heart was bursting with pride, and still is. ●

A final few words from KATY CAMPBELL

I was a triathlon novice when I won the competition to be mentored by Chrissie and coached by Matt. Despite being excited about the opportunity, I was also worried when we first started working together. Scared that I would embarrass myself, frightened of cycling uphill, worried about what people would think . . . the list goes on! I would never have dreamed of doing Alpe d'Huez, yet as the months went by I started to believe that it would be possible. No detail was left to chance; we addressed everything. I learned the incredible power of consistency, finally recognised the importance of rest and prioritisation, delved into the finer points of nutrition, and even started listening to my body – although the rather dramatic finale suggests I still have work to do on this aspect! Just as importantly, they took all the stress out of training; I understood the plan, so just had to get on with it. I grew hugely in confidence in all aspects, whether it was tackling the hills in Devon or taking to the open water – two things that I never expected to feel comfortable doing! Chrissie and Matt turned me into an athlete I barely recognised and enabled me to cross that finish line to achieve more than I ever thought I could. I will draw on and value the lessons I learned through this fantastic journey (not to mention the inspiration of having a sporting superstar as a good friend!) for my future sporting adventures . . . whatever they may be! ●

TURNING TURDS INTO TRIUMPHS: BOUNCING BACK FROM RACE DISAPPOINTMENTS

Although I was undefeated at Ironman distance, I certainly wasn't undefeated as a triathlete. I suffered 'losses': times when I wasn't atop the podium or didn't reach my own personal goals. In some respects, it's those times that I value as much as the victories, as they taught me more than a win ever could about effective preparation, dealing with difficulties, the importance of a great support network and the power of positive thinking.

There's no doubt that such instances can knock you for six, given everything we invest in getting to that start line. I've included two examples to hopefully demonstrate that everyone can bounce back from race-day disappointment.

In 2006, I lined up for the National Age Group Sprint Championship in Redditch. From the outset, it was a miserable, rainy day and it didn't really improve. Having been away from the UK for the best part of two years, working in Nepal and then cycle touring in New Zealand, Australia and Argentina, I didn't own a wetsuit. My solution: borrow from a friend. I tried it on the day before and it seemed, to my untrained, un-tri-educated eye, to fit. When I wriggled into said suit on race morning it was obviously too big. I climbed into the non-tropical lake just before the cannon fired and the wettie immediately filled with water. I couldn't swim, I couldn't breathe and I could barely lift my arms. As my competitors disappeared I realised I wasn't even going to be able to finish the swim. Maybe I should have persevered, but it would have taken me an age to complete the 750m and I wasn't altogether passionate about drowning in 14°C water in the pouring rain with an ill-fitting wetsuit. So a kayaker pulled me to the side. Race over. I was mortified and embarrassed, yet humbled and determined to learn from my mistakes and try again.

Three weeks later, I took part in the Shropshire Olympic Distance Triathlon. In the preceding weeks, I practised in a more suitable wetsuit, bought a new (albeit second-hand) bike that was also the right size and harnessed the power of positive thinking with ample encouragement from my BRAT Club teammates. I managed to win the race and qualified for the World Age Group Championship that year. If it hadn't been for Redditch, I may never have revaluated and changed my race preparation or had that added drive and determination to succeed.

> " It's often with hindsight that we realise that low points are actually the opposite: they strengthen and empower us in ways we might never have imagined. "

Another example is the Columbia Triathlon in 2009. I went into it wanting to win. Not expecting to win, but aiming for the top nevertheless. And what happened? I felt flat for the whole race. I saw the splash of feet as the main pack got away and when it came to the bike I urged my body to break into the next gear. It wouldn't respond. On the run, I pushed hard, but my pace didn't equate to the effort exerted. I crossed the line in sixth. Smiling, but inside incredibly disappointed because I knew that, if I had performed to my potential, I could have contended for the victory.

As a triathlete you'll have to deal with such disappointment, especially sessions or races that have been total – for want of a better word – turds. Yes, sh*t happens to all of us. At such times, we can throw our tri toys out of the pram, stamp our feet and let the flames of disappointment consume us, or we can emulate a phoenix – that mythological bird which rises from the inferno, emerging stronger and more powerful. So how do we ensure we take the latter path?

Wallow, then move on

Cry, stamp your feet, rant, rave and throw your heart-rate monitor out of the pram. It feels good. And then stop. Remember that the feelings of despair or frustration are temporary and they are under your control. You can either choose to wallow and hence prolong the agony, or else make that conscious effort to replace them with 'cup half-full' feelings. Smile, laugh: it's easier than frowning.

Lean on others for support

Admitting to 'failure' is not weakness so talk to friends, family, teammates, a coach, counsellor or Jeremy Kyle. They will provide a shoulder, an objective assessment and opinion and/or give you a sharp kick up the posterior, tell you to kindly zip up your (tri) suit and remind you that you are so much more than simply a swim, bike and runner.

Review the positives

You may not have had the overall performance you wanted, but you may have had a great swim, or a superb run, or you might have finally managed to learn how to pee on the bike without having to duck behind a bush. With every shocker, there has to be some element of success: you might just have to dig beneath that melancholy mud a little to find it. Write those positives down, and focus on them. You can also reflect on why you did the race in the first place – and then try to make a more objective judgement call on winning and losing, success and failure. For example, in doing the Columbia Triathlon, I took myself out of my long-course comfort zone, and yes – it hurt. But that's a good thing. I visited a part of the USA that I had never been to before, met some fantastic people and put medals around the necks of the finishers. I was able to support an event organiser whose philanthropic work I admire and consolidate a friendship that endures to this day. There is always a plus side.

Review the negatives and your weaknesses

To plunder the words of the Japanese poet, Masahide: *The barn has burned to the ground. Now I can see the moon.* Having set alight the barn, the 'failure' gives you clarity to look at the lunar landscape, so take time to learn the lessons: did you consume one too many kebabs in the lead-up? Did you have an argument with a loved one that preoccupied your mind? Did your equipment choices bite you on the backside? Or was your backside looser than you would have wanted it to be as a result of some nutritional faux pas? Work out which of these, if any, were under your control and which were not. For example, for Redditch, getting a suitable wetsuit and practising in it beforehand would have been an extremely good idea. And in Columbia, I didn't give myself space to truly focus my mind but rushed around like a headless chicken. I let my nutritional strategy slip by going out for huge buffet meals during my taper. I didn't wear enough clothes for the cold and wet conditions. And I admit to approaching the race with a degree of arrogance, not giving it the deserved respect. These are all lessons from which I learned, and used to make me a stronger and better athlete, and person.

> 66 Remember that the feelings of despair or frustration are temporary and they are under your control. Smile, laugh: it's easier than frowning. 99

Address the causes

Minimise the risk of history repeating itself by working on the facets that are under your control. If nerves were debilitating, develop a strategy for coping with anxiety. If you were stuck by the roadside unable to change a flat tyre, get someone to teach you how to deal with a puncture. If you suffered from cramp on the run, look at hydration/nutrition or inadequate S & C work as possible causes. Get help from trusted sources, including a coach if possible, to work on your weaknesses. And yes, controlling the controllables also means trying on your kit beforehand.

Be inspired by others

Read about people who have successfully surmounted hurdles. If they can do it, so can you. Even J. K. Rowling admitted she reached rock-bottom before Harry pottered along. Remember the likes of Alistair Brownlee, Sir Steve Redgrave and yours truly didn't always travel along a path paved with roses. Sir Steve, for example, overcame illness, disappointment and self-doubt to win his five Olympic gold medals. Indeed, one might argue that it was precisely because he endured those turd-filled troughs that he was able to rise to greatness.

Celebrate the journey

We must enjoy the process of preparing for a race, rather than our emotions being tied to a very specific race outcome. Remember all the good times and high points you've had along the way, and make sure you value and treasure those as much as the result itself.

Recall the 'good races'

Having a clunker of a race makes you appreciate the good times even more. Look at your previous winner's medals, watch old race videos or, outside of triathlon, remember the promotion you were awarded at work or a successful presentation you gave. Remind yourself that you have achieved past goals and will do so again.

Set a new goal

While sometimes we need to pause and reflect, when the time feels right I would fire up the mojo by giving yourself a new, realistic yet ambitious goal and begin working towards it.

Triathlon is a journey, a challenge, an amazing adventure. We invest a huge amount of time and energy in achieving our goals and the race result is a really important, visible marker of our efforts. However, it's often with hindsight that we realise that any 'low points' or 'bad performances' are actually the opposite, and strengthen and empower us in ways we might never have imagined. As the late, great Muhammad Ali said: 'Success is not achieved by winning all the time. Real success comes when we rise after we fall. Some mountains are higher than others. Some roads steeper than the next. There are hardships and setbacks but you cannot let them stop you. Even on the steepest road you must not turn back.'

Life Changing: My Post-race Speech at the Ironman World Championship, 2007

What follows is the transcript of my speech from the Ironman World Championship in 2007, the year I first won and the event that changed my life for ever.

Aloha.

I am more nervous now than I was before the race. When I raced nobody knew who I was, now all eyes are on me . . . and I have a whole heap of butterflies that have decided to dance the tango inside of my stomach!

It is a privilege and an honour to qualify for, and race here in Kona – to have the opportunity to compete on the hallowed turf of so many triathlon legends and to compete against the best athletes in the world.

To stand up here and wear the Ironman crown is something that hasn't quite sunk in yet. I am amazed, overjoyed and incredibly, incredibly overwhelmed.

And as for England winning the rugby *and* the football – now that's just the icing on the cake!

Also have to mention that I am least US$10 richer. My two so-called friends each bet me $5 that I would finish in 9 hours 35 minutes. I haven't forgotten and will be collecting the winnings at the end of the night. Or at least make them buy me a beer!

I understand that I caused a few problems for the commentators during the race because nobody knew who I was. My friends at home tell me that the only thing the commentators had to say about me was that I wasn't wearing a hat or a visor. I'll tell you why I wasn't wearing a hat or visor . . . that's because I don't have a hat or visor sponsor!

As some of you know, I came to the sport relatively late. I was always a sporty kid, swimming, playing hockey, running, but never excelling and always more interested in the social side of the sports scene. I went to university at 18 and then travelled the world for two years, which opened my eyes to the many problems that exist, but also the opportunity that there is for positive change. I knew then that I wanted to work in international development, I did a Masters and got a job working for the UK government on international development policy for three years. In 2004 I left to work in Nepal for 18 months, and returned to the UK and my old job last year.

As for triathlons, I did a few in 2004 – on a shitty, ten-year-old borrowed bike with pedal cages and a surf wetsuit. I wondered why I sank or came out of the swim in about 35 minutes! And when I got back to the UK in 2006 I entered a few races – one of which was the very famous Shropshire triathlon. Which you should all do if you are ever in the UK. I surpassed all my wildest expectations and managed to qualify for the World Age Group Championship in Lausanne. I got a coach, trained like a beast for ten weeks and managed to win the World Age Group title.

Then I had big decisions to make.

I never want to look back and think 'what if'. You only get one chance at life and the most important thing for me is to know that I have given it everything and been the best that I can be. I didn't know where that would take me in terms of triathlon, but unless I gave it a shot at going pro I would never really know.

So, I was put in touch with the well-known coach, Brett Sutton. He took a look at me one wintery week in Switzerland. And by February I had quit my job and was making plans to join my new team at our training camp in Thailand.

It's been a great first season! Highlights would be: winning my first ITU race in the Philippines, the Alpe d'Huez Long Course race where I crashed and punctured and won by . . . well, a margin! and Ironman Korea, my first ever Ironman race.

I never thought then that I would be standing here now. Part of me keeps thinking that it has all just been a dream, but then I feel the pain in my legs and I know that the race actually happened!

I wasn't actually that nervous before the start. My coach had told me to see it as just another race. The swim was below average for me. Three minutes down from what I wanted but the scenery was good, and when I wasn't looking at the soles of people's feet I could look at the beautiful fish and coral!

On the bike, it took me about 30km to get going; after that I found my rhythm and felt stronger as the race went on. I almost got blown off my bike coming back down from Hawi and had to hang on for dear life! I caught the leading girls going on to the Queen K highway, and had to decide whether to stay with them or go past. I felt I had more in the tank so I took off. Was surprised but happy to see that they didn't go with me! I guess it gave me a bit of confidence, and I continued at that pace and rode up to Leanda Cave and Dede Griesbauer about 20km later: I really couldn't believe that I was leading the Ironman World Championship! And it was incredibly embarrassing because I didn't even have a cool-looking aero helmet on!

Once I had the lead I wasn't going to let it go easily. I was just hoping that I remembered to pack my run legs in my transition bag. Luckily for me they were there, and I felt strong going out on the run. There were a few niggles on various parts of my legs, but I had the gels and the amazing support of the crowd lifted me and seemed to take the pain away!

I guess I never really thought I was going to win until the last 10km. My coach always says that the race doesn't start until 30km into the run. It's often true, and I was just hoping that I had enough left to finish strongly. I think I only started to believe it in the final 5km; although I do wish I had checked the course map before the race! I thought the finish was at the end of

Surprise and elation at winning my first Ironman World Championship in 2007.

Palani Road, when the motorbikes took a sharp left and along Kuakini. Oh bugger, I thought, I've misread the mile signs. I had my Union Jack flag ready and had to carry it another kilometre until the real finish line!

It was worth the wait though.

So where next?

The most important thing for me is to seize the wonderful opportunity that I have to combine my two passions in life: sport and development.

I worked as a swimming teacher at a day school in Boston, Massachusetts, back in 1997; at a school called Beaver. I always thought it was amusing to wear a swimsuit with Beaver written across the front!

At Beaver, I saw first-hand what a difference sport can make to children's lives, and again in Nepal, where sport was one thing that could bring conflict-affected communities together.

Sport has a tremendous power – and can be a force for considerable change.

I hope that through my victory here, I can inspire and encourage people – young and old – to take up triathlon and other sports and to galvanise interest and support among the media, government and business, both in my home country the UK, but also all around the world, and particularly developing countries.

I want to finish with some thank yous.

First, a big 'cheers' to my coach Brett Sutton and the rest of the team for giving me that chance. I am able to train with one of the best triathlon coaches in the world and with many of the world's best triathletes, two of whom I am proud to say join me on the stage today. Belinda Granger and Rebecca Preston. I have learned so much from them, and it is a vindication of Brett's coaching that we are up here on the stage.

To Ironman and all the other race sponsors for their unwavering support to the sport.

And thank you so much to the thousands of volunteers who give up their precious time to help. I spoke just now to a lady called Sammy and she said 'we are proud to help you realise your dream'. Well, without people like Sammy the event would not be able to take place. I know I speak on behalf of all the athletes here when I extend my sincere gratitude to you all.

I also want to say thank you to the thousands of supporters who lined the streets from start to finish. You are the real endurance athletes! The atmosphere was absolutely electric, not just when I was coming down Ali'i Drive, but for every single athlete that crossed the finish line. To be there at midnight to watch the last finishers was amazing and something I will never ever forget.

I also want to say congratulations to all of the other pros, and of course to give a mention to Natascha Badmann, and wish her a really speedy recovery.

For us professionals, this is our job, we can dedicate our lives to it. I want to save the last word for the 1,600 age groupers who swam, biked, ran, walked and crawled their way over the finish line. From the youngest to the oldest. To double amputee Scott Rigsby and all those who have overcome adversity and won – you are the true Ironmen and women: an inspiration. Mahalo! ●

Dealing with a DNS: Thoughts Following the Ironman World Championship, 2010

On the morning of Saturday, 9 October 2010, I made the difficult decision not to start the Ironman World Championship. What follows are two blogs from that time. I hope they give a healthy dose of inspiration and motivation to those who have also been beset with disappointment and are wondering if they will ever shine again.

On Saturday I had to make one of the hardest decisions of my life – whether or not to start the Ironman World Championship. In the end, I didn't race. However, before I try and explain the decision that I made I want to start off with a huge congratulations to the amazing Mirinda (Rinny) Carfrae. Her performance on Saturday was nothing short of remarkable. She truly is a worthy World Champion.

So many thoughts are going through my head at the moment, and it will take time to sift through them all. I'd like to quickly elaborate on my physical and mental state leading into the race and why I finally took the decision I did.

I started feeling slightly ill on Friday lunchtime, with a sore head and throat. I did my usual three short sessions but on the run particularly I knew something wasn't quite right. My legs were like jelly and I was sweating much more than usual. My tired head hit the pillow at 7 p.m. and I woke up several times during the night literally drenched in sweat, my head pounding and my throat constricted. I got up at 3.45 a.m., had a shower, and went through my pre-race routine hoping that I would feel better. However,

nothing improved. It was then that the thought of DNS'ing first crossed my mind.

I tried to tune into my body and listen to the signals it was giving. I sought counsel from those closest to me, including Tom, my manager Ben and Dave. Dave asked me, quite simply, whether I would go out and do a session if this were any other day. I said no.

I had my answer.

At around 5 a.m. the decision was made. There was no going back.

Like all the other athletes, I invest so much time, passion, energy into getting myself in the best possible shape for the World Championship. I have so much respect for the race, and the toll it can take on your body. It is demanding and brutal, and competing when ill risks greater health problems. Furthermore, I believe I owed it to myself and all the other competitors to give the performance I had trained so hard for.

Those that know me will understand how incredibly difficult, frustrating and heart wrenching it was to make that call. Two days later, and although I am starting to feel physically better, I know I made the right decision for me at that particular time. Yes, I could sit here feeling sorry for myself, reflecting on what might have been, but ultimately wallowing in self-pity doesn't help me, or anyone else. I will look to the future and all the opportunities it will bring – putting Saturday behind me and moving on to fight another day. This is sport. As I have always said, it has ups and downs. Highs and lows. It is a mountain I must climb. No different from any other I have climbed, and scaled, before.

I will spend the coming days with my family and friends, seeing some of this amazing island and tomorrow will head back to Boulder.

The journey to the World Championship in 2011 begins here and the fire in my belly is already burning.

This was followed by the following blog a few weeks later . . .

I contracted my fair share of nasties during the time I spent travelling to far-flung, and decidedly unsanitary, places around the world. I have had rabid dog bites, infected leech wounds, and more bouts of Giardia than Muhammad Ali had in the boxing ring. I have learned to read my body relatively well and listen to the signals that it gives me. In Nepal I suffered the repeated Return of the Giardia Parasite (sounds like a dodgy remake of a *Star Wars* film) and spent half my waking hours with my backside attached to a toilet (aka a hole in the ground); however, sometimes the feelings of ill health are subtler and less palpable. The day before the World

Championship was one of these. I couldn't quite put my finger on it, but I knew something wasn't quite 'right'. I felt off. My throat was sore, my head heavy and I had a general feeling of malaise and lethargy: hardly an ideal platform on which to fight a 9-hour, 140.6-mile battle on the lava fields.

Since my DNS I have had various blood tests: one for the anti-doping authorities and more to check for underlying causes of my persistent ill health. With all those needles, I felt a bit like a human pin-cushion but at least I have found the answer. According to the doctors I have been afflicted by the following: bacterial strep throat, bacterial pneumonia and to top it all off a little mosquito-spread blighter by the name of West Nile Virus (I am not sure of the origins of the name, although Boulder is definitely geographically west of the said river). For the symptoms to manifest themselves the day before the biggest race of my life was clearly suboptimal timing; however, it is not altogether surprising. Preparing for the World Championship is stressful to body and mind and can increase your vulnerability to contracting various illnesses. However disappointing and heart wrenching it was not to start the race, I know – even with hindsight – I made the right decision.

I am now popping bullet-sized antibiotics like they are Halloween treats, and am focusing on getting myself healthy enough to compete at Ironman Arizona on 21 November. So, there you have it. Contrary to the many (some laughable and some more insidious) rumours, I am not pregnant, I didn't have a nervous breakdown, and nor did I deliberately try to avoid the rigorous drug-testing procedures. I simply got sick.

DAVE SCOTT on my DNS at the World Championship

I knew that Chrissie was going to do herself serious damage if she raced feeling like she did. However, it's not for the coach to tell the athlete what to do, but to discuss the options, ask the right questions, eliminate any background noises or influences and provide unconditional support.

Any Ironman race, let alone one in Hawaii, is extremely taxing even with a body at 100 per cent. For Chrissie, the DNS was the right decision to make, and remained so when we learned of the viruses she was contending with. Yet not starting a race is incredibly difficult for any athlete. Chrissie also felt a huge amount of external pressure to perform for the fans and for sponsors, but ultimately you have to bring it back to yourself and do what's best for you and your health.

I reflect on my own experience, when I pulled out the night before the October 1988 World Championship. I was six-time and reigning World Champion but in the July of that year developed a slight knee injury and, despite my best efforts to deal with the problem in the intervening months, by race week nothing had improved. Pain shot through my knee with every foot strike. I am pretty adept at reading my body, and knowing when to push through discomfort and when to back off, and I decided that this was a raw, unbearable pain that I could not compartmentalise or manage. I made the difficult choice not to start and nearly 30 years later I know it was the right decision – as Chrissie's was in 2010. Heavy sweating, a sore throat and an internal thermostat that was off – it was not a day to tackle the lava fields.

We learned a lot from this experience, not least the need for her to up her intake of some immunity-enhancing vitamins and nutrients and to also pay close attention to her taper to ensure that she remains healthy. It was a tough time, but she bounced back to fight another day with a resounding win at Ironman Arizona six weeks later. ●

I also refuse, however, to see it as just 'bad luck'. I am responsible for my overall well-being and need to get to the start line, not only fit but also healthy. Hence, Dave and I will examine why I succumbed to these illnesses and whether there is anything we can do going forward to boost my immunity and ensure it doesn't happen again.

Although I'm no longer reigning World Champion I will use this experience to make me stronger and more determined – and I will continue to champion the sport of triathlon, and the causes I care about, in any way I can. In the words of the lesser known, but decidedly catchy 1990s musical masterpiece 'Tubthumping' (which, incidentally, had nothing to do with tubs or thumping) 'I get knocked down, but I get up again, you ain't never gonna keep me down.' ●

The Perfect Race: Thoughts Following the Ironman World Championship, 2011

Below is the report from my last race as a professional triathlete: the World Ironman Championship in 2011. It was my 13th Ironman and, in this case, 13 did (eventually) prove to be very lucky!

Every once in a while you are blessed with a very special day when history is rewritten, records fall and you surpass your own notions of what is possible to achieve. On 8 October, Craig Alexander broke the long-standing course record to take his third World Championship win, age group records tumbled, athletes overcame personal struggles and euphorically crossed the finish line. I am so proud to have been part of that historic day.

This race report reiterates, and augments, the messages I tried my best to convey at the awards ceremony. I apologise for my tardiness in putting fingers to keyboard, but there were some serious celebrations to take care of, some luxuriating to be done and some tree-trunk-like cankles [swollen ankles that merge with the calf] to offload. With the benefit of the passing of time (and sobriety as the effect of the champagne wears off) I have been able to better reflect on what was the most exciting, challenging and best race of my career.

Last year I was devastated to succumb to illness and be unable to defend my title.

That day Rinny gave everyone a show to remember, especially with her record-breaking 2 hour 53 minute run split, to be crowned World Champion. My non-start, however disappointing, instilled in me a hunger like never before. As the saying goes, you don't know what you've got until it's gone. The fire and desire to regain the World Championship title burned all the more brightly.

Every athlete, myself included, wants perfect race preparation, great training sessions and no injuries. Two weeks prior to the World Championships everything was looking rosy – I was on track and determined to give my best-ever performance. However, this was due to be my 13th Ironman race and on Saturday 24 September it seemed like 13 was living up to its superstitious reputation for bringing bad luck. I was doing my last long ride with a group of friends in Boulder and, after about 30 minutes, approached a left-hand bend that I have taken a million times. I started to turn and then suddenly – bang! – body hits tarmac. Unknown to me I had a flat rear tyre, causing the wheel to lose traction and skid. The result?

A sizable donation of skin and blood from my left leg, hip, ankle and elbow to the Colorado asphalt. The abrasions were akin, the doctors said, to third-degree burns. I also had deep bruising to my left side, a damaged pectoral muscle and, to top it off, contracted a serious infection in my left leg, which became swollen and red and rendered me unable to walk. I was put on a course of antibiotics and my wounds were dressed so extensively that I resembled an Egyptian mummy.

I rested for a few days and then, letting panic and fear get the better of me, stupidly decided to go for a swim. I managed one lap of the pool before having to be lifted out, with Tom and Dave carrying me to the car in my swimsuit. I remember shaking and sobbing and hardly looking like a three-time World Champion about to head to Hawaii!

To be honest I think I was still in shock. The trauma and the huge mental pressure of getting ready for the race was so all-consuming and overwhelming – I just wasn't thinking rationally. I was so anxious about the disruption to my preparation I let the compulsion to train override the obvious need for rest.

I delayed my flight to Kona, arriving on the Saturday instead of the planned ten days prior. I was greeted at the airport with open arms and a Hawaiian lei by my 'Kona mum and dad', John and Linda, and struck as always by the smell of tropical flowers, the warmth of the humid air and the energy that the island exudes. Hawaii has a very special place in my heart and arriving there never fails to excite me.

But the joy was short-lived. I spent race week unable to swim and as an impatient patient at the Kona Hospital. I had Active Release Techniques (ART) therapy from the ceaselessly supportive and sanguine Mike Leahy, as well as my acupuncturist who had only come out for a holiday, but was put straight to work. The care I received was outstanding – but the disruption and continued discomfort all added to the weight on my shoulders.

Of course, I'm no hero and many other athletes have endured – and overcome – far more serious illnesses and injuries than I had. I am not recounting what happened in the weeks preceding the race to elicit sympathy, or make excuses, but rather to share the most important lesson that I learned: to never let my head or heart drop.

So yes, life threw me a curve ball. I could either be crushed by that ball or I could throw it right back and, to follow the advice of a friend, rise like a phoenix from the ashes of the crash. But I would be lying if I said that I wasn't scared, nervous and apprehensive, and physically traumatised, coming into the race.

I always say that Ironman is 50 per cent physical and 50 per cent mental – all the preparation in the world will not carry you to victory if your mind is not prepared. To plunder the words of Muhammad Ali, 'the will must be stronger than the skill'. I was scared of the pain, scared of not being able to do my best and yes, scared of losing. The solution was to change my expectations for the race, adjust my approach to racing and change my perception of success.

Rather than focusing on a desired outcome (winning) I focused on the process (doing the very best I could every minute of the race).

So Saturday 8 October dawned and the cannon fired into the clear, morning air. I was in pain, I was nervous, I lacked power in my left arm and didn't have the initial speed to position myself in a fast swim pack. But I had Dave's wise words ringing in my ear. 'Don't worry if your swim is slow, it's better to take it steady and be able to complete the race, than to put yourself in a hole you can't get out of.' And so, 1 hour 1 minute later I exited: a nine-minute deficit to Julie Dibens and four minutes down from Rinny. I had a lot of work to do.

I named my bike Phoenix, for obvious reasons, and once aboard I tried to quell any rising panic, keep my head and slowly try to reel in those ahead of me, as well as resisting the charges from behind. I overtook Rinny on the climb up to Hawi, where I gained an additional boost from seeing 'Team Welly' on the sidelines. Despite their smiles and cheers I knew they were concerned about the deficit mounting between Julie and me. Soon after I was overtaken by super-cyclist Karin Thürig. I managed to stay with her for about ten miles, until I had to concede that her pace was above my capabilities. I ignored the aches and pains that racked my body, preventing me from ever really feeling comfortable. I sat up at every aid station and incline to try and open up my hips, and ease the numbness that had developed in my lower back. Expletives were uttered every time urine trickled down my leg and into my wounds (making sure the television crews weren't there to capture such profanities).

Off the bike, I proceeded to run like I had a firework up my backside: determined to make hay while the sun shone (and it was definitely shining with no cloud cover and temps of about 90°F plus). Once again, I had Dave's voice in my ears, 'Focus, focus focus, I know you want to smile and wave, but you need to devote every ounce of energy to your performance.' So yes, there were a few less smiles than normal that day!

My body and mind alternated between feeling OK and then screaming in agony. The pain in my left hip was excruciating, my form was poor and other areas of my body felt the effects of a changed gait. My hamstrings, calves, even my shoulders were begging me to stop. I had that ugly voice on one shoulder suggesting I quit and take the easy route. But I hate the easy route. So I ignored the pain. I ignored the internal whispers. It was the other voice, the louder one on the opposite shoulder, which gave me the will to continue: which enabled me to keep my head to, as Kipling says, force 'heart and nerve and sinew to serve your turn long after they are gone, / And so hold on when there is nothing in you / Except the Will which says to them: "Hold On!"'

I let the cheers of the crowd propel me forwards. I had the sight of my boyfriend Tom, en route to an amazing 11th place, to give me a boost. As I overtook Julie Dibens, Rachel Joyce, Leanda Cave and finally Caroline Steffen at the entrance to the famous Energy Lab, my confidence soared but, unlike the name of the Lab, my energy levels were waning with every step. 'Just keep your head, keep your head' rang in my ears. 'Never ever give up.' I recalled times in training and

> **Of all my Ironman victories this was the performance – the moment in my sporting life – that I am the most proud of.**

racing when I have suffered and endured pain, I recalled Jon Blais and others who have shown what it is to be truly courageous, and I thought of my family and friends and my desire not to let them, or myself, down.

Back on Queen K I embarked on the last 10km or so, with my strength fading with every incline. I was given all manner of splits: 'Four minutes from Rinny, five minutes from Rinny, Rinny is only three minutes behind!' I knew I couldn't let up, not even for a second. I couldn't think of the finish. I couldn't think of the possible victory. I focused solely on what was happening in that moment. I was finding it hard even to smile, even when a man in a huge sumo outfit ran with me in the final few kilometres. Only as I descended Palani Road and let the downhill momentum carry me did I believe that my body would hold out, and that I would win my fourth World Championship.

As I ran the final metres along Ali'i Drive, waving to the crowds and finally allowing myself to smile, I felt utterly overwhelmed by what I had managed to achieve. Comparable to 2007, when I won the World Championship for the first time, it seemed so surreal to have achieved something that nine hours previously I could never have imagined. I heard the Hawaiian conch shells being blown, the noise of the huge crowds, the sound of the drums and the voice of

the announcer, Mike Reilly. I reached the finish tape, hoisted it over my head, and then rolled in memory of Jon Blais; overcome with a sense of pride, satisfaction, relief and unadulterated joy that I had won: that I had defied what I had thought possible.

I left everything out there on the course that day: including blood, sweat and tears and a few bits of skin. I conquered my demons, the course, the brutal conditions, my injuries, my doubts, and all the other amazing athletes to win that race.

I have often said that I wanted to finish an Ironman feeling emotionally and physically spent. On that day, my wish came true. People sometimes say to me that I make winning Ironman races look easy. This was anything but. I hope I showed that I am human. I get injured, I cry, I even curse, but I will dig to the depths to give everything I have to this wonderful sport, to realise the potential inside myself. The finish time was irrelevant as a criterion by which to judge success. Success in this context was giving it everything – doing the very best with what I had. This race taught me a valuable, simple lesson: never to stop believing. It should teach you all never to stop believing too. Of all my Ironman victories this was the performance – the moment in my sporting life – that I am, without a doubt, the most proud of. ●

Insight

DAVE SCOTT on the World Championship, 2011

This experience aged me about 30 years! Prior to the accident everything had been going so well. I thought we were going to smash the World Championship: that it would be her best ever race. As it turned out it *was* her best race ever, but not for the reasons we could have predicted! It's one of the greatest athletic feats and I was intimately involved as the action unfolded.

We had a plan going into the final two weeks, and I had to throw that plan out of the window: we had to take it hour by hour, day by day. Four days after the accident I remember asking Chrissie whether she wanted to race. Her response was categorical: she was going to start. I never asked again.

We both landed in Hawaii a week before the race and slowly pieced the schedule together, depending on how she was feeling. In Boulder she could hide away, but in Kona all eyes were immediately on her. The media and the public weren't really aware of what was happening, and repeatedly spoke of victories and records. Yet, she looked like a cheese-grater had gone over her! She was nervous, worried and in considerable pain, and the only people she could share her true feelings with were Tom, her family and me. I know what she was going through, because I'd felt that pressure and weight of expectation as an athlete, even without injury.

Then on Wednesday she had intense pain in her pectoral muscle and had to get an MRI to check for any blood clots, which fortunately came back negative. She also had to go to and from the hospital to get her wounds scrubbed out and re-dressed every other day. Training wise she did a few light bike and run sessions, but didn't swim for three days before the race to rest the pec muscle and give the wounds the chance to heal.

Although she began feeling better she ideally needed at least another four weeks: to rehab and build back up to the phenomenal level of fitness she was at before the accident. She had been swimming faster, biking faster, running faster. I believed she could go sub 8 hours 40 minutes, breaking the course record that would stand for a long time to come. That wasn't to be, but time isn't everything in triathlon.

In the days before a big event I always remind my athletes about the simplicity of racing: encouraging them to stay calm and concentrate on maximising their performance at that very moment. With Chrissie I tried to eliminate her self-doubt, with large doses of positivity and encouragement. She didn't need worrywarts or pessimists and she didn't need to focus on winning or worry about the pressure or expectations. I did advise her to conserve as much energy as she could in the days before the race, instead of always trying to give back with a photograph, interview or autograph, as well as during the race itself, by not waving and smiling quite so much as normal.

The cannon fired on race morning and I was biting my nails with nerves watching the swim. Mirinda exited in 57 minutes and every second was agonising. I was looking out to the bay, trying to spot Chrissie's stroke. It's very distinctive. Finally, I saw her . . . A few minutes later she climbed out, in a much slower time than previous years, but she had at least finished the swim and, despite my pre-race advice, had this big smile and I think 'Well, OK – now the game really begins!'

She came into T2 three minutes in front of Mirinda, with Julie Dibens 22 minutes down the road and about five other women in between. Everyone expected Mirinda to catch Chrissie, but I'm thinking, 'No, the run can still be your weapon, let's do it!' She opened up a lead right from the start, ignoring her battered body: she was racing, she was in her element. At that moment, I knew Chrissie could dictate what would happen, whether her destiny or her demise in that race. The gap grew to five minutes and I knew how much she would be hurting. I was thinking: 'You're going to have to draw energy from everywhere, including under your toenails, to pull this thing off!' Everyone, including me, was holding their breath and Chrissie was just a mess; her running form was a complete shambles. But it didn't matter – she simply had to be as efficient as possible with the

mental and physical fatigue and injuries she had sustained.

I could hear the cheers as she approached the finish line, and had to fight my way through the crowds to meet her . . . I was this sweating, stinking mess, wanting to get there for my athlete. It was so overwhelming. Tom was there, crying and hugging her, her parents were there, also in tears. Finally, I managed to wrap my arms around her – she was completely spent and could hardly stand up. I was so proud. She'd played her best game that day. And what a game it was.

My day wasn't over though, as I headed back out to cheer for my son Drew, who had fractured his wrist in the same crash as Chrissie. He finished and I couldn't have been happier.

It had been an overwhelming, difficult but incredible day. And yes, Chrissie was finally able to give back with that huge smile of hers, as she always did! ●

TO THE FINISH LINE AWARDS: TRI ANECDOTES

Two things I love about triathlon are, first, that professionals and amateur athletes race on the same course, at the same time, on the same day, in pursuit of the same goal – the finish line. We share smiles, grimaces, grunts and groans and sometimes expose parts of ourselves that even our loved ones might not see. Second, the spectators who line the course are so close that you can, and often do, touch them. Given this intimate interaction, it's not surprising that I've been witness to a variety of amusing images and incidents over the course of my career that are worthy of recognition. I have therefore decided to bestow a few awards in honour of these rib-tickling moments.

Best post-race party

The Mekong River Triathlon in Thailand in 2007 when I danced funky-chicken style to 'It's Raining Men' with a group of Thai ladyboys and Stephen Bayliss. It wasn't raining, and Stephen was the odd one out given that he was, in fact, the only male among them.

The proposing bananas on the sidelines of the World Ironman Championship.

Best-dressed athlete

The competitor at Challenge Roth in 2009 who chose to don a white banana hammock, which unfortunately revealed his banana and more. It put me off my stride, but his fruit-filled package definitely made me smile.

Best-dressed male spectator

Once again, the yellow fruit tops the podium. This award goes to the banana at the Ironman World Championship in 2009 who held up a sign saying 'Will You Marry Me?' At that point I was somewhat preoccupied with trying to get to the finish line, otherwise I might have stopped and accepted his (or maybe her?) kind proposal. A special commendation also goes to the stripper at Ironman Australia in 2008, although he clearly wasn't best dressed.

Best-dressed female spectator

A toss-up between the woman dressed as the policeman from the Village People, complete with moustache, oversized 'assets', a truncheon and high heels, at Ironman

Arizona 2010 and the near-naked blow-up doll in Kansas. The latter was a little deflated by the end.

Best race appendage

Aside from the banana in the hammock, it has to be the doll strapped to the saddle of a competitor's TT bike at Ironman Arizona. Clearly dolls, in all their forms, are an essential piece of kit for any discerning triathlete.

Best post-race tourist attraction

I did some sightseeing after Ironman Korea in 2007 and discovered a Sex and Health Museum, Loveland, Happy Town, the Teddy Bear Emporium and the Chocolate Museum. Spoilt for choice, I ended up being happy in love and surrounded by chocolate teddy bears.

Best chat-up line at a race

A British age-grouper at the ITU Long Course World Championship in 2008 who wooed me with the smooth-talking chat-up line: 'Haven't I seen you in a magazine?'

Best pre-race cuisine

It has to be Ironman Korea in 2007 where they served pickled cabbage, salty dried fish and dubious meat products that used to bark. Enough said.

Best request

This award goes hands down, literally, to all the women (note: plural) who've asked me to sign my name where marker pens have never gone before (I abbreviate my signature for fear of losing the nib).

Best pre-race party

Challenge Roth in 2011 where most of the pros wore the traditional lederhosen and dirndls (renders breathing almost impossible), and where Belinda Granger and I arm-wrestled and then went hammer-head to hammer-head in the typical Bavarian 'hammering nails into a piece of wood contest'. I lost both.

So that's about it. Congratulations to all the winners – you're what makes triathlon so special, memorable and downright amusing. The sport wouldn't be what it is without you!

With the wonderful Walchshöfer family before Challenge Roth, 2010.

CHAPTER TEN
REST AND RECOVERY

OPPOSITE: Serenity as I swim with dolphins in Kona, Hawaii.

In January 2007, I went for a trial week with Mr Brett Sutton at his training base in Switzerland. 'Do I have what it takes to be a professional triathlete?' I asked. His slightly macabre answer being: 'Physically yes, but I need to cut your head off.' Wishing to avoid decapitation, I asked him to elaborate. 'You are like a bull in a china shop and you don't know how to rest your body and mind. Unless you change you will never be a successful athlete.'

Headless? He was right. I was that proverbial chicken. Given that 'rest' only entered my vocabulary as the beginning of a word ending in 'aurant', I nearly reached for the carving knife and performed the decapitation there and then. Yes, I could swim/bike/run until I was falling over with exhaustion. But this wasn't enough. No amount of logbook ticks, no number of 'eyes popping from head' sessions, would create a champion. The puzzle would always be incomplete unless I prioritised the vital and missing piece of the jigsaw: rest and recovery.

This chapter covers some of the most common techniques and strategies for optimising your ability to rest and recover – mentally and physically – from training and racing. It also includes a separate section on one of the most important times of the season – the period when you 'have it off': the end-of season break in which you allow your body to rejuvenate sufficiently in order to come back firing on all cylinders.

HEAD CHOPPING: REST AND RECOVERY FUNDAMENTALS

We are creatures of habit, we love routine, some of us are obsessive-compulsive perfectionists, who come out in hives at the thought of an easy session, a nap or, heaven forbid, a rest day. But I cannot say this clearly enough. It is not the swim/bike/run sessions or races that will make you fitter, it is the recovery – the adaptation and regeneration – from the stress caused by those activities. And it is

> **It is not the swim/bike/run sessions or races that will make you fitter, it is the recovery.**

not just about physical recovery, it's mental recovery and relaxation too. That's why I say that as a professional I trained 24/7. Rest and recovery is part of training my body to be the best that it can be. It can take a wide variety of forms – physical and psychological. There are many different methods and techniques, and this section will cover the most important.

Reduced intensity (easy training/active recovery)

Reducing the intensity of your sessions can help limit stress on the body and facilitate recovery. The emphasis is on the word easy. If you are not being overtaken by a shopper bike when cycling then you are not going easy enough. If it goes from being a 90-minute spin to a two-hour ride with a few hills then you have totally changed the nature of the session – and its purpose. A five-minute cool-down at the end of a hard workout will also begin the recovery process. The cool-down can be followed by some targeted, light stretching.

Reduced volume

A reduction in your training volume for a given period of time can give more time for rest and help with recovery. This includes the need to have a full day off . . .

Full rest days

As a professional athlete, generally I had one or two total rest days a month. This may not sound like a lot, but pros have the indulgence that most age groupers don't: they can rest in between training sessions. There is no hard-and-fast rule but, as I said in Chapter 2, if you generally train every day I would suggest incorporating a rest day once every seven to ten days at the very least. The key is to listen to your body and its signals, irrespective of your planned training schedule. To maximise the opportunity to actually get some physical rest, try to stay off your feet as much as possible, although, as we will see, it's also important that this downtime doesn't make your mind go into triathlon overdrive. It is *not* wasted time, so quell any unnecessary and self-destructive feelings of guilt or laziness and trust in rest days to make you stronger and more resilient.

SOME TOP 'SLEEP-INDUCING' TIPS

> Use the bedroom for sleeping only.

> Have soft lighting.

> Have a nice warm bath before going to bed.

> Light reading (maybe not triathlon guides or magazines though!).

> Turn off your phone – checking the internet right before you sleep is a sure way to stimulate your brain with new information, which can keep you awake.

> Don't finish a training session right before going to bed.

> Try to eat at least 90 minutes before hitting the hay.

> Drink some warm milk.

> Cut out caffeine (especially after midday).

> Limit alcohol consumption.

> Invest in good-quality bedding.

Sleep

We don't all have this luxury but as an athlete, and pre-motherhood, I tried to get eight to nine hours of shut-eye a night. Having a routine was key – I went to bed and woke up at the same time each day. A quality bed and bedding and a non-snoring partner/earplugs were also beneficial. If my sleep was broken it was one of the first signals that I needed more, not less. As a parent, eight hours of uninterrupted sleep is something I can only dream of!

Nutrition

As Chapter 7 makes clear, effective recovery is only possible by eating the right foods before, during and after training. Overall, you should aim to eat a healthy, well-balanced diet with sufficient calories to sustain your training and lifestyle; consume foods that are rich in carbohydrates before higher intensity workouts or those lasting over about 90 minutes, and then refuel with carbs and protein afterwards. There are foods and spices that allegedly help reduce inflammation, such as beetroot, fish, ginger, pineapple, turmeric, cloves and garlic; but maybe not together. Antioxidants are also important, so try to consume a rainbow of vegetables and fruits, nuts and, for non-vegetarians, oil-rich fish.

Compression

A few decades ago people wouldn't be seen dead wearing tight garments that resembled an Edwardian corset. Times have changed. Now athletes the world over squeeze their muscles into a wide variety of skin-tight attire without anyone batting an eyelid. These garments supposedly increase the velocity of blood flow in and to the muscles, enhance the removal of waste products and reduce muscle damage. I used to wear compression socks and shorts/quad guards during some run sessions, especially hill repeats given the higher impact nature of downhill running (see page 147 for details). Just make sure that you choose a brand that actually compresses (especially after a few wears and washes), rather than ending up like baggy MC Hammer pants. Also note that, despite being de rigueur in the triathlon world, you may wish to hide your compression attire underneath other clothes while at work/weddings/job interviews. I was also a huge fan of the multi-segment inflatable pneumatic boots that, when connected to an electric pump, rhythmically inflate and deflate – thereby compressing and releasing – in a peristaltic movement. They aren't cheap, but perhaps a group of you could club together and get a pair, or else see if they can be hired at a local sports facility or medical centre.

Leg elevation

Elevating your legs by lying on your back and extending them vertically against a wall can help to drain the blood from lower limbs and encourage fresh, new blood to flood in when you stand up. I suggest doing it for three or four minutes.

Massage

As a professional athlete, I had a weekly deep-tissue massage, and then a light massage two days before a race. They are great for loosening muscles, increasing flexibility and providing a mental boost by allowing you to switch off for an hour (in between screams of pain as the therapist's hands knead your knotted hamstrings). In a perfect world, I would suggest all triathletes invest in a monthly massage with a trusted therapist, but they can be pricey so a foam roller is a good second option (see page 161 for more details). I also had regular Active Release Techniques (ART) therapy, which is soft-tissue movement massage that treats muscles, tendons, ligaments, fascia and nerves, and which I found highly effective.

Ice and heat

Many athletes choose to use ice or cold baths after hard sessions to reduce inflammation and muscle soreness and promote recovery. The jury is out as to their effectiveness. I enjoyed jumping into a tepid shower or the swimming pool after a long run when training in hot climes simply to cool off. However, I never regularly used cryotherapy (cold therapy) and so can't speak from experience as to whether it works. Be careful if you are taking a hot shower immediately following a cold swim. When you are cold, your body protects itself by concentrating the blood around the vital organs and away from the extremities (such as fingers and toes). An immediate hot shower will shock the system and, in extreme cases, can lead to fainting. Take it slowly and if in doubt warm up first and then start showering at lukewarm temperatures. If you're keen to try such methods it's best to experiment during training (although not in the weeks preceding a big race), being conservative with the temperature initially (e.g. cold baths rather than ice baths); don't overexpose your body (maybe stick to five minutes at first) and closely monitor your body's response.

Relax your mind

As my coach Brett Sutton implied when he told me to 'chop my head off', you have to recover mentally as well as physically, clearing your mind of clutter, worry and stress. Watch television, play Scrabble, cook a delicious meal, meditate, read a book, pet your pet, go to the movies, spend time with family and friends – anything that gives your brain a break from training, work and the stresses of everyday 'headless-chicken' life.

Some athletes and coaches like to use Training Stress Scores (TSS) to track the impact of training. TSS is a factor of duration and intensity that can be based on a number of metrics including RPE, heart rate or power on the bike. The general premise is that TSS is a better indicator than hours trained or miles completed of how much you are loading your body. A red flag can be raised if the cumulative stress is rising above the desired level (i.e. higher in a heavy training block, lower during a recovery week). There is plenty of information online for those who love this kind of number-crunching analysis, but even if you don't want to – or cannot

> " You have to recover mentally as well as physically, clearing your mind of clutter, worry and stress. "

– follow the maths, every athlete should regularly monitor themselves for signs and symptoms related to fatigue. Tiredness is something that we all experience; however, it can occasionally develop into something more serious. My coach Dave Scott describes short-term overload as 'over-reaching'. This fatigue can be managed within a few days through total rest or doing very low-intensity sessions. However, continuous over-reaching can develop into 'over-training'. Chronic over-training takes much longer to recover from and may require weeks or months of zero, or extremely minimal, volume and low-intensity training. In this extreme case, it is always best to seek medical advice.

Experiencing some/all of the following markers for more than a few days is likely to mean that your body needs more rest and recovery:

> a trending decline in the quality of your training sessions;

> elevated resting heart rate, and inability to raise the heart rate during workouts;

> broken sleep;

> lost appetite;

> irritability;

> lack of motivation;

> a feeling of being rundown;

> prolonged or frequent illness and injury;

> prolonged feeling of muscular heaviness or overload.

Whether you are flying or feeling like you're slightly flopping, rest and recovery is a fundamental pillar of triathlon success. When I finally learned to 'chop my head off' and put my feet up, my triathlon performance and overall health was all the better for it.

Give It a Rest – Post-race Recovery

Q 'What should I do when my Ironman is over? I know I need to recover but I'm worried about going stir crazy.'

ABI WHITE

A First of all – congratulations in advance for what you will achieve. It will be a marvellous, life-altering experience – and will give you memories to draw on for ever. It's all too easy to cross the line and immediately focus on the next goal, yet effective recovery is vital in order to fight another race day. You're right to think about this even before the event gets underway.

Preparing for and completing an Ironman have physical and psychological impacts. Overwhelmingly the experience should – and no doubt will – be a positive one. However, we have to accept that irrespective of the finish time, our muscles and tendons will take a battering, our immune system might be shell-shocked, we're likely to be in calorie and fluid deficit – and our undercarriage will have seen better days.

Race recovery depends on many factors, including the race distance (recovery is still important for those not doing an Ironman) and the intensity you raced at, the course, weather conditions, travel to and from the event, your taper, nutritional strategy, other life stresses, your physiology and conditioning, age and level of experience. It also depends on your post-Ironman training and racing goals.

Despite these variables, there are some general principles that triathletes should adopt to promote physical and psychological recovery.

> **It's all too easy to cross the line and immediately focus on the next goal, yet effective recovery is vital.**

PHYSICAL RECOVERY

Q&A

Some practical steps to help your physical recovery include:

> Refuel and rehydrate as effectively as possible in the hours, days and weeks after the race, so as to replenish lost calories and fluids. See Chapter 7 for more information about nutrition. That said, the days following your A race are also a time to let your hair down and indulge in whatever culinary delights you might fancy, preferably without an energy gel/bar/drink theme. My post-Ironman Arizona indulgences of burgers, chips, onion rings and donuts are testament to this philosophy.

> We all feel stiff and sore to varying degrees following a race and often want to collapse in a heap, but continuing to move after you have crossed the line can help prevent you from seizing up completely. Those doing shorter races may want to do a short cool-down in the form of a gentle jog, swim or bike to facilitate the recovery process.

> I liked to immerse myself in water after a race to take the weight off my aching body. Some athletes swear by ice baths to help reduce inflammation although I wasn't partial.

> Compression attire can help promote blood flow and reduce swelling (e.g. of your post-race 'cankles'). They are useful when travelling – especially on aeroplanes – when your body has a tendency to swell still further. Leg elevation can also help with this, although perhaps not during a flight. I even found that my face became puffy after an Ironman; however, I'm not sure the compression clothing manufacturers have developed a mask to specifically address this problem!

> Sleep is also important, although adrenalin, euphoria, sugar and over-tiredness can make it difficult to get decent shut-eye in the days after a big race.

> Massage is often available at the end of a race and can help flush out some of the waste products and promote recovery, but make sure it's very light with no pummelling.

> Nothing helps more than time: the essential ingredient for post-race healing, repair and rejuvenation.

In terms of training, one of the most common mistakes athletes make after a big race is to return too quickly to full training. It's often due to fear of losing fitness or of

 Q&A

changing a familiar routine. However, there is far greater risk of doing too much too soon than of doing too little – especially after a long-course event. 'De-training' is vital for recovery and ensuring longevity in the sport.

If the Ironman is the last race of your season, you could use the opportunity to have an off-season break (a subject covered in detail on page 300). If you have more races you should still have a period of recovery. After an early or mid-season Ironman, I would take three days almost completely off training with some light walking to loosen the legs and perhaps an extremely gentle swim/float. For the next week, I would do some easy, low-intensity recovery activities to de-train my body from the high workload. These might be short swims, bike rides or even hikes all kept at recovery or cruise intensity. I didn't run for six to seven days following an Ironman, given its high-impact nature, and waited a couple of weeks to start S & C exercises. If it hurt, I would stop. If I didn't feel like doing anything, I wouldn't. The key is to listen to your body and obey its commands. I would get back to full training about two weeks post-race unless I was having an off-season break.

If you were doing a shorter race instead of an Ironman, I would suggest having at least three to four days to recover from an Olympic distance and a week to ten days for a half Ironman.

If the Ironman doesn't go to plan, resist the urge to punish yourself through training; which is exactly what I did after the Columbia Triathlon in 2009. I had a sub-par performance, and tried to compensate by smashing myself in training in the days following the race. I dug myself a hole – and it took a while to climb out. Irrespective of the race result, we have prepared for and competed in a triathlon and this will have taken its toll.

PSYCHOLOGICAL RECOVERY

You have invested considerable time, energy and emotion planning and preparing for this race. You may have fought pre-race anxiety and nerves. Considerable concentration is also needed during the Ironman itself. All this can be mentally taxing and draining. Oft-forgotten mental rest and rejuvenation is as important as physical recovery.

See page 296 for the steps to take if you don't achieve your desired result. But if, as will hopefully be the case, you do achieve your goal, you will doubtless experience an array of emotions upon crossing the finish line: elation, relief, joy, pride and

Q&A

satisfaction are just a few. Make sure you celebrate how much you have achieved, especially with those who helped you on your journey.

The feeling of euphoria may never fade; however, please don't be alarmed if you suffer from the post-race blues and feel slightly glum, negative or anxious at some point. After the emotional high of my biggest victories, I often felt an ensuing slump – an aching void where my goal once stood. I had worked so hard and focused on the race for so long that I felt, in some way, lost. If you experience these emotions, trust that they are normal, but also ephemeral. In time, the feelings of jubilation will return.

> " After the emotional high of my biggest victories, I often felt an ensuing slump – an aching void where my goal once stood. "

Post-race is the time to switch off mentally from triathlon for a while by exploring the non-sporting side of life and reconnecting with people and activities that you may have sidelined. Don't be in too much of a rush to set a new goal either. All too often, I went straight into preparing for the next race, without reflecting on – and even basking a little in – what I had achieved. Given my time again, I would certainly have had a longer recovery period after each Ironman to give myself that mental space to rejuvenate fully.

Sport and training are important components of all our lives, but so are rest, recovery, balance and perspective. Make sure the few months after the race are replete with large doses of these. In time, you can take off your hard-earned medal, remove your race wristband and hang up your finisher's T-shirt – but carry the memory of your success with you for ever. ●

HAVING IT OFF: THE OFF-SEASON

Picture this. You've completed your A race. You've celebrated, partied and worn the finisher's T-shirt until it's threadbare. It's now approaching the time of year when the events section of the *220 Triathlon* website is as sparse as toilet paper on race morning; your clothing has the words 'long', 'warmer', 'fleece-lined' in the name and the shorts you have worn every day for the past year have started to reveal cracks that shouldn't be made public.

It's winter. It's cold. It's rainy. It's rainy and cold. It's cold and rainy. Good for ducks; suboptimal for triathletes. Luckily, this dismal meteorological state coincides with the end of the racing season. For many athletes, this means only one thing – 'having it off'. Any wife/husband/partner reading this might jump for joy at these three words (rarely used in the life of an exhausted triathlete). However, celebrations may be short lived. For I'm not referring to nocturnal gymnastics, but the so-called off-season: the period after your last race when triathlon goes from a hugely important focus of your life to having a back seat in day-to-day existence.

It sounds so easy to do. Stop or reduce the volume and intensity of your training, and instead see your non-tri friends or your spouse, spend quality time watching *The Jeremy Kyle Show*, eat food products whose labels don't begin with the word 'energy' and celebrate the return of a non-chafed posterior. But, as the saying goes, if it were that easy we'd all be doing it. The reality is that too many athletes eschew time off and, instead, plough on with their usual training programme without even stopping to wash their Lycra.

> " The reality is that too many athletes eschew time off and, instead, plough on with their usual training programme without even stopping to wash their Lycra. "

Many triathletes – myself included – are creatures of habit; we love a regimen and we crave control (without sometimes realising that the desire for control is actually controlling us). We are often fearful of taking a break from this routine, worrying over lost fitness and added waistline insulation and dreading the endorphin cold turkey. But listen loud and clear, folks. It is not the swim/bike/run sessions that will make you fitter – it's the recovery, the adaptation and regeneration from the stress caused by those activities.

And it is not just about physical recovery: it's mental rejuvenation too. Computer geeks tell me that, plugged in for long enough, eventually your laptop battery will wear out. Our bodies and minds are the same. We need to be unplugged in order to come back firing on all cylinders. The key to the off-season is to recharge not only your physical but also your mental batteries – leaving you invigorated, motivated and ready to give 100 per cent once more.

Often the fitter we become and more experienced we are, the greater our end-of-season recovery needs. It's like an interval session: the intense effort must be followed by a proportional period of recovery/rest. I know it can be psychologically difficult, and we have to suppress self-destructive feelings of guilt or laziness, but know that this is NOT wasted time: it's a vital bedrock to success and longevity.

The first question I am often asked is how long this off-season should last. I used to take around four to six weeks after the Ironman World Championship. But it is really up to the individual. So much depends on your training volume, level of fitness and health, and your state of mind. One thing is for sure, though, there are much greater risks from having too little rest than a bit too much.

I would personally divide my four-to-six-week off-season into three stages: 'unplugged'; then 'a little bit of what you fancy does you good'; and, finally, 'turn it back on'.

UNPLUGGED

First, spend about two weeks doing absolutely nothing that resembles training. On the weekends, rather than meeting Lycra lovers for the five-hour smash fest, turn your alarm off, consume breakfasts with 'fry' and 'up' in the name, read a book (training bibles – aside from this one – don't count), wear clothes that flap in the wind, stay up after 9 p.m. (kebab shops are at their best after this time anyway). Joking aside, try not to gain more than a few kilograms, but definitely don't starve yourself as punishment for not training. Believe me, an extremely lean body is not always optimal year-round in terms of building and maintaining physical and immune strength.

Spend time honestly evaluating the previous season in all its multifaceted glory while it's still fresh in your mind: make a note of the good and bad; the highlights and the lowlights; your strengths and weaknesses. Your logbook is a great place to start, but don't just focus on training and races – also think about wider lifestyle issues, like how much sleep you've been getting, the state of your relationships, what stresses you may have had in your life, how you feel at work. Second opinions can be garnered from your coach, teammate, drinking partner. Then close the notebook and put it on the shelf with your training log to gather dust for a few weeks.

A LITTLE BIT OF WHAT YOU FANCY

As much as you might have enjoyed becoming a couch-loving King Edward, once this initial period is over it's time to embark on the 'a little bit of what you fancy does you good' stage. Introduce some activities to elevate your heart rate slightly. Variety is the key here. Maybe try a new sport. Lawn bowls, tiddlywinks, yoga, skiing/après skiing, table tennis, rock climbing, belly dancing, bog snorkelling – anything that will invigorate you and get the aerobic system firing again (engaging in the implied activity in this section's title may also do this). Team sports are a good antidote to the oft solitary nature of triathlon training. Dragon-boat racing could be amusing. The key is fun, unstructured and non-triathlon focused. Don't keep a log. Don't wear a heart-rate monitor. Don't train. Exercise.

After a few weeks of spicy variety, you might a) realise that you much prefer bog snorkelling or b) have severe triathlon withdrawal symptoms. There is no harm in reintroducing swim/bike/run activities. Just keep it fun, unstructured and low in intensity. You don't have to get up for the 5.30 a.m. swim session. Try different strokes. The lifeguards are on hand should you drown attempting 25m butterfly. Take the dog for a walk. Poop-a-scooping adds that extra bit of flexibility work. Go running. But leave the all-singing, all-dancing, wrist-based computer at home. For example, I spent the end of the 2008 off-season in Argentina. I went for a friend's wedding, arriving at the nuptials in my cycle kit having biked all day to get there. We then spent their *luna de miel* – or honeymoon – cycle touring around and across Andean mountains that had never even seen a bike – and for good reason given we had to skid across glaciers, cross rivers and push over rocks. It wasn't training, but kick-started my body and was the making of my 2009 season.

At this stage I would also see a physio. A biomechanical assessment helps highlight strengths and weaknesses, with your kindly physio prescribing gym exercises involving the words squat or downward dog. You don't have to start them right away, but the early season is a great time to build structural and functional strength (see Chapter 6 for more details). Also take a look at your equipment. For example, a year of saddle sores indicates a bike fit may be needed and now's the time to do it (see page 124 for more details on bike fitting).

You can then dust off those books and start to think about next year's goals, again sitting down with your coach, friends and family to make sure their views are taken into account. After all, none of us get to the finish line alone, and significant others should be involved in our journey from the outset. What changes would you like to make? What weaknesses do you want to address? What places do you hope to visit? What would you like to achieve?

TURNING IT BACK ON

After a transition period of two to three weeks, re-inject some structure. Remember, your body has undergone many physiological adaptations and needs to be nursed back. You cannot pick up exactly where you left off, in either volume or intensity. Focus on developing a sound structural base (which means following the prescribed 'single-legged' squat programme); start gently and avoid grunting. Think about doing drills to improve your swim, bike and run technique, giving yourself time to develop the skill-specific strength early on.

Initially your swim, bike and run programme should focus mainly on aerobic base training. After a few weeks – unless you are a beginner – inject a few higher intensity efforts to kick-start the body. Resist the urge to punish yourself for time spent 'detraining'. Be patient. I would start with one to two weeks at 50 per cent of the volume you were doing before your time off, then go to 75 per cent and by three to four weeks you will be back at normal volume. Yes, it will hurt. You'll doubt your ability to run for the bus, let alone 10km. You will compare yourself unfavourably to others. Your motivation may even have waned. Be kind to yourself. Your body will return to its former glory, you won't be beaten in the pool by that 90-year-old breaststroker and you will develop a taste for tuna pasta rather than tubs of Ben & Jerry's Phish Food.

And when you wonder, 'Will I ever get fit again?', trust that the answer is yes. In fact, not only will you get fit again, the obligatory off-season will make you faster, stronger and more resilient. So, here's to having it off during the wintery triathlon barren spell. And enjoying it!

Off-season push biking, literally, in Argentina, 2008.

CHAPTER ELEVEN

TRI-NATAL

This is a chapter I didn't know whether I'd ever write. I wasn't sure I wanted children. After all, Tom and I were happy with life as it was. We relished spontaneity and our independence, loving the outdoors, socialising, doing a variety of sports, travelling, eating out and getting eight hours of uninterrupted sleep a night. All our boxes were ticked. Until I reached the age of 38 and it dawned on me, like being hit by a juggernaut, that the biological clock was ticking rather loudly: the Big Ben clock of ticks, rather than a nice silent stopwatch. If Tom and I wanted to have children the time was now. Having um-ed and ah-ed for years, the choice ultimately was easy. Not wanting to live with regret, we decided to start a family.

We were worried. Concerned about losing our independence, of being tied down and unable to spontaneously take up any endurance challenge. But upon talking to parents who'd had similar thoughts, we realised that, although changing immeasurably, our life would be enriched, not hampered by the arrival of a baby – aka our 'Bean'.

This chapter looks at how I prepared myself physically for the arrival of the Bean, as well as post-natal life, as seen through an athlete's – albeit a professionally retired one – lens.

PRE-NATAL PASSIONS: EXERCISE IN PREGNANCY

We conceived our daughter in March 2015. The Bean was the size of a grain of sand when I embarked on extensive research into exercise in pregnancy, specifically from an athlete's perspective.

I have to preface the text below with the caveat that this is my experience and the information I have gleaned. The first port of call for any advice regarding sport and pregnancy is your own antenatal team, your GP, an obstetrician or, failing that, Paula Radcliffe's autobiography.

It's worth mentioning that all women approach and experience pregnancy in different ways. I was fortunate to have an uncomplicated pre-natal period, with no adverse issues or side effects. Aside from excessive snoring. Which was fine for me, but a pain in the lugholes for my other half who had the unenviable options of a) sleeping with his head under a pillow and risking asphyxiation, b) sleeping in the spare room, c) getting arrested for bashing me with a large, blunt object, d) gritted-teeth style grinning and bearing my nocturnal grunts or e) divorce. Fortunately he opted for d).

> All the available evidence suggests that exercise is important and overwhelmingly beneficial to mother and baby.

Aside from the grunting, I had an uncomplicated pregnancy and wanted to remain as active and healthy as possible. This would ensure I stayed in my happy place mentally, could give myself the best foundation for a trouble-free labour and speedy post-natal recovery and, most importantly, benefit the health of the Bean, both in the womb and after her arrival.

Midwives, prenatal groups and the internet are replete with information about the different stages of pregnancy, how you (and the father) will feel, how your body will change, what to eat, what to drink, how to lift things, what equipment to buy, what colour the nursery should be. However, as an athlete I specifically wanted to know about exercise and pregnancy. All the available evidence suggests that exercise is important and overwhelmingly beneficial to mother and baby. But questions remained: how much should I be doing? What sports could I do and at what frequency and intensity? When should I ease off? Should I swim, bike and run, or simply run a bath and relax?

Most of the literature suggested, generically, that pregnant women do 30 minutes of exercise three times a week. That's a lot for some people, but for me it's tantamount to hibernation. I initially struggled to find information, grounded in science, targeted at people on the more athletic, obsessive end of the spectrum whose 'normal' is two hours of training a day. Luckily, quite a few sportswomen (and their partners) and obstetrically qualified friends could help shed light. Below is what I gleaned, and applied, when growing the Bean.

Don't start anything new

Pregnancy is not the time to start a new sport. I have done a bit of running, swimming and cycling in my time, and so those activities had the green light (having never successfully pole danced, this activity was shelved – for now). I chose to power/Nordic walk and swim during the first eight weeks of the first trimester (pre-natal lingo for the first three months), which was a pivotal time in the Bean's development and hence not the time for me to be pushing myself athletically. Swimming, especially, is an absolutely fantastic activity for any pregnant woman, provided they can actually swim beforehand. Water running could also be an option, although I didn't try it. I then introduced running – up to 75 minutes at a time – and cycling as I approached the second trimester. I did swap the road bike for the more upright/stable position on the mountain bike at week 28 – but stayed off the rocky, technical trails; and stopped cycling at about week 32. I ran a week before giving birth, tapering for labour with swims and power walks. I had a rest day once a week.

Activities to avoid include: contact sports where there's a risk of being hit, such as kickboxing, judo or squash; scuba diving, because the baby has no protection against decompression sickness and gas embolism (gas bubbles in the bloodstream) – bog snorkelling is OK; and exercising at heights over 2,500m above sea level unless fully acclimatised.

Stay at a lower intensity

I wanted to err on caution's side and not raise my heart rate significantly during pregnancy. Although I know others who have retained some intensity with no ill effects, I decided to veto hard intervals. Anything that made me red in the face or caused me to pant (nocturnal snoring doesn't count) was out. No hill repeats, no track sessions, no 25m sprints in the pool.

THE PELVIC FLOOR

The pelvic floor can be strengthened with very subtle, easy exercises:

> Close up your anus as if you're trying to prevent a bowel movement.

> Simultaneously draw in your vagina as if you're gripping a tampon, and your urethra as if to stop the flow of urine.

> Do this exercise quickly, tightening and releasing the muscles immediately and then more slowly, holding the contractions for as long as you can before relaxing.

> Do three sets of ten squeezes every day.

> 66 Hopefully there will be times when you can savour and celebrate the miraculous experience that is carrying and bearing a child. 99

Reduce training volume

Prior to conception I was doing about two to two-and-a-half hours of exercise a day. I reduced this to a maximum of 90 minutes, with a few sneaky three-hour rides between 12 and 20 weeks on the weekend.

Core is crucial

A strong pelvic floor is paramount. Not something you find in B & Q, this floor comprises layers of muscles that stretch like a supportive hammock from the pubic bone (in front) to the end of the backbone. Weak pelvic floor muscles can cause you to leak urine when coughing, sneezing or straining. It's known as stress incontinence and it can continue after pregnancy (stress incontinence wasn't to blame for me peeing on the bike during a race – that was just bad manners).

Totally disregarding what I just said about not trying anything new, I started doing Pilates in pregnancy. I was examined by a women's health physiotherapist and attended her classes twice a week, also doing exercises at home. Pilates focuses on subtle, slow movements that are totally alien to my frenetic, bull-in-a-china-shop personality. With hindsight, it was the best thing I could have done to enable me to enjoy – yes enjoy – pregnancy and labour and facilitate post-natal recovery.

Be in tune with your body

Listen to your body, gauge how it is responding and understand your personal limits. This is important even if you aren't expecting a Bean. Many are deaf because they don't want to hear the signals, often resulting in injury or illness. If it hurts: stop. If you feel like something isn't right: stop. If you are concerned: stop. Now isn't the time to be taking risks.

Enjoy being active

You'll have to reduce and moderate your training but this shouldn't prevent you from embracing and enjoying being active. I relished being outside, even in the pouring rain, and moving my expanding body; especially given the imminent sedentariness and sleep deprivation. My friend's advice was to play the pre-natal game while you can, as the post-natal months are a different ball game altogether!

Be positive

I know that for many women pregnancy is not easy: you may spend hours hugging the white elephant with sickness that strikes not only in the morning, but all day; or you're so tired you can't keep your eyes open; you wee yourself because the bump presses down on your bladder; or you have stretch marks where you never had before. Despite this, hopefully there are still times when you can savour and celebrate the miraculous experience that is carrying and bearing a child.

Wear comfortable clothing

Maternity Lycra doesn't seem to exist and I simply bought clothes and swimsuits a size or two bigger than normal. For cycling, I found a great range of bib shorts that were not tight around my belly and had a zip at the back so that I could pull them down (for the obligatory pees) without having to take the shoulder straps and jersey off. While running, I wore a special maternity belt to support my waist and hips. Well-fitting, supportive and comfortable sports bras were an absolute must.

Embrace physical changes

Of course, my body changed and that can be hard for someone who has always been lean and angular rather than soft and curvy, but I viewed pregnancy not as something to be endured or as an affliction but something to embrace. I loved seeing my body growing a new life and felt sexy – yes, sexy – with a rounded belly and boobs that were more padded than the pancake variety I had before.

And yes, we welcomed our wonderful Bean – our little girl, Esme Grace Lowe – into the world in December 2015: healthy and, from the outset, incredibly happy. We already know that she's changed our lives for the best; even my Pilates-fortified pelvic floor would agree.

POST-NATAL PASSIONS: BEING A 'FIT MUM'

You enter a race and prepare for months on end. You watch your body alter, you eat different foods and try to get as much sleep as possible. You buy new clothes and equipment, and chat to friends and relatives about what's happening and, to more experienced people, about what to expect. You're excited yet nervous, especially when the time comes to pack your bags and get ready for the start. And, finally, the day arrives. It's harder, tougher, more strenuous but more gratifying than anything you've ever done. You are overwhelmed with unbridled happiness when you reach the grand finale . . . and hold your child in your arms.

In many respects pregnancy and childbirth are analogous to doing a triathlon, albeit ten times as hard and without the finisher's T-shirt. Instead of a medal and lukewarm pizza, you are presented with a new life: one that turns your world upside down, but gives you more joy, pride and satisfaction than anything you could have ever imagined.

Despite the huge changes that took place – physically, emotionally and practically – we wanted exercise to remain an important part of our lives. In addition to the personal benefits, we wanted Esme to grow up with physical activity being the norm: for her to love being outside; to be healthy; to be confident in herself; and for her mum and dad to be the role models for this. Doing sport, we felt, would also make us better, more relaxed and fulfilled parents.

So how do you recover from this endurance feat and return to non-nappy/change/ feed-related activities, while accepting that your life, body and perspectives have greatly altered?

This section recounts my experiences as Tom and I journeyed along this new path as a family of three. Given that the father's perspective and experiences can differ from the mother's, I asked Tom, who's also a retired professional triathlete, to contribute his thoughts on life post-birth (see page 316). Even if your pre- and post-natal experiences bear no resemblance to ours, the advice below should prove useful for any new parent, or parent to be.

Research

I researched the subject of post-natal exercise even before Esme arrived. I spoke to the midwives, health visitors and obstetricians and ploughed through books and the internet. You may struggle to find advice specific to the more athletic, endurance-sport-focused mum, but one thing the literature does say, and which is valid no matter who you are, is that you have to listen to your body and, if anything, be conservative.

Physical impacts

The first few post-natal months are shaped by the nature of your pregnancy and labour. Both have a range of physical impacts, from loose joints and ligaments, especially around your pelvis, to separation of your abdominal muscles, bleeding and anaemia. These, compounded by sleep deprivation, increase the risk of injury and illness. I was fortunate that my labour, although eye-poppingly painful (I even burst a blood vessel to prove it!), was uncomplicated and I gave birth without incisions or drugs, aside from a dose of nitrous oxide, aka gas and air. I was also able to breastfeed, with Esme taking after her mother and guzzling food at 100km/h.

I did have a small separation of my abdominal muscles, and also suffered from sheet-drenching night sweats in the weeks after the birth, both of which are very common.

Start slowly: don't rush or panic

Aware of the potential for injury, the first week was largely spent in bed or on the sofa. I walked 1km (for hot chocolate) on day four, but crawled home and realised that I probably should have waited a few more days. After day seven, I walked progressively longer distances, with Esme in the sling or buggy, but always culminating in a chocolate-flavoured beverage. Cake, too, was obligatory and entirely justified given that breastfeeding necessitates an increased calorific intake (not that I needed an excuse!).

For someone so used to being outside and getting an endorphin fix, it was hard to be housebound and I felt claustrophobic and a little frustrated at times. I was also (irrationally) fearful of never looking or feeling the same again. It was therefore a relief when, at four weeks, I began power walking for up to 60 minutes between feeds but, following the advice of the midwives and health visitors, dutifully waited six weeks to increase the intensity to a gentle 30-minute run. I built this up over subsequent weeks, running up to about an hour by week eight or nine. I kept the intensity low and favoured slightly softer surfaces to minimise the impact. I did do a few turbo sessions, and included some slightly higher intensity intervals, but swimming was logistically harder to fit in because the pool opening times didn't fit with Esme's breastfeeding routine. Six months post-birth, however, I had an ankle injury that, on reflection, was a result of doing too much running too soon. Given the time again I would have been more conservative with the run volume, rather than succumbing to the temptation to rush and 'get my body back'.

Keep the core

I resumed pelvic floor exercises a few days post-birth to minimise any 'post-natal-peeing-yourself-when-you-sneeze' problems – doing them while I breastfed. Having consulted a women's health physio, I did (modified) Pilates exercises after three weeks.

Get the right clothing

A well-fitting sports bra was, and still is, essential given my breasts had burgeoned. In the first few weeks I was so well endowed that I wore two bras, and I know some of my sporty friends have done the same. You may need to get measured post-birth to ensure you're wearing the right size. I also wore a thin sanitary towel in case of urinary accidents, and donned my maternity clothing for comfort.

Focus on nutrition and hydration

I ensured my nutrition was spot on and that I stayed hydrated by having a bottle of water beside me at all times. Snacks were really important to maintain my energy levels, and I found myself eating countless plates of corn cakes with peanut butter and honey at night. I stayed off coffee, as I didn't want the caffeine to enter my breast milk. In the first few weeks, friends kindly brought us pre-cooked dinners, which was a fantastic help. We also batch-cooked and froze meals, so that we didn't have to prepare something every night. And yes, we did enjoy a post-natal glass of bubbly to wet Esme's head!

Reprioritise

Esme remains the utmost priority when planning and scheduling any activity. I wanted to be available to feed on demand, and didn't want my milk supply to be negatively impacted by exercise. This meant that some days I couldn't leave the house, and on others I adapted my plans to fit. Given that babies are 'sleep thieves', it's important to get shuteye when you can. It was frequently more important to have that 20-minute nap than it was to spend the equivalent time pounding the pavements. Time pressures have limited the post-exercise stretching, and I find it increasingly hard to fit in S & C sessions as Esme naps far less than previously. Hence, I had to devise an S & C routine that I can do as part of everyday life, rather than as a standalone session.

Focus on what you can do

There are ways to combine motherhood and exercise. For example, we have a running buggy so that Esme can come along for the ride. The same goes for a bike seat or bike trailer, which can be a great way to get kids involved in outdoor activity, even if the km/h isn't quite what it once was. Many parents also put their baby in a chair or on a mat beside them when they turbo, although out of the range of any perspiration showers. Long walks with the buggy or baby carrier are great ways to be active in the fresh air. Once the baby gets heavier, carrying them really is a workout! Exercise videos make it possible to train at home and parent–baby yoga and Pilates classes also exist in some areas. I have also exchanged childcare with sporty mothers; they look after Esme while I run and I reciprocate the favour. Although I haven't done so, many friends have joined gyms with crèches and work out while their child is cared for in a safe and secure environment.

Time efficiency and organisation

In my pre-parent life, I took spontaneity for granted: generally training when I wanted, where I wanted and for as long as my heart desired. I also faffed a lot, wasting time getting my clothes sorted, downloading podcasts to listen to on my runs or chatting in the swimming-pool changing room. Since becoming a mother, I'm increasingly time efficient and organised, and seize small windows of opportunity with both hands. If it's pouring with rain I still get on my bike. And it's worth going for a run even if I can only do 15 minutes. Bang for buck has never been more pertinent.

All smiles at the finish line of the London Marathon, 2017.

Enjoy being active

In the 12 months post-birth, I didn't set myself huge outcome (performance) goals, but simply enjoyed being active; even entering a few run races, as well as a cycle sportive and the cycle portion of a half Ironman relay, to get my racing fix. My eye was less on times and positions, and more on having fun with my friends and being in that familiar competitive environment. It was hard to race knowing that I had lost fitness and strength, and that people were still watching to see how I would perform, but I didn't want to let that pressure or fear stop me. I might not be the level of athlete I once was, but I am now a mother with more balls to juggle. Training and racing are all the more gratifying as a result and, most importantly, I can finish races like the London Marathon in April 2017 and hold our daughter in my arms.

Lean on others

I couldn't have done this without Tom's empathy and unwavering support, emotionally and practically. We are a team – and now a family. Our friends and family have also been incredibly supportive, which I appreciate so much more than the independent side of me would like to admit!

It's a hard juggling act, but when I question whether or not I can be a mum and continue to be active, I look to other female athletes who have given birth and managed to get back to pre-birth fitness and glory. Take British athletes Dame Jessica Ennis-Hill and Jo Pavey MBE, for example. Both mothers and both Olympians at Rio 2016, with Jess getting a silver medal having also been crowned World Heptathlon Champion a year previously when her son was just 11 months old. And Swiss triathlete Nicola Spirig, who had a baby soon after becoming Olympic champion in 2012 and achieved silver four years later in Rio.

> **When I question whether or not I can be a mum and continue to be active, I look to other female athletes who have given birth and managed to get back to pre-birth fitness and glory.**

I am encouraged and inspired, too, by friends who have been through the same process and continued on their sporting journeys. Myself and a few crazy, endurance-athlete buddies have set up our own little informal 'Fitmums' WhatsApp group where we arrange get-togethers to talk about sport, nappies, sleep deprivation, crying, teething and what races to enter – all over good food and a glass of wine. They have helped motivate me and convince me that you can be so much more than simply a mum. You can be a Fit Mum, and help inspire the next generation as you do so.

And Esme: I look at her and am filled with love. She is my proudest achievement. She makes everything worthwhile, and I will do whatever I can to be the role model she deserves.

Insight

TOM LOWE on being a father

Watching my daughter come into the world was undoubtedly the best moment of my life. As a new father, I felt my main role was to support our family, and make life as easy as possible for Chrissie and Esme. I wanted to be as helpful and hands-on as I could; changing nappies, cooking meals, keeping the house tidy or taking Esme out for a walk so Chrissie could have a 20-minute nap, eat a meal or have a shower. My wife and child come first and taking care of them is my main priority.

In the initial few weeks my training was significantly reduced, as I wanted to be present as much as possible and also due to tiredness from the sleepless nights! After a few weeks, I started going out for rides and runs, but kept them short. My work schedule is flexible, and pre-fatherhood I was able to fit training in relatively easily. However, as a father time is limited, so I have become a lot more efficient and organised. Mornings are the best time for me to train and I often get out of the door before Chrissie and Esme wake up, and return soon after the first feed finishes. Esme was born in December and so I needed a good set of lights for cycling in the dark. I also do bike sessions at home on the rollers; if you have a suitable area, you can leave them set up with bike atop and jump straight on. It was, and is, a case of adapting and doing what I could when I could.

> My workouts are a lot shorter than they were before, but incorporate more intensity meaning I maximise the limited time available.

Training on my own is most time-efficient, and due to the nature of long-distance triathlon I've learned to be happy with my own company. Where possible, I've included sessions with other fathers who are also trying to fit sport into family life. My workouts are a lot shorter than they were before, but incorporate more intensity, meaning I maximise the limited time available. I am struggling to find the time and motivation to do regular S & C work, which makes the risk of injury that bit greater, especially when compounded by a poor night's sleep – although I can't complain, I'm not awake all night nursing a baby!

Chrissie loves being with Esme. Being largely sedentary in the first few months didn't come easy and, although she wanted me to be happy, she was slightly resentful that I could train. I, in turn, felt guilty for having the freedom to run or bike. While it never led to any arguments, it was something we had to discuss to make sure that it didn't become the elephant in the room.

At the six-week point, Chrissie was able to exercise, and I wanted to facilitate this as far as Esme's two-hourly feeding schedule would allow. I tend to be a lot more conservative and cautious than Chrissie when it comes to training, especially when returning after injury or illness, and would have preferred that she had taken things a little more slowly in the first few months. Despite my urging, her temptation to train won the day and she probably overdid it after the birth, leading to an ankle injury. Fortunately, it was nothing serious, but it did mean she was slightly more willing to take my advice afterwards!

While we are no longer professional athletes, sport remains an important part of our lifestyle. There's no reason for this to change now that we have become parents, we just have to adapt things to fit around our number one priority: our daughter. Chrissie and I have managed to establish a training routine that seems to work and we're at the stage where we can set some bigger racing goals and develop a programme to work towards them: with Esme as our number-one cheerleader. ●

chapter title

CHAPTER TWELVE

TRIATHLON TITBITS

All the other sections in this book fit neatly under different chapter headings. This chapter is the mongrel, comprising an unrelated and random assortment of articles that don't go anywhere else. It includes my musings on how to make triathlon as easy on the wallet and financially friendly as possible, advice on how to acclimatise in the heat, a tongue-in-cheek dictionary covering popular triathlon parlance and a tongue-in-the-other-cheek look at what it takes to be a bona fide triathlete. I felt it was important to include them all, both to inform and amuse – adding a few light-hearted high-fives as you head to the book's finish line.

Tri on the Cheap – Making Your Money Go Further

Q 'I'd love to do a triathlon but am concerned by its reputation of being an expensive sport. What advice can you give to someone on a budget?'

ANNIE VERNON

A There's no doubt that triathlons are harder on the bank balance than some other sports. However, please rest assured that you can do the sport without breaking the bank. I won the World Age Group Championship in 2006 using a borrowed wetsuit and a second-hand road bike with normal wheels; and won the Ironman World Championship in 2007 wearing my friend's race shorts and a £15 pair of sunglasses bought from a petrol station three years before.

Ultimately you compete using your heart and head, not your wallet. That said, it's hard to ride without a bike and birthday suits aren't overly popular, so how can you make triathlon as inexpensive as possible?

You can use most of the kit in racing that you wear in training and, as long as it fits, it can be rented, borrowed, bought second-hand or in end-of-year/ex-rental clearance sales. The essentials are: a swimsuit; goggles; swim cap (if your hair's long) and a wetsuit if you plan to race in open water. Bikes range from a few hundred pounds to the price of a car. There's nothing stopping you using a hybrid or mountain bike, as long as it passes a safety inspection. Chunky tyres can be swapped for skinnier slick versions, while superfluous paraphernalia like mudguards, chainguards and pannier frames can be removed. If you have a spare £300 lying around, an entry-level road bike would be a good investment – for training, racing and even commuting. Using normal pedals (or those with cages) means you can use the same shoes for biking and running. A regular helmet is a no-brainer.

Despite the barefoot-running fad, the rules necessitate that running shoes are worn in races, so don't skimp on buying a good pair. You can use the same shoes for training and racing, though.

Q&A

Instead of a race-specific tri-suit, a swimsuit can be worn from start to finish (although it's not always pleasant for your nether regions), or you can slip into a pair of shorts and a T-shirt/cycle jersey/running vest post-swim. A set of £5 elastic laces can save you more time in the bike/run transition than a £150 aero helmet might on the bike.

Creativity is cost-effective. An inflated bag from inside a wine box is an effective substitute for a swim pull-buoy (and you get to drink the contents!), while free online tools plan and measure training runs and rides with no need for fancy computers.

Running and biking outside are free, while public pools are much cheaper than private gyms. Consider joining a local tri club for a nominal fee and accessing their free coaching. Club members sometimes get discounts at local tri stores and often have equipment exchanges or second-hand sales. To access more advice and information, buying this guide is probably the best investment you can make (borrowing from a friend or library can help you stretch those pennies that little bit further though!) and there is a wide range of online resources that offer free content on every triathlon issue under the sun.

Good nutrition doesn't mean spending a huge slice of your salary pie on sports-specific products. You can make many of your own portable foods and drinks (see recipes on page 193). Oats, nut butter, honey and dried fruit make for great energy bars and recovery smoothies can be as simple as combining milk, peanut butter and banana.

Bigger, high-profile races generally involve road closures, mass stewarding, security and a pro field, so they're also expensive to enter. Opt for smaller, lower profile events with lower entry fees, accepting that they might not come with all the bells and whistles. Travel may be cheaper if booked well in advance. Could you combine your annual holiday with a race to get bang for travel buck?

Like you say, the issue of triathlon expense is as much about the perception and reputation as the actual cost. Once you fall in love with the sport – and your wallet can handle the pressure – you can add optional extras or upgrade. Ultimately, though, the best investment is in the form of hard work, drive and huge doses of free determination! ●

Me on the bike on my way to victory at the World Age Group Championship, 2006.

TAKE THE HEAT: STRATEGIES FOR HEAT ACCLIMATISATION

You've entered, or qualified for, a race where high temperatures are likely. Your support crew is delighting in the chance to bask in the sun's rays, working on their suntans while sipping cocktails to rehydrate. That's what my family and friends did in Hawaii. While I pounded the streets, sweltering in the 35°F heat, they went to the beach, donned their bikinis/mankinis and drank Mai Tais.

It's all very well for those who live in places where a big yellow ball dominates the forecast, as they are accustomed to such conditions, but it's a different story for those whose meteorological norm is rain/snow/cloud. So, if you're in the latter category, what strategies can you adopt to best acclimatise to the heat and ensure you can maximise your race-day performance?

> 66 Training in the same conditions that you will be racing in builds confidence that you will be able to deal with such conditions come the Big Day. 99

The best way to acclimatise, for hot or for cold, for that matter, is to train in locations characterised by similar weather conditions to those in which you'll be racing. As a professional, I loved competing in the heat and tended to enter races where warm temperatures were almost guaranteed. I was fortunate to be able to follow the sun and train in climes that were warmer than your average British summer, whether that be Thailand, the Philippines, Spain, South Africa or Boulder, USA. After a week or so, my body physiologically adapted to the conditions and, come race day, I coped well when the temperatures soared.

The next best thing for amateurs who haven't got the luxury of travelling the world in search of a training-tan is to spend a few weeks holidaying – preferably a swim-bike-run-focused vacation – in hot places. Bear in mind, though, that it can take about 10–14 days to acclimatise and the benefits start to dissipate after a week or so of returning to cooler conditions.

If heat-oriented holidays aren't possible, then the other option is to simulate the conditions at home – through training on a treadmill or turbo in a warm room, maybe even next to a radiator or heater and/or by overdressing when training indoors and outdoors. Sitting on your turbo in your wetsuit is probably a step too far, so instead of all-over rubber outfits, I would opt for layered, breathable fabrics. Some athletes also like to sit in saunas or steam rooms. I don't think it can do any harm for 10–15-minute blocks, but taking a treadmill in with you is probably not advisable.

Whatever method you choose, ensure you take things slowly for the first three to five days, being especially cautious with intensity. Yes, expose yourself to the heat on a daily basis for increasing amounts of time, but do your higher intensity work closer to dawn or dusk, in cooler conditions. After three to five days, you can do progressively more sessions at hotter times of the day. If you do decide to travel to the event before race day, avoid the temptation to cram your acclimatisation and compromise your taper in order to train in the heat. Instead, walk around to allow your body to adjust, and only do your lower intensity sessions when the sun is at its highest.

Don't forget the importance of hydration. Make sure you consume enough fluids and electrolytes to replace those lost in sweat, but don't overhydrate. Additionally, employ thermoregulation strategies to help keep cool; such as throwing water over your head, wearing a visor or cap, carrying ice in your hands/under a cap/down your top/in your shorts, and wearing light colours and/or technical cooling and wicking fabrics.

Maximising the physiological adaptations to heat will obviously be important, but training in the same conditions that you will be racing in also has psychological benefits because it builds confidence that you will be able to deal with such conditions come the Big Day. And, if nothing else, console yourself that once the race is over you'll finally be able to don the beachwear and celebrate the fact that the only umbrella you'll see is the one sticking out of your cocktail!

A SPECIAL BREED: TRIATHLON'S RULES OF ENGAGEMENT

Triathletes are a unique species. Of course, there are many sub-categories – the 'gottahavealottagear-asaurus', the 'whatsabrick?-rookie', the 'seemybumcrack-whiteLycraworshipper', the 'statisticsavvy-logbooklover'. But despite this cross-section there are a number of commonalities that the majority of us share or, in the case of the 'whatsabrick?-rookie', will soon adopt in order to be truly initiated into the fold. For triathlon is not simply a sport. Oh no. It is a religion with rites of passage and traditions that all disciples must follow to earn the right to call themselves a bona-fide 'triathlete'. So, without further ado, here are some of the most important ones:

> Your Christmas present list is comprised solely of wicking-, compressive-, aero- or carbon-related products. Opening such gifts causes the recipient to pant/ moan/drool/give out more kisses than a mistletoe-holding Hugh Hefner. All other non-go-faster gifts will be sold before you can say 'eBay'.

> Beauty products are rendered obsolete. Sweet-smelling perfume or manly cologne are replaced by the distinctive, slightly overpowering L'Eau de Chlorine that never needs reapplying, and has the bonus of acting as hair dye (the over-chlorinated green low-light being a particular favourite). Red-rimmed eyes replace eyeliner. Roll-on deodorant is pointless. The spray-version is, however, extremely useful as a means of disinfecting unsanitary shoes.

> Your elderly neighbour takes a heart-attack-inducing glance at your figure-hugging attire, and politely asks if you are auditioning for the role of Peter Pan in a Christmas pantomime or *Swan Lake*. You laugh, and reply that the only lakes you have ever heard of are the open-water variety, and you hope that they don't include any species of vicious waterfowl.

> Your New Year's resolution is to shave ten seconds off your finish time. Failing that, you solemnly swear to shave all bodily foliage in order to achieve your personal best time without actually having to train at all.

> Your idea of haute cuisine is a gloopy glucose solution in a foil packet. This 'banana-strawberry delight' is washed down with a fine bottle of red: a full-bodied beverage with a rather overpowering aroma of cranberry and

pomegranate, a splash of sodium and a large mound of undissolved glutinous powder at the bottom.

> You buy your loved one a box of chocolate-flavoured delights on his/her birthday: they come in a pack of 20, have 50 per cent protein, a rubbery texture that resembles eating a flip-flop, and have 'energy' and 'bar' in the name.

> You look like a zebra-cum-badger, with white feet, torso and 'full moon' due to the triathlon tan lines. You can also be identified by the 'temporary' race number tattoo on the back of your calf or upper arm that, despite a week of showering and scrubbing, lingers like a tri badge of honour.

> Every room in your house has a shrine to triathlon. The living room serves as a turbo/sauna, the kitchen is a well-stocked aid station, the hallway has long since become a mud- or oil-laden 'T1 and T2'. You park your bikes in the garage and use the driveway for your car. You are lulled to sleep by windchimes: aka your finisher's medals hanging on the bedpost.

> Becoming an octogenarian is something that you look forward to, given the increased probability that you will finally qualify for the World Age Group Championship. Your free bus pass will only be used as a bookmark in your training bible.

> You remain dry-eyed while watching Christmas re-runs of *Watership Down*, but reach for the nearest box of Kleenex during Ironman World Championship videos. Those with the most watery of triathlete works can repeat the commentary verbatim, but are unable to remember the date of their wedding anniversary or best friend's birthday.

> During dinner parties, saucer-sized saddle sores, buttock numbness or nipple chafe are deemed some of the most defining issues of our time and the subject of much debate. Remedies for such war wounds are received with rapture and unbridled celebration.

> You played truant from maths classes at school, but think nothing of using Stephen Hawking-style equations to calculate accurately your run splits or calorie intake.

> Your bookshelf is collapsing under the weight of *Joe Blog's Training Bible How to Swim Like a Shark*, (dog-eared copies of) my autobiography and the entire *220 Triathlon* back catalogue. You use the *Encyclopaedia Britannica* to prop up the front wheel of your turbo-mounted steed and your favourite bedtime reading material is the self-help tome *Ten Top Tips to Avoid Bonking*.

> Talking of the 'Bonk': this is a nightmare-inducing scenario to be avoided at all costs. And all other forms of bonking are now out of the question given your perpetual state of exhaustion.

> You occasionally resemble a beetle: cramping so badly that you lie on your back, and wriggle your arms and legs in the air to relieve the offending muscle spasm. Passers-by ignore your protestations that, rather than resulting from over-consumption of cheap cider, this is due to the under-consumption of apple-flavoured, electrolyte-enriched Special (Sports) Brew.

> You spend hours moaning about a (needless to say) unfair drafting penalty, yet you pay your £100 speeding ticket without so much as one complaint. In addition, you think it is daylight robbery to be charged £70 for a pair of jeans, but think nothing of forking out £170 for postage-stamp-sized shorts that come with promises of speed, PBs and freedom from chafing.

> An ability to perform every bodily function while simultaneously partaking in swim/bike/run becomes your favourite party trick. These on-the-go multi-tasking talents include: robing and disrobing; eating your own bodyweight in calories; showering yourself with any available fluids; blowing snot rockets; and occasionally watering the race course and/or the inside of your neoprene.

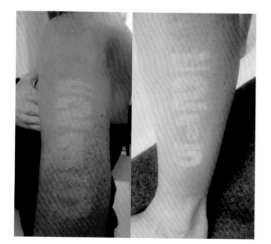

If you recognised yourself in the majority of these descriptions – 'congratulations!', you can now call yourself a fully fledged, bona fide triathlete! As a member of this prestigious club, hereby resolve to convert as many unsuspecting friends, colleagues, family members and total strangers to this wonderful sport as possible: breeding the next generation of Special Sports Brew-drinking, -swimming, spandex-wearing worshippers of the altar that is the triathlon finish line.

LEARNING THE LINGO: AN ALTERNATIVE TRIATHLON GLOSSARY

Triathlon has its own language. It doesn't just require a new wardrobe, a new diet, a new personal hygiene routine, a new circle of wetsuit-wearing, leg-shaving friends, new tan lines and a maxed-out credit card, it also requires the participant to diligently learn the lingo if they are to be fully accepted into the fraternity. Yes, the triathlon vernacular is worthy of its own Collins (a Jim Collins Dictionary that is, named after the founder father of Ironman).

I thought it might be worthwhile to create a handy little glossary for the non-triathlete whose idea of meeting a 'stripper' has little to do with the removal of neoprene.

Aerobars: A tasty chocolate bar with lovely little bubbles, but also a type of handlebar (not the moustache variety) or pair of sticks that attach to road-bike handlebars, with padded places to put your forearms and soak up substantial puddles of sweat. Such bars allow triathletes to maintain an excruciatingly uncomfortable, aerodynamic position while also looking very mean and aggressive.

Bonk: When you suddenly lose energy and experience a crushing fatigue. At such time glycogen stores are depleted, your brain chastises you for even entering the race and suggests that stepping to the side and eating pizza is a preferable option. Also known as, and feels like, 'hitting the wall'. With your head. Best avoided.

Brick: Commonly, a combination workout that includes a bike and run back to back. It's also what your legs feel like afterwards. 'Having a brick planned' does not mean that an athlete is about to perform some kind of colonic evacuation.

Century: Completing 100 miles on two wheels. It furnishes the finisher with substantial bragging rights . . . and Mount Vesuvius-sized saddle sores.

Chamois cream: A non-greasy lubricant placed between your bits and your cycling shorts. In addition to making biking more comfortable, it reduces the chances of sores. The whipping variety is not recommended.

Chip: A device worn above the ankle or on the shoe that allows timing during a race or event. Despite such technical advancements, it is still common for athletes to look down and stop their watches at the finish line rather than getting a good, celebratory photo. The potato variety is eaten in excess by yours truly after a race, best accompanied by a burger or ten.

Compression: Not ideal attire for work or weddings, these skin-tight items of clothing help with recovery and stop wobbly bits from wobbling. Can be borrowed by your children for fancy dress or pantomime costumes.

Disc: Not the compact, musical version popular in the 1990s, but a solid wheel that is supposedly very aerodynamic. They look cool. Sound cool. Can cost a small fortune and cause carnage in crosswinds.

Double-up: The practice of doing two sessions of the same discipline in the same day. In no way related to tri-polygamy.

Drafting: When one cyclist cycles right behind another with the latter gaining an advantage by doing less work but still travelling at the same speed as the lead athlete. It's illegal in age group races, except in some ITU sprint-distance events, as well as many professional races. Warning shots can be fired if you think someone is getting too close. Read my autobiography for more details on the technique (as a spoiler, it involves the release of bodily fluid). It can also be legally used in swimming but practise beforehand otherwise you might resemble the losing opponent in a boxing match.

Expo: The site, at a race, where obsessive, frenzied bargain hunting and freebie collection takes place. Such freebies can then be hoarded and given as Christmas/birthday gifts (nothing like out-of-date energy gels poured over Brussels sprouts to get your grandparents jumping). Despite the fact you should never use anything new on race day, many a triathlete can be found at the expo purchasing everything they need for the race the very next day. Buying speed is popular at such a site (not the illegal purchase of dodgy pills, but the common tactic used to compensate for a lack of actual training).

Half wheeling: Usually used in the cycling context, this is when you are riding two abreast, yet your partner keeps their front wheel slightly in front of yours, making you puff and pant like a 40-a-day smoker to keep up. Incidentally, I first learned about half-wheeling etiquette from a teammate. He said to me, 'Chrissie, do you know what half wheeling is?' To which I replied, 'Umm. No.' He responded, 'It's what you're doing right now and it's p*ssing me right off.' I now try to keep a respectful 10m distance. In front.

Hammer time: To pedal very hard, typically for an extended period. Also the words uttered in the 1980s by an MC of the same name while wearing dubiously coloured ill-fitting trousers. I doubt he did much of the triathlete-style hammering, though.

Hangry: The state of being hungry and angry. This usually occurs after a long session when you discover your housemate, spouse, partner, gerbil has eaten the last of your Shreddies, Quaker's (oats, not the religious sect) or BOGOF packets of muffins. You are left having to refuel on a tin of tuna with tomato ketchup, out of the can. Or you eat the gerbil.

Lube: The difference between a smooth winner and a sore loser.

Runner's high: An intense feeling of exhilaration or being 'in the zone' that can occur during a run, usually due to the release of endorphins. Can also be experienced when 'buying speed' at the expo. Followed by a 'runner's low' when you get your credit-card bill.

Slot: Triathletes love getting a slot to compete. Especially at the first time of trying. They will then part with large sums of money and purchase lots of new clothing with their national flag or the words 'Kona, Hawaii' written all over it. Bragging rights increase in proportion to each slot obtained.

Snot rocket: Swimming, cycling and running makes everyone have a runny nose. It's a biological fact. Rocketing is the art of removing the nasal river while on the move. The technique is simple, but must be practised otherwise you risk giving your training partner a snail trail to take home.

Stripper: A special type of volunteer who keeps their baggy T-shirt on, but helps to remove your wetsuit after the swim. They also deserve a big smile.

Transition: Part of the course where a triathlete keeps their belongings and switches from one discipline to another. Also the site where athletes drool over bikes that are considered 'bling' (aka very expensive and fast-looking). It is also the place where you will perform the funky-chicken dance in trying to rid yourself of your neoprene.

Triathlete: A person who spends all their spare time and money swimming, biking, running and shaving. Talks about nothing but said activities. Wears nothing but tight clothing. Loves an energy-related bargain but, thankfully, has enough spare cash to purchase this guide.

Triathlon widow: The male or female spouse of the triathlete. While they are technically still married, they either don't see their partner at all, or when they do the said partner is in a fully comatose post-training stupor and is unable to perform normal bodily functions, let alone engage in non-grunting conversation.

Volunteer: These individuals devote their time to helping you get hot and sweaty. They are very nice people who wear brightly coloured T-shirts. They don't get paid. Make sure you smile and thank them.

There you have it. Not exhaustive, but hopefully a good starter for developing your triathlon vocabulary, which will grow in proportion to your level of experience and ludicrous triathlon tan lines. For further definitions, you could also pop to the Annex where the less tongue-in-check triathlon glossary is located.

CHAPTER THIRTEEN

THE FINISH LINE: A CONCLUSION

T raining guides cannot possibly solve all triathlon-related conundrums, but hopefully the experiences of yours truly and the wisdom of the trusted experts bestowed throughout this book will assist your endeavours in this wonderful sport.

I've talked much of finish lines, but starting is often the hardest part – whether a training session, a different sport or a new direction in life. Don't let fear of failure or of what people might think put you off. Your limits extend far further than you realise, but to discover them you have to step outside your comfort zone. It's only by pushing that little bit further that you will you break down your own barriers or raise your own bar. Sometimes that challenge feels too big, but in doing so not only

OPPOSITE: Euphoric relief at my final Ironman finish line: the Ironman World Championship, 2011.

will you find much personal reward, but you'll also inspire those around you; those you love and those you may not even know. Strength breeds strength. Fortitude breeds fortitude, and passion breeds passion. You can realise your goals, and also be a shining light for others to follow.

Yes, triathlon can be daunting. The sport is replete with unusual terminology, conflicting training philosophies and endless choices of go-faster kit. Gadgets are available to monitor our every move. Magazines and websites promote the latest fad, and more always seems to be better. But stop. If you take one word of advice, it is to keep things simple. Focus on the basics of swim, bike and run, do the best you can in the context of your life and everything will fall into place. I promise.

 You can realise your goals, and also be a shining light for others to follow. 99

There will be euphoric highs. Make sure you celebrate them, sharing the joy with those who have trodden the tri-path with you. But the journey – and it is a journey – will no doubt be peppered with a few lows that make you question who you are, why you are putting yourself through this and whether you are good enough. We all experience lapses in motivation, of discomfort, of fear and of self-doubt. You have the capacity to endure these and to conquer any hurdles that might lie in your path. It's the lows that make the successes sweeter and galvanise you for the battles to come, not just in sport, but in life itself.

This is your triathlon journey. To your triathlon finish line. Never stop believing in all you can achieve.

OVERLEAF: Fireworks at the finish line of Challenge Roth.